RETAIL AND COMMUNITY

Business, Charity and the End of Empire

Edited by
George Campbell Gosling,
Alix R. Green and Grace Millar

BRISTOL
UNIVERSITY
PRESS

First published in Great Britain in 2024 by

Bristol University Press
University of Bristol
1–9 Old Park Hill
Bristol
BS2 8BB
UK
t: +44 (0)117 374 6645
e: bup-info@bristol.ac.uk

Details of international sales and distribution partners are available at bristoluniversitypress.co.uk

British Library Cataloguing in Publication Data
A catalogue record for this book is available from the British Library

ISBN 978-1-5292-3524-1 hardcover
ISBN 978-1-5292-3525-8 ePub
ISBN 978-1-5292-3526-5 OA PDF

Cover design: Andrew Corbett
Front cover image: Piara Singh Hayre at his corner shop on Knox Road,
Wolverhampton, c1969 / Black Country Visual Arts © Apna Heritage Archive
Bristol University Press uses environmentally responsible print partners.
Printed and bound in Great Britain by CPI Group (UK) Ltd, Croydon, CR0 4YY

FSC
www.fsc.org
MIX
Paper | Supporting
responsible forestry
FSC® C013604

Contents

List of Figures and Tables

Figure

Tables

Notes on Contributors

Nadia Awal is Researcher at the Black Country Living Museum. She has been working on *BCLM: Forging Ahead* since 2018. Her work focuses on researching and interpreting the 1940s–1960s historic town, and her interests lie in representing inclusive histories. She has worked in museums since 2009, with extensive experience in interpretation, research and exhibitions.

Ben Curtis is a historian of the South Wales coalfield, the British coal industry, industrial disability and de/industrialization. He is Honorary Research Fellow at the University of Wolverhampton on the 'On Behalf of the People' project on British coal industry and its coalfield communities, 1947–1994, History Tutor at the Department of Professional and Continuing Education at Cardiff University, and author of the 2013 monograph *The South Wales Miners, 1964–1985*.

Jessica Field is a researcher, writer and educator. Her academic work examines the politics and history of humanitarian action, particularly in the United Kingdom and India. Jessica also writes about housing inequality in Britain and, in 2022, she won the Dawn Foster Memorial Essay Prize for her writing on a large-scale eviction of tenants in Yorkshire.

Triona Fitton is Senior Lecturer in Sociology and Student Success at the University of Kent. Although she has researched and written more generally on the topics of charity, philanthropy and the teaching of non-traditional and practitioner students, her main area of academic interest is charity shopping, and second-hand consumer practices. She was co-editor of a 2022 special issue of *JOMEC* journal entitled 'Second-hand Cultures in Unsettled Times' and has published both methodological studies and empirical analysis of the charity retail environment and its politics.

Marjorie Gehrhardt is Associate Professor in 20th Century French History at the University of Reading. Her research focuses on the history of philanthropy, particularly in the late 19th and early 20th centuries. Her recent publications examine the role of charities in supporting disabled veterans, the evolution of fundraising methods and the impact of the First World War on philanthropic activities.

Jenny Gilbert is Knowledge Exchange Manager for Social Sciences at the University of Sheffield. She previously worked as a researcher for Black Country Living Museum and managed the partnership between the museum and the University of Wolverhampton. She holds a PhD in history and has undertaken wide-ranging teaching, partnership, public engagement and media activity.

Keith Gildart is Professor of Labour and Social History at the University of Wolverhampton. He has published widely on working-class history, labour politics, youth culture, popular music and deindustrialization. His books include the 2001 *North Wales Miners: A Fragile Unity, 1945–1996*, the 2013 *Images of England through Popular Music: Class, Youth, and Rock 'n' Roll 1955–1976*, and the 2020 *Keeping the Faith: A History of Northern Soul*. He is also editor of the multi-volume *Dictionary of Labour Biography*.

George Campbell Gosling is Senior Lecturer in History at the University of Wolverhampton. He is the author of the 2017 book *Payment and Philanthropy in British Healthcare, 1918–1948* and a series of journal articles on the history of the voluntary sector in modern Britain. More recently his work has focused on the various ways British charities have engaged in retailing since the 18th century.

Nick Gray spent most of his working life in UK public sector administration. He is a PhD researcher at the University of Wolverhampton, with an interest primarily in 19th- and early 20th-century social history, and in retailing and consumption in particular.

Alix R. Green is Reader in History at the University of Essex. A historian of contemporary Britain, her particular interests lie in politics and political culture and the uses of history and historical records. Since her 2016 book, *History, Policy and Public Purpose: Historians and Historical Thinking in Government*, she has been focusing on collaborative research with archivists, mobilizing historical collections in operational businesses and organizations.

Harshad Keval is a writer, academic and activist, with special interests in race-critical and decolonial social theory, knowledge and practice. He writes, teaches and consults across institutions, disciplines and platforms, and is currently finishing a new book on Whiteness, coloniality, racialized systems and institutional power. He is currently Lecturer at Edinburgh Napier University.

Ruth Macdonald is an archivist with an MA in cultural memory from the University of London. She is currently Archivist and Deputy Director of the Salvation Army International Heritage Centre and chairs the Religious Archives Group. Her research interests lie in social and working-class history and the politics of memory.

Grace Millar is a labour historian. Her PhD was on families during the 1951 New Zealand Waterfront Dispute. She is an Honorary Research Fellow at the University of Wolverhampton, working on 'On Behalf of the People', a project which studies the history of the British coal industry and its coalfield communities, 1947–1994.

Ian Mitchell is Honorary Research Fellow at the University of Wolverhampton. His main area of research has been retailing and consumption in 18th and early 19th-century England, with particular interests in the book trades and retailing beyond the shop. He published *Tradition and Innovation in English Retailing, 1700– 1850: Narratives of Consumption* in 2014. He is now focusing on shopping in the 1850– 1914 period.

Massimiliano Papini has recently completed a doctoral degree at Northumbria University. His research is concerned with the transcultural interaction between Europe and Japan through art and artefacts during the 19th and early 20th centuries, to better understand the ambiguous representation and perception of Japanese culture outside of Japan from 1854 to this day. His publications appeared in the *Journal of the Art Market, History of Retailing and Consumption* and *Museum History Journal*.

Andrew Perchard is an honorary Research Professor at Te Whare Wānanga o Ōtākou – University of Otago. He is the author of *The Mine Management Professions in the Twentieth Century Scottish Coal Mining Industry* (2007) and *Aluminiumville: Government, Global Business and the Scottish Highlands* (2012) and co-editor of *Tin and Global Capitalism: A History of the 'Devil's Metal'* (2014) and *The Deindustrialized World: Industrial Ruination in Postindustrial Places* (2017). He was previously head of energy supply policy at the Scottish Executive (now Scottish Government).

Preface

The face looking out from the cover of this book is that of Piara Singh Hayre, photographed in his Knox Road shop in late 1960s Wolverhampton. His lived experience and the wider history of the British Asian shopkeeper sits at the confluence of the local and the global, which is a prominent theme in this book. Yet this is not where the idea for the book began. First came a rather different question: where does the emergence of the charity shop so familiar on British high streets today fit into the history of retail and consumption? As a charity historian turning his eye to the various ways charities had entered the world of retailing over recent centuries, I could find little trace of them in the historical scholarship. Things were very different for the co-operative movement, another case of retailing with a social purpose, the importance of which had long been recognized alongside supermarkets, chains and department stores. Once I started engaging with these wider histories, it was clear there was a bigger question in play: in the case of retailing – whether charitable, co-operative or commercial – what did it mean to be *modern*? A focus on either connection with, alienation from or exploitation of various communities, from the local to the global, can render very different ideas of what we understand to be modern retailing, the modern consumer or indeed the modern age.

To explore these questions, I gravitated towards the Centre for the History of Retailing and Distribution (CHORD) at the University of Wolverhampton. Founded in 1993, this continues to be a major hub for retail history scholarship, and most of the chapters in this collection began as papers presented at CHORD workshops by academics and PhD students from a host of disciplines, as well as archivists and heritage professionals. Five of them were given at the May 2019 workshop on the theme of *Retailing and Community: The Social Dimensions of Commerce*, which ended with plans for a collection of some kind to be headed up by myself and Grace Millar, who was working in the department as a researcher on a major project on the oral history of mining communities. We brought in a number of other contributors and set about pinning down the common themes and threads that ran through our eclectic set of case studies. This was a deliberately collaborative process, with every contributor reading other chapters and helping with the broader task of sensemaking that shaped the collection as a whole.

Global connections and contexts emerged as one of the major themes shaping our English retail histories. This ranged from real and imagined global connections to post-imperial encounters and comparisons. We slowed down the process to allow for Commonwealth migration and the end of empire to receive greater attention from chapters being refocused and reimagined as well as a new addition to our slate of contributors. The COVID-19 pandemic then slowed us down further, providing some contributors with time for writing while preventing others from visiting archives. The project was then re-energized when contributor Alix Green joined the editorial team. Where Grace was central to the task of organizing the collection and establishing its core themes, Alix took the lead on how they speak to us today. Alix's work on tightening the chapters and Grace's on sharpening the writing and getting the manuscript ready for publication have been invaluable. Without either of them, this book would likely never have been realized.

We would like to thank the anonymous readers and the editorial team at Bristol University Press, who have helped to strengthen the book and brought it to publication as speedily and smoothly possible. We are also grateful to Anand Chhabra of the Apna Heritage Archive project, who supplied the cover image, and all the archivists who have enabled the research presented in this book. Finally, we would also like to acknowledge that open access publication of this book would not have been possible without the generosity of both the Library and the Centre for Historical Research at the University of Wolverhampton.

George Campbell Gosling
University of Wolverhampton

Retail and Community: English Experiences and International Encounters in the Long 20th Century

George Campbell Gosling, Alix R. Green and Grace Millar

Introduction

'A good position is one of the great secrets of success in business', declared Gordon Selfridge at the 1922 grand opening of a new shop on Regent Street, less than a mile away from his famous department store in London's fashionable West End. This was the new flagship store of the charity St Dunstan's, which had been providing rehabilitation and retraining for blind veterans since the early days of the First World War. The mats, baskets, wooden trays and other craft items made by St Dunstaners were sold from this prime location until the 1960s, and of it, said Selfridge, 'no organisation in the country is more deserving'.[1]

At the turn of the 20th century, many charities ran workshops training the disabled or the poor in handicrafts and helped sell the items made.[2] St Dunstan's was notable for two reasons. First, it was a remarkably successful high-end example of this model, combining modern retailing with elite philanthropy. Their business-like approach embraced contemporary styles for store design, lighting and window displays while emphasizing the quality of products for sale. Aristocratic and even royal endorsements reinforced the clear message presented in shop windows and mail order catalogues alike that being a customer was a way of living up to the community's responsibility to aid 'victory over blindness'.[3] St Dunstan's usually avoided saying explicitly that buying from them was an act of charity. Yet that would have been clear to passers-by reading:

All the goods in this window have been made by Sailors, Soldiers and Airmen blinded in the Great War: they are strong, well finished and good value: the proof by sales that their work is appreciated is a great encouragement to them

BUY SOMETHING TO-DAY
ONE GOOD TURN DESERVES ANOTHER.[4]

The second reason St Dunstan's is a notable example is that it not only trained its charitable recipients but often set them up as small shopkeepers. Whenever possible St Dunstaners were expected to open their own shops, using their new artisan skills to serve local communities around the country, while the charity found ways 'to sell those goods which cannot be disposed of locally'.[5] By 1951, the After Care Department was paying regular visits to 140 shopkeepers. Many had branched out beyond selling their own craft goods, with picture framers selling art supplies and others trading as confectioners, newsagents and tobacconists. Only rarely were these stores owned by the charity, yet photographs show it was common for a sign over the door to announce that the shopkeeper had been 'trained by St Dunstan's'.[6] The reputation of the charity was thus traded on and customers made aware of the social purpose of lending their support, not to a fundraising effort but to a commercial venture in which the St Dunstaner was working to make a profit just like any other shopkeeper.

Across much of the early and mid-20th century there were a significant number of blind shopkeepers all around the country being supported by the charity. At a time when the presence of broken and brutalized men was widely seen as posing a moral threat to the community, there was a further dimension to supporting blind veterans to set themselves up in business. Where disabled and unemployed veterans might constitute a radical political force in other countries, St Dunstan's was part of a wider effort that sought to re-establish them as 'breadwinning fathers and husbands'.[7] Yet in the case of the shopkeepers, cultural reassurance went beyond breadwinner domesticity, with the St Dunstaner as head of both a household and a small business. The new identity and social position offered was not that of the respectable worker, aligning instead with an old idea of England as being traditionally a 'nation of shopkeepers'.[8] The long-serving chairman of St Dunstan's, Ian Fraser, himself blinded at the Somme, hoped the St Dunstaner opening his own shop would have 'the added advantage of stimulating local interest in his welfare'.[9] Setting up shop in a community was assumed to be one and the same as establishing oneself as a member of that community.

Such close and complex interrelationships between retail and community more widely are at the heart of the following chapters, which present some of the latest research on the histories of retailing over 150 years, from the late 19th to the early 21st centuries. The focus here tends to be on small-scale, urban retailing. It was in urban settings that we find the key developments in the emergence of modern retail, while in small-scale retailing we find the clearest evidence that the dramatic changes of the 20th century were only part of the story. Meanwhile, the chapters' specific case studies are drawn from across England, rather than the Four Nations. This allows for a complex and diverse picture to be presented without any implication that the distinctiveness of Irish, Scottish or Welsh retail was a mere variation of a shared retailing culture.

Each of the following chapters speaks to one or more of our three overarching themes. The first of these is how social contexts and networks have influenced and in turn been influenced by retailing. Trading initiatives as social projects to aid the disabled or the poor place this front and centre, but they can also be seen in retailers' practices of employment, payment and credit, and their relationships with the local communities within which they operate. As a multidisciplinary collection, the chapters here engage with a variety of ways in which community has been understood. This includes the investigations of sociologists and others into networks of kinship and explorations of who has historically belonged or been excluded. We also contribute to debates rooted in human geography and community studies on what has been lost as the social consequences of economic change – and importantly what was *not* lost.

The second theme brings together the emergent scholarship on the history of charity retail with new thinking in more established areas of retail history. The St Dunstan's case shows a different kind of *charity shop* to that which is familiar today, neither selling second-hand goods nor trading as a form of fundraising, and offers a glimpse into a longer and more varied history of charity retail than is often imagined. The prominence of charity retail in this collection, with case studies including but also going far beyond the late-Victorian bazaar and the postwar charity shop, is a conscious effort to redress an imbalance. Bringing histories of charity retail into conversation with those of co-operative and commercial retailers' social aims and interconnections invites a rethinking of familiar narratives of ever-increasing depersonalization and instrumentalization in modern retail.

Third, our analytical frame embraces both the local and the global. Some chapters emphasize the importance of local communities, bringing politics, class, race and gender to the forefront. Specific case studies are drawn from London and Leamington Spa, the Black Country, Manchester and the North East of England, and are all located within a broader frame. This framing recognizes the ways in which local stories play out against much wider backdrops. Britain's place in the world and how this was understood at home were central to the local-to-local cultural transmission evident in exotically themed markets or in the neo-imperial project to export the Oxford charity shop tradition to a former colony. St Dunstaners lived this complexity, establishing themselves as shopkeepers in local communities, supported by a national charity working with imperial veterans in the aftermath of two world wars. These chapters demonstrate the potency of retail to explore historical connections between the local and the global.

While the chapters in this collection share these core concerns, they approach them in a variety of ways. As a multidisciplinary collection, the contributors employ different methods, draw upon different types of sources and use different scholarly languages to make sense of the multifaceted historic relationship between retail and community.[10] In some cases, this means making explicit the sociological or ethnographic nature of the research presented, or its relevance to the heritage industry or archival contexts within which the research was conducted. In others, it is implicit in the routine use by historians of theories developed in other disciplines, reflecting the fact that, as Ludmilla Jordanova has convincingly argued, 'history is profoundly interdisciplinary'. 'Thematic overlap, shared concepts and broad approaches' are at the heart of a deep-rooted 'kinship' between history and the social sciences, which might be expected given the 'absence of watertight categories, and the subject matter, approaches, concepts and themes shared between the many fields that concern themselves with human existence, individual and collective'.[11] We do not take interdisciplinarity to mean the subsumption of history; if anything, the interdisciplinary enterprise relies on a keen sense of *disciplinarity*: what is distinctive about a field's approaches and methods. This might be the historian's preoccupation with disrupting or complicating too-neat structures of time or her attentiveness to archival sources in the contexts of their production and retention, resisting conceptualizations of the archive as a site of data extraction and of the archivist as gatekeeper.[12] Record creation, organization and retention require our critical attention – not just the content we can glean from their present-day presentation. This applies across retail settings to the records produced by charities and voluntary organizations, co-operative societies and commercial retailers large and small, and is a task immeasurably enriched though engagement with archivists.

This collection takes a porous understanding of historical practice as both necessary and generative for the study of retail and community. Beyond informing individual chapters, the involvement of scholars from a range of disciplines, working in a variety of academic and other research environments, has been integral to the dialogic development of the book and its treatment of its overarching themes. The remainder of this chapter serves to locate the following chapters within the scholarship on each of these three themes: the community and social dimensions of modern retailing, the place of charity retail within this, and the significance of wider global contexts in influencing the development of retailer–community relationships.

Community in retail history

This collection contributes to a strand of scholarship that complicates the dominant narrative of a transition from traditional to modern retail by challenging the assumption that the social dimensions of retailing were left behind in the process. In presenting case studies of continuity and adaptation, rather than decline, we break from views of modernity that draw binary distinctions between traditional lives, deeply embedded within a series of social relationships and rooted in a specific place, and unrooted modern lives. As far as there was any clear transition from the traditional to the modern, it was more than a matter of shedding social entanglements and did not always render encounters between increasingly atomized individuals ever more transactional. The history of modern retail – as of modernity itself – is not one in which *community* is simply something lost. A fuller understanding requires us to ask questions about the changing nature of belonging and the boundaries of inclusion and exclusion.[13] In order to understand how the social dimensions of retail played out over the long 20th century, we must first trace the changes seen in the world of retail during this time.

The emergence of modern retail has traditionally been seen as beginning in the late 19th century. Although historians have been keen to highlight earlier innovations, the notion remains influential that there was a change across Western Europe and North America around this time when, as Selfridge put it, 'a few shop-keepers became inoculated with the spirit of enterprise' and 'grew beyond the little shop'.[14] He saw 'the modern spirit of organization' represented by the new department store, both through the scale of its operation and its impact in the locality: 'It is intimately associated with every family in the community in supplying them with the necessities of life, and thus by force of circumstances enters into the daily life of the city in which it is.'[15] Historians have tended to agree that department stores had a significant impact in a number of respects. For retail historians, they relocated consumption to city centres and were instrumental in the establishment of new practices for displaying, advertising and pricing the goods on sale, alongside rationalization and a 'managerial revolution'.[16] Meanwhile, cultural histories of *the* department store have explored the extent to which it was architecturally and symbolically something new and exciting, promising democratized luxury and the opportunity to browse as a form of leisure activity.[17]

Writing in the 1950s, James B. Jefferys identified the emergence of the department store alongside two other defining trends over the late 19th and early 20th centuries. One was the growth of the co-operative movement, strongest in its industrial heartlands in the North West and East Midlands.[18] Local societies typically established themselves by selling groceries and provisions, always adhering to the model set out in 1844 by the Rochdale

Pioneers which saw surplus profits returned to members in the form of a dividend.[19] The other trend was the rise of multiple store retailers (or chains), whereby expansion was made profitable through economies of scale, standardization and prioritizing low prices over luxury. By 1914, both the newsagent WH Smith & Son and the Singer Sewing Machine Company had over 1,000 sales outlets, with the likes of Lipton Ltd, the Home and Colonial Tea Company and the Boots Pure Drug Company not far behind.[20]

It was only over the middle of the 20th century, however, that these and other new forms of retail became the norm. Mass retailing and mass consumption developed less rapidly over this period than it did in the United States, though the transformation was still dramatic.[21] As John Benson noted, by the 1980s 'British shoppers [had] transferred the bulk of their custom from small, local retailers ... to larger, more centralised, and more impersonal outlets'.[22] At the forefront of retailers adopting the practice of selling pre-packaged branded goods at a fixed price were the new self-service supermarkets.[23] Increasingly the customer's guarantee of quality came from the standardized product and the way it was mass advertised, rather than through negotiation and relationship with a specialist retailer. What might be celebrated as greater freedom for the consumer could also be regretted as a loss, though felt differently according to class. This might be a loss of the economic advantages of credit and bargaining for working-class consumers, and equally a loss of the subservience displayed to middle-class customers.[24]

If the mid-20th century saw the relationship between buyer and seller depersonalized and disentangled from local relationships, then the past half-century has seen it commonly relocated from localities altogether. By the 1990s, out-of-town British versions of the North American shopping mall were being developed.[25] Retailing moved further away from traditional urban sites when it then migrated online more dramatically in the United Kingdom than elsewhere in Europe. This was evident long before the COVID-19 lockdowns, with one in five Britons having bought food online by 2012, and 15 per cent of all retail sales taking place online by 2014.[26] These changes combined have prompted an existential crisis for the high street and bricks-and-mortar retailing more generally.[27]

The core narrative of these changes is one in which retailing has been standardized, depersonalized and essentially uprooted from the communities within which it operates. Where historians have explored the limits and counternarratives to this, they have tended to do so with a focus on credit.[28] For Margot Finn, 'Victorian and Edwardian tradesmen remained hostages to traditions of consumer activity rooted in credit, character and connection', which worked against the emergence of economic relationships entirely defined by the cash nexus.[29] Sean O'Connell has seen some continuity despite the further developments of the 20th century, as 'agents from within working-class communities made many business decisions on behalf of mail order catalogue companies or the large-scale moneylenders'.[30] Meanwhile, in his study of working-class credit in Tyneside, Avram Taylor looked to 'the interpenetration of instrumental and affectual spheres of action' to explain the apparent contradiction that small shopkeepers 'were part of the communities that they exploited'.[31] The chapters in this collection consider credit as one of a variety of ways to explore the place of retailers within those communities.

This is clearest when looking at small-scale retailing, which has, despite the modernizations and consumer revolutions of the 20th century, remained an important part of the retail landscape. Michael Winstanley acknowledged this for the early part of the century, noting that the great many independent traders and small shopkeepers who survived tended to be skilled specialists rather than the general stores more easily displaced by the supermarket.[32] Moreover, and significantly for our purposes, he found they often 'value[d] social and psychological rewards which find no place in the balance sheet or the economic textbooks', placing independence and respectability ahead of a simple calculation of profits made.[33] The tendency to overlook small-scale retailing continued into the 21st century, as John Benson and Laura Ugolini noted: 'The hawker and peddler, the Saturday-night market, the corner shop and even the specialist grocer, clothes shop and off-license can all too easily be relegated to a sepia-tinted, Christmas-card version of the world we have lost.'[34]

These traders have undoubtedly had to operate alongside increasingly large-scale, automated and depersonalized alternatives, but small-scale retailing – often with a local and personal character – has never stopped being an important part of *modern retail*. Indeed, in 2018, those with fewer than five employees accounted for three-quarters of VAT (Value Added Tax) or PAYE (Pay As You Earn) based enterprises in the UK retail sector.[35] Despite the challenges and disruptions of the COVID-19 pandemic, discussed in Chapter 14, small traders are still an important part of contemporary retailing. We therefore cannot understand retail, historically or today, if we overlook small-scale and local retailers.[36] And it is the tailor in Leamington Spa, the fundraising bazaar in Darlington, the womenswear shop in the Black Country, the charity shop in Manchester, the fish and chip shop in County Durham and the British Asian corner shops up and down the country which occupy much of this book.

'Successful small shopkeeping' in the early 20th century, as Christopher Hosgood put it, 'demanded an investment by the proprietor in the social life of the community'.[37] In Chapter 7, Nadia Awal and Jenny Gilbert document this in the cases of two small female-owned clothing retailers trading throughout the 20th century. As brought to the surface in a new heritage project at the Black Country Living Museum, the buying and selling of women's clothing was and continued to be social, tactile and embedded in community networks, deeply rooted in place and regional identity. Meanwhile, it is local contexts and cultures that Ian Mitchell tells us, in Chapter 4, explain not only the business success or otherwise of individual co-operative societies, but also the choices made in balancing paying out the members' dividend and funding a range of educational, social, cultural and political projects. In doing so he adds to our understanding of both co-operative retailing and the political movement.[38]

Credit was often central to a small shopkeeper's standing in their community. In Chapter 3, Nick Gray sheds new light on its social dynamics at the turn of the 20th century, focusing on a Leamington Spa tailor shop as a case study. He shows how important male, middle-class social relationships were to credit, and credit to the business, with customer loyalty more significant than social status for understanding business practices. In working-class communities, shopkeepers have been described as 'bankers of the poor', with a moral obligation to support regular customers through times of hardship.[39] Mitchell tells us in Chapter 4 that similar practices were to be found in local co-op stores, despite their supposed insistence on cash payments. Meanwhile, in Chapter 12, the authors find this to be true on the other side of the world in 1950s New Zealand and at the other end of what might be called *the short 20th century* during the 1980s Miners' Strike. Prolonged industrial action in each case led to credit and other forms of economic and material support being provided not only by small shopkeepers and co-ops, but even supermarkets, presenting a challenge to typical narratives of the impact of supermarkets on the relationship between retailers and the communities within which they operate. Rather than it being customers who maintained older modes of shopping and forms of social relationships, the authors find times of widespread hardship revealing that retailers continued to be rooted in community networks of solidarity.

Large-scale retailers' histories of community relationships also include the co-operative John Lewis Partnership. As Alix R. Green discusses in Chapter 10, John Lewis found the racial politics of Commonwealth immigration complicating its principles of 'colour-blind' recruitment. Through relationships with their staff and local communities, large-scale retailers found they were not so insulated from the political environments they operated in. Meanwhile, geographers have identified cases where consumers have come to treat out-of-town shopping centres as in some senses a 'new town centre', suggesting a greater degree of continuity in the relationship between retail and community spaces – even if relocated – than critics envisaged.[40] Optimistic impressions of this kind run counter to Robert Owen's initial scepticism about the precursors of the Rochdale movement two centuries ago, paraphrased as the view 'that a community might set up a shop, but a shop could never set up a community'.[41] In contributing to this literature, the chapters presented here suggest that the ways retailers engaged with their social contexts was far from unaltered by the changes of the modern era, but neither were they entirely swept away.

Charity retail

This collection addresses the very limited inclusion of charity retail in retail history scholarship. This is especially striking given the attention from scholars across a wide range of disciplines prompted by the growth in the number of charity shops in the final decades of the 20th century. These were retail outlets run usually as one of a number of shops trading to raise funds for the same charity, typically staffed at least in part by volunteers and primarily selling donated second-hand goods. At the time of writing, there are over 10,000 such shops in the United Kingdom.[42]

Charity shops are not an exclusively British phenomenon, although the latest available figures do show the United Kingdom to have more per head than any other country in the world, at 15.22 charity shops per 100,000 population in 2023.[43] This is significantly more than the equivalent figures for North American charity-run *thrift stores*, which (even grouped together with other kinds of resale retailers) would be roughly half the UK rate in the United States and only a quarter in Canada.[44] The only other countries to come close are New Zealand (12.56) and Australia (9.60), where they tend to be called *opportunity shops* or *op shops* for short, and the Republic of Ireland (10.42).[45] The most common charity-run stores across the rest of Europe are the *world shops* (previously *third world shops*) selling foodstuffs and craft items produced ethically in the Global South. Germany leads the way with 900 of Europe's 2,500 world shops today, though compared to population this is only around one per 100,000 people.[46]

Most of the United Kingdom's charity shops are in England, along with the vast majority of the population. However, pre-COVID-19 figures showed that, of the constituent Four Nations, England in fact had the lowest number of charity shops per head (at 16.61 per 100,000), behind Wales (17.86) and Northern Ireland (17.83) and noticeably lower than Scotland (18.48).[47] An independent Scotland would therefore have the highest number of charity shops per head in the world. This stands in stark contrast to only 68 South African charity shops listed by Charity SA (1.13 per 100,000).[48] In Chapter 9, Jessica Field looks to the 1970s as a time when there were efforts to export the British model of the charity shop to the former colony. The difficulties these efforts ran into offer some insight into the geographical boundaries of this retailing phenomenon.

It is this distinctly, though not uniquely, British form of charity retail that first came under serious investigation from a range of disciplinary perspectives in the 1990s, led initially by retail and marketing researchers. The reasons for growth were identified as both the increased popularity of supporting charities as customers and donors, and the willingness of charities to embrace the fundraising opportunities presented by turbulence across the retail sector, including vacated premises.[49] In 1992 researchers found that 41 per cent of charity shops were run by medical or disability charities, 18 per cent by international development organizations and 14 per cent by children's charities.[50] Detailed surveys profiled the charity shopper, finding that more than half the population had bought from a charity shop, and investigated how distinctions of class, education, gender and generation played out in patterns of and motivations for charity shopping, donating and volunteering.[51] Contemporary charity shop retailing and consumption was mapped out.

Sociologists and geographers were among those who brought a heightened focus on the charity shop as a site of alternative modes of consumption, with the commodification of donated and sold items complicating the supposedly linear process of production and consumption. This means that 'goods are not only potentially resaleable but are open to re-enchantment; they have consumption histories and geographies just as much as production histories and geographies'.[52] The motivations for consumers to engage in this process can range from affordable provisioning to using obscure purchases for positioning themselves within subcultures or as a political choice to engage in 'alternative economies' as a way of 'fighting against the capitalist system'.[53]

By the turn of the 21st century, the distinctiveness of this model of retailing, and the tax advantages it brings, were widely seen as being undermined by the increasing professionalization of the charity shop.[54] Suzanne Horne mapped this onto a continuum, whereby the development of a charity retailing operation entailed moving from a 'social service orientation' to a 'commercial service orientation', resulting in 'a retail sector which at one end of the scale shows unrivalled retail professionalism and at the other a safety net for the socially excluded in society'.[55] The social and community functions that a charity shop might leave behind in its *professionalization* were listed by Elizabeth Parsons as including 'providing a contact point between the parent charity and the general public, providing clothes and household goods cheaply for customers, providing useful employment, support and training for a range of volunteers, and recycling unwanted household items'.[56] Researchers emphasized the complexity of these developments.[57] Richard Goodall noted that 'professionalisation and commercialisation' were accompanied by 'alternatives and counterposed resistances'.[58] Equally, Parsons' typology of charity shops revealed that the most profitable were not always the most professionalized, with community-rooted local hospice shops a clear counter-example.[59]

This debate took place during a temporary decline in the number of charity shops, which was widely mistaken for the onset of a period of retraction after decades of growth. As growth returned, there was a let up in the pressure to address the 'unusual cocktail of values' informing the retail practices of what had become 'a hybrid sector'.[60] Triona Fitton's ethnographic participant observation research set out to observe *in situ* the ongoing and unresolved heterogeneity of everyday practices in charity shops, moving the discussion on from 'top-down processes' to 'how these are played out by actors within the physical space of the charity shop itself'.[61] She found professionalization's bureaucracy, rationality and impersonality countered by price negotiations, the continued importance of unpaid staff's informal obligations, and connections with the public and private sectors.[62] It is the last of these which is the focus of her contribution here (Chapter 13), historicizing this changing aspect of charity shop retailing practices not only in relation to developments in the sector but also the wider political and economic context of the period following the global financial crash of 2008. In doing so, she documents the sometimes-perverse implications recent practices have had on the *gift relationship* in the charity shop, establishing a 'subversive moral economy' that reveals the complexities of interactions between social and economic goals in charity retailing.

More widely, this collection locates the charity shop of recent decades within a longer and more varied history of charities engaging in retail. In the 1970s, Frank Prochaska identified bazaars as a notable aspect of middle-class women's involvement in 19th-century public life, as seen in the fact they were sometimes referred to as 'ladies' sales'. He traced the growth of the charity bazaar, in parallel with the commercial bazaar, between the 1810s and the 1840s. Estimating there were still annually over 1,000 bazaars across the country at the end of the century, he projected tens of thousands raised over the century as a whole by bazaars ranging from the grandest which might be patronized by the Duke of Wellington or Queen Victoria to small rural sales, of which little trace has been left behind.[63] The Anti-Corn Law League Bazaar of 1845, which Prochaska thought 'probably the most profitable and long-lived fancy fair of the century', was said by Peter Gurney to have 'collapsed consumption and politics together and perfectly captured, both materially and symbolically, the ultimate ambition of the League: to turn the whole world into a giant bazaar'.[64] By the end of the 19th century, organizers had moved beyond exploiting the 'captive bazaar audience' for fundraising purposes to work with commercial partners on developing the charitable commodity on offer, which was one of many ways the likes of Dr Barnardo and the Salvation Army have been seen as leading the way in the emerging 'charity market'.[65] In these changes the elements of spectacle and entertainment increasingly took on international and 'exotic' themes, as explored by Massimiliano Papini in Chapter 2, focusing on the Mikado Festival in the North East of England in the 1880s.

The contemporary scholarship on charity shops occasionally briefly acknowledges bazaars as part of a longer history of fundraising retail, including the earliest incarnations of Salvation Army thrift stores.[66] A more comprehensive account of Salvationist retailing is offered here across two chapters. The idea of retailing that not only adheres to the values and principles of the Salvationist movement, but also raises funds that can be reinvested into growing that movement, is discussed in Chapter 5 by Marjorie Gehrhardt. She traces the impact of the 1890 'Darkest England' social scheme on the various retailing operations run by the Salvation Army's Trade Department, which developed beyond fundraising initiatives to become a vehicle for the Army's core social mission. The fact that some of its schemes were highly profitable exposed it to fierce criticism, to which the response was partly an argument that consumption of the goods for sale was the material embodiment of belonging to the Salvationist community. This rationale could apply beyond the central Trade Headquarters, to the early thrift stores attached to local social centres and the retail activities run from the women's rescue homes. In Chapter 6, Ruth Macdonald explains that it was keeping these trading operations separate that allowed them to remain so firmly embedded in the social mission to *rescue* women from lives of poverty and immorality, restoring them to *respectability*. Beyond the moral environment of the homes as sites for needlework, the production and sale of the items they made were opportunities for the women to build connections and strengthen their membership of the Salvationist community, reinforcing their newfound respectability. As with the St Dunstaners running shops, economic considerations were not unimportant, yet they were firmly enmeshed with the social and moral dimensions of buying and selling that meant charity retailing was never simply transactional.

It is within this diverse history of charity retailing that we ought to see the development of the modern British charity shop, charted by George Campbell Gosling in Chapter 8. Whereas developments since the 1990s have been well documented, significant contributions on the preceding decades have been notably rare and tend to focus on the retailing operations of the international development charity Oxfam. 'Business acumen and concern for social change became tangibly entwined' when the charity's flagship store opened on Broad Street in Oxford in 1947, Jessica Field has argued, constituting 'consumption and giving as mutually reinforcing ethics' and 'charity shopping as a key form of popular philanthropic action'.[67] Between its shops and its trading company, established in the mid-1960s, Tehila Sasson has gone as far as to suggest that 'Oxfam changed consumerism into an ethical act, a choice that went beyond what one *wants* to what one *ought* to purchase'.[68] Yet the same connection between items for sale and the social projects from which they originate, fusing charity and consumption, might be seen in the 'one good turn deserves another' sales pitch of disability charities like St Dunstan's or the retailing linked to the Salvation Army's rescue work and other job creation schemes discussed in Chapters 5 and 6.

When our focus shifts from consumption to retailing, Gosling suggests, we find postwar charity shops rooted in the associational culture of local communities, largely independent of the fundraising or fair trade aims of the parent charity.

All of which suggests the need to locate Oxfam and the contemporary charity shop in the context of a wider history of charity retail, something to which numerous chapters in this collection contribute. It is equally enlightening to bring the history of charity retail into conversation with the histories of commercial and co-operative retailing, as this collection does. Offering historical perspective sheds new light on more recent concerns in relation to charity retail: assessments of the relative merits and dangers of replacing charity shop volunteers with paid staff, reducing the predominance of second-hand goods in the merchandising mix, and implementing more business-like and commercially oriented retail practices. Doing so reveals that these all echo the tensions, discussed earlier, which characterized the (supposedly linear) transition from *traditional* to *modern* retailing.

From the local to the global

The chapters in this collection respond to the call of Benson and Ugolini that historians 'should look to the broader economic, political and social environment within which retailers (and potential retailers), customers (and potential customers) found themselves'.[69] Those environments, and the factors that shaped them, did not stop at the water's edge. For this reason, the following chapters consider the international and global dimensions of modern retail's social embeddedness alongside the local, the regional and the national. They are therefore in step with a broader disciplinary shift that recognizes the extent of transnational connections; no longer treating national borders as stable, inevitable markers of historical analysis nor of human organization or identity.[70] Efforts by British historians in the 1990s 'to recast the nation as an imperialized space ... materialize[d] the traffic of colonial goods, ideas and people across metropolitan borders and indeed [threw] into question the very Victorian distinctions between Home and Away that defined the imaged geography of empire'.[71] Gregory A. Barton's favoured response was a 'British World model' focused on the 'elite transformations, trading patterns, and cultural exchange that gave rise to a single global culture'.[72] Although critiqued for its lack of engagement with the diversities and power dynamics of imperial history, this scholarly project has shed new light on the histories of global Britishness and Britain's place in the world through its networks across the globe.[73] This adds to the longer-running explorations of imperialism as a cultural phenomenon, focusing instead on the impact of the world, including the British Empire, on Britain itself.[74] In keeping with this diversity of scholarly approaches, various chapters in this collection adopt different ways of exploring the movement of people, practices and products in, to and from modern English retailing.

Within retail histories at the local level, we can see wider global entanglements playing out through the impact of migration. It was not uncommon historically for migrants to secure an income from itinerant trading as hawkers or pedlars. As Benson and Ugolini have noted, 'the economic disadvantages and cultural discrimination faced by many working-class and minority families encouraged them to enter trades like hawking and peddling and small shopkeeping, which demanded only a small initial investment and provided the opportunity to turn their working-class/ minority identity to economic advantage'.[75]

Mui and Mui drew a distinction between 18th-century hawkers and pedlars in the North of England, whose trading they saw as complementing the range of goods on sale in local shops, and those in the South who were widely perceived to be in more direct competition with local shopkeepers.[76] It was those southern concerns that prompted reforms in 1832, whereby acquiring a licence required character references to prove local connections and social standing. Among those who suffered were the Scottish and Irish itinerant sellers identified by Alison Toplis as filling a gap in the rural retailing of non-elite women's clothing in early 19th-century Herefordshire and Worcestershire.[77] The same can be assumed of the Jewish traders commonly associated with the itinerant selling of second-hand clothes by this time.[78]

Historians and migration scholars, as Léa Leboissetier has noted, have viewed the more recent history of itinerant trading differently. Historians have typically written it off as a form of retail that fell into decline over the 19th and 20th centuries and was not a significant part of *modern retailing*, while migration scholars have recognized its continuing significance for those seeking to make a living in a new place.[79] Despite this, the opportunity dramatically declined over the postwar period as traditional door-to-door sellers lost out to the new mail order catalogues, whose part-time agents were more often women drawn from the local community than offering an entry point into it.[80] At the same time, other forms of employment were becoming easier to find. For the first generation of postwar Commonwealth immigrants, as Kennetta Hammond Perry has noted, manual work was both easy to find and assumed by employers and the state to be suitable for Black workers.[81] By contrast, the widespread manufacturing redundancies in the 1970s prompted growing numbers of Sikhs and other Punjabi migrants to pool family savings and purchase a shop.[82] These patterns and the wider relationship between retail and migration over the 20th century remain ripe for further study.

One area of immigrant retailing which is better addressed in the scholarship (more often by migration studies scholars than historians) is that in relation to food. 'Historically', as Marta Rabikowska and Kathy Burrell have noted, 'food has always been central in maintaining ethnic identity away from the original homeland, and an important means of asserting a presence on the new landscape through market stalls, shops and restaurants'.[83] As Anne Kerschen observed:

> [I]t is not only hunger which impels the migrant. Perceived economic opportunity either in the exporting or importing of 'exotic' foodstuffs or in the transportation of culinary cultures has been a determining factor in the migrant's rationalisation of destination. The burgeoning of ethnic food purveyors and restaurants bearing witness to this phenomenon of voluntary migration. Within the British context it has to be recognised that, allied to the beacon of upward economic mobility has been the legacy of imperialism which set in place the chain migration of immigrants from Pakistan and Bangladesh, countries which today provide the bulk of Britain's Indian restaurant owners and workers. It is a chain forged out of a British colonialism which employed Indian lascars, mainly from east Bengal, to work on the ships that carried the spices, fruits and tea – that most English of drinks – from lands far away to the heart of the Empire.[84]

The association between food selling and Italian immigrants in London had grown from the ice cream street vendor to the many restaurants serving Italian and other cuisines by 1928, when the first Indian grocery shop was opened to serve the growing number of Indian students, businessmen and officials in the city.[85] Nearly a century later, Rabikowska and Burrell have noted that 'the need for Polish food has dominated business activities among and aimed at the new immigrants' of the early 21st century.[86] In the decades in between, historian Panikos Panayi has traced a shift from the era of 'the foreign restaurant', when relatively small numbers of migrants opened shops and restaurants, to a 'culinary revolution' in the postwar period.[87] This included the proliferation of Indian and Chinese restaurants which provided an opportunity for (often exploitative) employment through family and networks of newcomers.[88]

The relationship between migration and retail work in the postcolonial period is the specific focus of two chapters in this collection. Alix R. Green, in Chapter 10, uses the John Lewis archive to explore racialized definitions of inclusion in different communities within and beyond the retailer's co-operative partnership. She explores moments of tension in the 1950s and 1960s when the exclusion of Black Commonwealth migrants from employment were discussed internally, revealing tensions between a rhetoric of equality and the power given to imagined customers and their imagined views. In Chapter 11, Harshad Keval turns his attention to both the lived realities and deeply embedded narratives of the postcolonial 'encounter at the counter' in the British Asian corner shop over the last half century. Together, these chapters shed new light on how the racial politics of Commonwealth immigration in the postwar period was inscribed onto the world of retail, ranging from the large multiple trader to the independent small shopkeeper.

Movement in the other direction is explored in Chapter 9, where Jessica Field considers efforts in the 1970s to export the British model of the charity shop to South Africa. The relationship she details is a paternalistic and a racialized one, reflecting the entwined histories of charity retailing and global humanitarianism. She also demonstrates the conflict between the imagined community that charities believed they were helping, and the much more complicated relationships that existed within. If Field finds the limits of a *British world of retail*, in Chapter 12, Millar and her co-authors identify similar retailing practices employed during times of prolonged industrial disputes in both 1950s New Zealand and the United Kingdom in the 1980s. Independent traders, co-ops, department stores and even supermarkets all contributed to networks of solidarity and support. Even if the methods for doing so might vary with changing business practices, their role within the community was similar in the industrial North of England and the farthest reaches of the Commonwealth. Both chapters, in different ways, contextualize and complicate narratives of British exceptionalism in modern retailing.

Two chapters, including the next, consider the transcultural significance of selling global products. In Chapter 2, Massimiliano Papini presents the 1887 case study of a charity bazaar in the North East of England, where the local steel industry's connections with Japan had little impact on the middle-class organizers' construction of an idealized imagining of pre-modern Japan. Papini's transcultural framing acknowledges the importance of imperialism alongside other discourses. For Gosling, in Chapter 8, it is the end of empire and the rethinking of British global responsibility that provides the context for international development charities' forays into alternative trading in the 1960s and 1970s. In both cases, the impact of international dimensions is limited, though from different directions. At the bazaar, the Japanese-themed fantasy to the setting and the goods for sale had a tenuous relationship to Japan itself and the money raised went to a local religious charity. For Oxfam, Christian Aid and others, the objective was to find new markets for craft items and later foodstuffs produced in the countries where they operated: the aim was global and charitable. These efforts, however, struggled to find a place within a domestic charity retail sector that was already well established as being geared towards local second-hand selling. The postwar charity shop was not a space where the local and the global found an easy accommodation.

Conclusion

Two decades ago, Benson and Ugolini made a strong case for 'a more nuanced approach to retail "patterns and processes", with a greater awareness of local circumstances, of small as well as large enterprises, and of the "traditional" alongside the supposedly "modern"'.[89] The chapters brought together in this collection do so in a variety of ways, drawing upon a range of disciplinary methods to engage with our three overarching themes of the social and community dimensions of retailing, the place of charity alongside commercial and co-operative retailing, and the significance of wider international connections and global contexts. They each explore different histories of retailers with significant community connections, though not only the local community within which they were geographically located. From the local to the global, social contexts and community networks have shaped and been shaped by retail operations, even as the development of the modern consumer society was thought to be leaving them behind.

The following chapters show, in different ways, that change in 20th-century retailing was about much more than ever-larger chains competing for their share of a globalized market. The changes in retail practice and technology were real and they transformed consumer culture.[90] They were, however, not the full story. By exploring retail and community, we hope to draw attention to socially contextualized experiences of buying and selling that defy easy attribution of scale. By looking beyond shopping malls and multinational chains, we find the spaces of personal interaction where global stories played out at street level.

Acknowledgements

This chapter has benefited from the advice of Laura Ugolini and the ongoing support of Rob Baker, archivist at Blind Veterans UK.

Notes

1   *St Dunstan's Review*, 67, July 1922, 2.
2   A. Borsay, *Disability and Social Policy in Britain since 1750* (Basingstoke: Palgrave Macmillan, 2005), 123–128.
3   St Dunstan's, *Annual Report*, 1923, 13. For a wider discussion of the role of philanthropy in this field, see D. Cohen, *The War Come Home: Disabled Veterans in Britain and Germany, 1914–939* (University of California Press, 2001).
4   Blind Veterans UK archive, image _2GA8233, view of shop window with handicrafts displayed (c.1920s).
5   *St Dunstan's Review*, 19, February 1918, 12.
6   See St Dunstan's, *Annual Report*, 1923, 6.
7   M. Roper, *Afterlives of War: A Descendants' History* (Manchester University Press, 2023), 203.
8   While the origins of the phrase are disputed, it was held up as a historical reputation to be celebrated by Margaret Thatcher, 'Remarks after speaking to National Chamber

of Commerce', 17/02/1975, https://www.margaretthatcher.org/document/102496 (accessed 07/07/2023).

9   I. Fraser, 'Carrying on: how the blinded soldier is helped when he has left St. Dunstan's', in *A Record of Victory*, Annual Report of St Dunstan's for 1920, 4–5.

10 B. Vienni-Baptista, I. Fletcher and C. Lyall (eds), *Foundations of Interdisciplinary and Transdisciplinary Research: A Reader* (Bristol University Press, 2023), 30.

11 L. Jordanova, *History in Practice*, 3rd edn (London: Bloomsbury, 2019), chapter 4.

12 M.T. King, 'Working with/in the archives', in S. Gunn and L. Faire (eds), *Research Methods for History* (Edinburgh University Press, 2012), 13–29.

13 For an overview of these fields, see G. Delanty, *Community*, 3rd edn (London: Routledge, 2018).

14 H.G. Selfridge, *The Romance of Commerce* (John Lane: London, 1918), 364. On earlier innovations, see, for example, N. Cox, *The Complete Tradesman: A Study of Retailing, 1550–1820* (Aldershot: Ashgate, 2000); I. Mitchell, *Tradition and Innovation in English Retailing, 1700 to 1850: Narratives of Consumption* (Aldershot: Ashgate, 2014); J. Stobart, *Sugar and Spice: Grocers and Groceries in Provincial England, 1650–1830* (Oxford University Press, 2016).

15 Selfridge, *The Romance of Commerce*, 363.

16 J.B. Jefferys, *Retail Trading in Britain 1850–1950: A Study of Trends in Retailing with Special Reference to the Development of Co-operative, Multiple Shop and Department Store Methods of Trading* (Cambridge University Press, 1954), 19–21 and 59–61; B. Lancaster, *The Department Store: A Social History* (Leicester University Press, 1995); P. Scott and J. Walker, 'The British "failure" that never was? The Anglo-American "productivity gap" in large-scale interwar retailing – evidence from the department store sector', *Economic History Review*, 65:1 (2012), 277–303; J. Stobart, 'Cathedrals of Consumption? Provincial Department Stores in England, c.1880–1930', *Enterprise & Society*, 18:4 (2017), 810–845. On department stores as a threat to local traders, see M. Winstanley, *The Shopkeeper's World, 1839–1914* (Manchester University Press, 1988 [1983]), 34–36.

17 See for example M. Naca, 'Modernity's disavowal: women, the city and the department store', in P. Falk and C. Campbell (eds), *The Shopping Experience* (London: SAGE, 1997), 56–91; G. Crossick and S. Jaumain, 'The world of the department store: distribution, culture and social change', in G. Crossick and S. Jaumain (eds), *Cathedrals of Consumption: European Department Stores, 1850–1939* (London: Routledge, 1999); E. Rappaport, *Shopping for Pleasure: Women in the Making of London's West End* (Princeton University Press, 2000).

18 M. Purvis, 'The development of co-operative retailing in England and Wales, 1851–1901: a geographical study', *Journal of Historical Geography*, 16:3 (1990), 314–331.

19 Jefferys, *Retail Trading*, 16–18.

20 Jefferys, *Retail Trading*, 21–28.

21 S. Bowden and A. Offer, 'Household appliances and the use of time: the United States and Britain since the 1920s', *Economic History Review*, 47:4 (1994), 725–748.

22 J. Benson, *The Rise of Consumer Society in Britain, 1800–1980* (London: Longman, 1994), 61.

23 On the complexities of these developments, see G. Shaw, A. Bailey, A. Alexander, D. Nell and J. Hamlett, 'The introduction of self-service: the coming of the supermarket: the processes and consequences of transplanting American know-how into Britain', in R. Jessen and L. Langer (eds), *Transformations of Retailing in Europe after 1945* (Aldershot: Ashgate, 2012), 35–54; L. Black and T. Spain, 'How self-service happened: the vision and reality of changing market practices in Britain', in D. Thackeray, A. Thompson and R. Toye (eds), *Imagining Britain's Economic Future, c.1800–1975: Trade, Consumerism and Global Markets* (London: Palgrave Macmillan, 2018), 159–180.

24 Benson, *The Rise of Consumer Society*, 69. See also R. Bowlby, *Carried Away: The Invention of Modern Shopping* (London: Faber & Faber, 2000); P. Lyon, A. Colquhoun and D. Kinney,

'UK food shopping in the 1950s: the social context of customer loyalty', *International Journal of Consumer Studies*, 28:1 (2004), 28–39; Black and Spain, 'How self-service happened'.

[25] M. Lowe, 'From Victor Gruen to Merry Hill: reflections on regional shopping centres and urban development in the US and UK', in P. Jackson, M. Lowe, D. Miller and F. Mort (eds), *Commercial Cultures: Economies, Practices, Spaces* (Oxford: Berg, 2000), 245–260.

[26] F. Trentmann, *Empire of Things: How We Became a World of Consumers, from the Fifteenth Century to the Twenty-First* (London: Allen Lane, 2016), 481–482.

[27] Although supermarkets are now returning to small-scale trading on high streets in addition to large-scale and online retailing. See R. Bowlby, *Back to the Shops: The High Street in History and the Future* (Oxford University Press, 2022), 64–65.

[28] For notable early works in this field, see M. Tebbutt, *Making Ends Meet: Pawnbroking and Working Class Credit* (Leicester University Press, 1983) and P. Johnson, 'Credit and thrift in the British working class, 1870–1939', in J. Winter (ed), *The Working Class in Modern British History: Essays in Honour of Henry Pelling* (Cambridge University Press, 1985).

[29] M.C. Finn, *The Character of Credit: Personal Debt in English Culture, 1740–1914* (Cambridge University Press, 2003), 280.

[30] S. O'Connell, *Credit and Community: Working-Class Debt in the UK since 1880* (Oxford University Press, 2009), 3.

[31] A. Taylor, *Working Class Credit and Community since 1918* (Palgrave Macmillan, 2002), 181.

[32] Winstanley, *The Shopkeeper's World*, 217. On the adaptations required for specialist retailers, see M. Hilton, 'Retailing history as economic and cultural history: strategies of survival by specialist tobacconists in the mass market' in N. Alexander and G. Akehurst (eds), *The Emergence of Modern Retailing 1750–1950* (London: Frank Cass, 1999), 115–137.

[33] Winstanley, *The Shopkeeper's World*, 218. See also J. Benson, *The Penny Capitalists: A Study of Nineteenth-Century Working-Class Entrepreneurs* (Dublin: Gill and Macmillan, 1983).

[34] J. Benson and L. Ugolini, 'Introduction: historians and the nation of shopkeepers', in J. Benson and L. Ugolini (eds), *A Nation of Shopkeepers: Five Centuries of British Retailing* (London: I.B. Tauris, 2003), 4. See also Winstanley, *The Shopkeeper's World*, 217.

[35] Office for National Statistics, 'Retail SMEs in England', 11/01/ 2018, https://www.ons. gov.uk/businessindustryandtrade/business/activitysizeandlocation/adhocs/007932retailsm esinengland (accessed 10/07/2023).

[36] Benson and Ugolini, *A Nation of Shopkeepers*, 4.

[37] C.P. Hosgood, 'The "pigmies of commerce" and the working-class community: small shopkeepers in England, 1870–1914', *Journal of Social History*, 22:3 (1989), 439.

[38] See P. Gurney, *Co-operative Culture and the Politics of Consumption in England, 1870–1930* (Manchester University Press, 1996) and N. Robertson, *The Co-operative Movement and Communities in Britain, 1914–1960: Minding Their Own Business* (London: Routledge, 2010).

[39] Hosgood, 'Pigmies of commerce', 439. See also Taylor, *Working Class Credit*, 69–73.

[40] Lowe, 'From Victor Gruen', 254.

[41] J. Birchall, *The International Co-operative Movement* (Manchester University Press, 1997), 4.

[42] Charity Retail Association, ' "Find a shop" data', January 2023. See Charity Retail Association, 'Key statistics', https://www.charityretail.org.uk/key-statistics/ (accessed 13/06/2023).

[43] UK figures: Charity Retail Association, ' "Find a shop" data, January 2023. See Charity Retail Association, 'Key statistics', https://www.charityretail.org.uk/key-statistics/ (accessed 07/03/2023); Office of National Statistics, 'Population estimates for the UK, England, Wales, Scotland and Northern Ireland: mid-2021', https://www.ons.gov.uk/ peoplepopulationandcommunity/populationandmigration/populationestimates/bullet ins/annualmidyearpopulationestimates/mid2021 (accessed 07/03/2023).

[44] NARTS: The Association of Resale Professionals, 'Industry statistics and trends', https:// www.narts.org/i4a/pages/index.cfm?pageid=3285 (accessed 07/03/2023); Statista,

'Second-hand goods in Canada – statistics and facts', https://www.statista.com/topics/2838/second-hand-goods-in-canada/#topicOverview (accessed 07/03/2023).

[45] New Zealand figures: Op Shop Directory, https://opshopdirectory.co.nz/ (accessed 07/03/2023); Stats NZ Tatauranga Aotearoa, 'Population', https://www.stats.govt.nz/topics/population (accessed 07/03/2023). Australia figures: NACRO, 'Fast facts about charity recycling', 2016, http://www.nacro.org.au/wp-content/uploads/2018/01/NACRO-Fast-facts-for-website.pdf (accessed 07/03/2023); Australian Bureau of Statistics, 'National, state and territory population', June 2022, https://www.abs.gov.au/statistics/people/population/national-state-and-territory-population/jun-2022 (accessed 07/03/2023). Irish figures: CNRI, 'Charity retail Ireland', https://crni.ie/our-members/charity-retail-ireland/ (accessed 07/03/2023); Central Statistics Office, 'Census of population 2022', https://www.cso.ie/en/releasesandpublications/ep/p-cpr/censusofpopulation2022-preliminaryresults/introduction/ (accessed 07/03/2023).

[46] Weltladen Dachverband, 'Die Weltladen-Bewegung: Daten & Fakten', https://www.weltladen.de/ueber-weltlaeden/die-weltladen-bewegung/weltlaeden-in-zahlen/ (accessed 10/03/2023).

[47] R. Osterley and I.D. Williams, 'The social, environmental and economic benefits of reuse by charity shops', *Detritus*, 7 (2019), 30.

[48] South Africa figures: Charity SA, 'Charity shops', https://www.charitysa.co.za/charity-shops (accessed 07/03/2023); South African Government, 'South Africa's people', https://www.gov.za/about-sa/south-africas-people (accessed 07/03/2023).

[49] E. Parsons, 'Charity retail: past, present and future', *International Journal of Retail & Distribution Management*, 30 (2002), 588–589.

[50] Corporate Intelligence Group, *Charity Shops in the UK* (London, 1992), 8.

[51] See for example A. Broadbridge and S. Horne, *Over the Counter: A Study of Charity Shop Volunteers* (Institute for Retail Studies working paper 9303, University of Stirling, 1993); R. Goodall and H. Blume, *The Public Perception of Charity Shops* (London: Charity Advisory Committee, 1996); 'Charity shop retailing', *Mintel Retail Intelligence* (1997); L. Parsons, 'New goods, old records and second-hand suits: charity shopping in South-West England', *International Journal of Nonprofit and Voluntary Sector Marketing*, 5:2 (2000), 141–151. See also S. Horne and A. Maddrell, *Charity Shops: Retailing, Consumption and Society* (London: Routledge, 2002), 38–54.

[52] N. Gregson, K. Brooks and L. Crewe, 'Narratives of consumption and body in the space of the charity/shop', in P. Jackson, M. Lowe, D. Miller and F. Mort (eds), *Commercial Cultures: Economies, Practices, Spaces* (Oxford: Berg, 2000), 101.

[53] N. Gregson and L. Crewe, *Second-Hand Cultures* (Oxford: Berg, 2003), 103.

[54] A special issue edited by Horne and Maddrell brought together some of the key aspects of this emerging debate. See R. Goodall, 'Charity shops in sectoral contexts: the view from the boardroom'; S. Horne, 'The charity shop: purpose and change'; A.M.C. Maddrell, '"You just can't get the staff these days": the challenges and opportunities of working with volunteers in the charity shop – an Oxford case study'; L. Parsons, 'New goods'; E. Chatto, 'Charity shops as second-hand markets'; A. Paddison, 'Charity shops on the high street: complementarity or unwanted neighbour?' – all in *International Journal of Nonprofit and Voluntary Sector Marketing*, 5:2 (2000). On charity shops and tax, see S. Horne, 'Charity shops in the UK', *International Journal of Retail & Distribution Management*, 26:4 (1998), 159.

[55] Horne, 'The charity shop', 120 and 123. This was based on the 'social enterprise spectrum' from 'purely philanthropic' to 'purely commercial' presented in J.G. Dees, 'Enterprising nonprofits', *Harvard Business Review* (January–February 1998), 59.

[56] Parsons, 'Charity retail', 589–590.

[57] On varieties of professionalization, see R. Goodall, 'Organising cultures: voluntarism and professionalism in UK charity shops', *Voluntary Action*, 3:1 (2000), 43–57.

58   Goodall, 'Charity shops', 110–111.

59   E. Parsons, 'Charity retailing in the UK: a typology', *Journal of Retailing and Consumer Services*, 11 (2004), 31–40.

60   Goodall, 'Charity shops', 111.

61   T. Fitton, 'Pricing up & haggling down: value negotiations in the UK charity shop', *JOMEC Journal*, 17 (2022), 55.

62   Fitton, 'Pricing up' and 'The "quiet economy": an ethnographic study of the contemporary UK charity shop', unpublished PhD thesis, University of York, 2013.

63   F. Prochaska, 'Charity bazaars in nineteenth-century England', *Journal of British Studies*, 16:2 (1977), 62–84. Inflation adjusted figures have been calculated using the Bank of England's inflation calculator.

64   Prochaska, 'Charity bazaars', 68; P. Gurney, ' "The sublime of the bazaar": a moment in the making of a consumer culture in mid-nineteenth century England', *Journal of Social History*, 40:2 (2006), 385–405.

65   S. Roddy, J.-M. Strange and B. Taithe, *The Charity Market and Humanitarianism in Britain, 1870–1912* (London: Bloomsbury, 2018), 36–37. On commercial bazaars, rather than the business partners of charity bazaars, see Ian Mitchell, 'Innovation in non-food retailing in the early nineteenth century: the curious case of the bazaar', *Business History*, 52:6 (2010), 875–891.

66   Horne and Maddrell, *Charity Shops*, 1–3.

67   J. Field, 'Consumption in lieu of membership: reconfiguring popular charitable action in post-World War II Britain', *Voluntas*, 27:2 (2015), 979–997.

68   T. Sasson, 'In the name of humanity: Britain and the rise of global humanitarianism', DPhil thesis, University of California, Berkeley, 2015, 107 (emphasis in original). For more cautious accounts, see M. Black, *A Cause for Our Times: Oxfam the First 50 Years* (Oxfam and Oxford University Press, 1992), 165–166; M. Anderson, 'The British fair trade movement, 1960–2000: a new form of global citizenship?', PhD thesis, University of Birmingham, 2008, 47.

69   Benson and Ugolini, *A Nation of Shopkeepers*, 10.

70   A. Iriye and P.-Y. Saunier, 'Introduction: the professor and the madman', in A. Iriye and P.-Y. Saunier (eds) *Palgrave Dictionary of Transnational History* (Basingstoke: Palgrave Macmillan, 2009), xvii–xx.

71   A. Burton, 'Who needs the nation? Interrogating "British" history', *Journal of Historical Sociology*, 10 (1997), 227–248.

72   G.A. Barton, 'Towards a global history of Britain', *Perspectives on History*, 01/10/2012, https://www.historians.org/research-and-publications/perspectives-on-history/october-2012/towards-a-global-history-of-britain (accessed 23/06/2023).

73   R.R. Bright and A.R. Dilley, 'After the British world', *Historical Journal*, 60:2 (2017), 547–568.

74   J.M. Mackenzie, *Propaganda and Empire: The Manipulation of British Public Opinion, 1880–1960* (Manchester University Press, 1984) and J.M. Mackenzie (ed), *Imperialism and Popular Culture* (Manchester University Press, 1986). For the counter-argument, see B. Porter, *The Absent-Minded Imperialists: Empire, Society and Culture in Britain* (Oxford University Press, 2004). On the influence of Mackenzie and his *Studies in Imperialism* book series, see A.S. Thompson (ed) *Writing Imperial Histories* (Manchester University Press, 2013); S. Barczewski and M. Farr (eds), *The Mackenzie Moment and Imperial History* (Basingstoke: Palgrave Macmillan, 2019).

75   Benson and Ugolini, *A Nation of Shopkeepers*, 11. See also Z. Lawson, 'Shops, shopkeepers, and the working-class community: Preston, 1860–1890', *Transactions of the Historic Society of Lancashire and Cheshire*, 141 (1991), 309–328.

76   H.-C. Mui and L. Mui, *Shops and Shopkeeping in Eighteenth Century England* (London: Routledge, 1989), 41.

77 A. Toplis, 'The non-elite consumer and "wearing apparel" in Herefordshire and Worcestershire, 1800–1850', unpublished PhD thesis, University of Wolverhampton, 2008, 110.

78 B. Lemire, *Dress, Culture and Commerce: The English Clothing Trade before the Factory, 1660–1800* (Basingstoke: Palgrave Macmillan, 1997), see Chapter 3.

79 L. Leboissetier, 'Explaining the enduring presence of migrant pedlars in late-modern Britain', CHORD blog, 18/05/2022, https://retailhistory.wordpress.com/2022/05/18/peddling/ (accessed 10/01/2023). For a traditionally declinist view, see D. Alexander, *Retailing in England during the Industrial Revolution* (London: Athlone Press, 1970).

80 O'Connell, *Credit and Community*, 26–54.

81 K. Hammond Perry, *'London is the Place for Me': Black Britons, Citizenship and the Politics of Race* (Oxford University Press, 2015), 87.

82 G. Singh and D. Singh Tatla, *Sikhs in Britain: The Making of a Community* (London: Zed Books, 2006), 155. On the exposure of these shopkeepers to racial harassment, see Taylor, *Working Class Credit*, 102–104.

83 M. Rabikowska and K. Burrell, 'The material worlds of recent Polish migrants: transnationalism, food, shops and home', in K. Burrell (ed), *Polish Migration to the UK in the 'New' European Union: After 2004* (London: Routledge, 2009), 211.

84 A.J. Kerschen, 'Introduction: food and the migrant experience', in A.J. Kerschen (ed), *Food in the Migrant Experience* (London: Routledge, 2002), 1.

85 See L. Sponza, 'Italian "penny ice-men" in Victorian London' and P. Panayi, 'The spicing up of English provincial life: the history of curry in Leicester', both in A.J. Kerschen (ed), *Food in the Migrant Experience* (London: Routledge, 2002).

86 Rabikowska and Burrell, 'The material worlds of recent Polish migrants', 211.

87 P. Panayi, *Spicing up Britain: The Multicultural History of British Food* (London: Reaktion Books, 2008).

88 See S. Chan, 'Sweet and sour: the Chinese food experience', in A.J. Kerschen (ed), *Food in the Migrant Experience* (London: Routledge, 2002).

89 Benson and Ugolini, *A Nation of Shopkeepers*, 15.

90 See R. Jessen and L. Langer (eds), *Transformations of Retailing in Europe after 1945* (Aldershot: Ashgate, 2012).

2

The Commodification of Japanese Culture in Transcultural Charity Bazaars: The Mikado Festival and Feast of Lanterns in Darlington, 1887

Massimiliano Papini

Introduction

On Wednesday 19 October 1887, Sir Joseph Whitwell Pease, a member of one of the great Quaker industrialist families of the 19th century, opened a charity bazaar at the Central Hall in Darlington with a speech:

> A little while ago [I] travelled with a gentleman who ... informed [me] that he was the English agent of the Canadian and Pacific Railway. He was a man who seemed to have been all over the world, and showed [me] a map of the route from England to Japan, how we could be taken by English steamboat to Canada, across that country by rail, and thence again by English steamboats be transported at once to where [we are] all supposed to be [today].[1]

Pease mentioned Japan because the fundraising event at which he was talking was arranged in order to resemble a Japanese traditional village.[2] The purpose of the Mikado Festival and Feast of Lanterns was to sell articles made or donated locally to clear the debts of the Paradise Chapel of Darlington and to collect funds to build the new Sunday School.

In exploring this local context, the chapter demonstrates the relationship between the cultural dynamics of local fundraising and commercial retailing practices. The opening of a retail premises named Japanese Shop by William Mossom two years after the Mikado Festival reveals the influence of fundraising events over commercial retail in a market town such as Darlington. In addition to signalling Victorian imperialism and cultural appropriation, this study also aims to investigate the commodification of the representation of Japanese culture for philanthropic ends, resulting in an ambiguous and manifold phenomenon that also impacted local retail practices.

This chapter employs a transcultural methodological approach. Originally, the term *transculturation* was coined in 1940 by the anthropologist Fernando Ortiz to identify 'the transitive process from one culture to another', involving both 'the acquisition of culture' and 'the loss of uprooting one's preceding culture'.[3] The transcultural approach advocates that cultural relationships are an ongoing unresolved negotiation rather than a static power relation. Monica Juneja has underlined that transculturality is a methodological tool to deconstruct concepts such as society, class or gender, while preserving the inner complexity and ambiguity of encounters between different cultures.[4] Mary Louise Pratt has argued that encounters occur in a specific environment, with the resulting social space functioning as a contact zone in which cultures 'meet, clash and grapple with each other, often in highly asymmetrical relations of domination and subordination'.[5]

Transculturality has often been employed to study extraterritorial environments at the margin such as Japanese treaty ports, but it has rarely been used to investigate cultural encounters that occurred in Europe and North America. For instance, Luke Gartlan reveals how Japanese photographers adopted what appeared to be an imperialist view of Japan while at the same time modifying 'such themes in subtle ways to challenge the visual primacy of their foreign counterparts'.[6] The present chapter transposes the methodology used by Gartlan to a different context. Rather than the city of Yokohama, which was the main Japanese gateway to the West and vice versa, the focus of this research is an English market town, which reveals that transcultural phenomena occurred even within a peripheral region of Britain.

The popularity of Japanese objects in Britain entailed another cultural phenomenon: the commodification of Japanese culture in public events. This chapter uses the definition of a commodity provided by Arjun Appadurai: 'commodities can provisionally be defined as objects of economic value'; however, the extent of their value is not 'the inherent property of objects, but is a judgment made about them by subjects'.[7] Appadurai underlined that consumption means both sending and receiving social messages.[8] This study asks what social messages were sent and received in the commodification of Japanese culture in Darlington at the Mikado Festival, and later in the Japanese Shop.

This chapter draws upon newspaper articles and archival materials to compare the complex transcultural encounter of a charity bazaar decorated to resemble a foreign location with a specific shop.[9] Thanks to the British Library's British Newspaper Archive, I was able to read newspapers published in Darlington and its surroundings from the late 1880s to the mid-1890s, which have been almost fully digitalized.[10] By using keyword searches including 'Japan' or 'Japanese' in combination with terms such as 'bazaar', 'festival' and 'shop' across multiple digitalized newspapers, it is was possible to unearth a great quantity of articles and advertisements which mentioned the Mikado Festival and the Japanese Shop. As a whole, these newspaper articles not only bring two forgotten examples of the late Victorian fascination with Japanese culture and aesthetic to light, but also show how Japan was discussed within provincial newspapers, providing a quite detailed case study of how Japanese culture was represented and commodified in peripheral Britain.

More specifically, newspapers have real advantages in studying encounters like this. The daily reports of the charity bazaar published in different newspapers offer multiple perspectives of the philanthropic event from its opening to the final day, shedding light on the ways Japanese-style decorations were arranged and how they were perceived by local journalists and visitors. Similarly, the numerous advertisements of the Japanese Shop that appeared in the local press allow to draw a significant picture of the commercial venture. While the advertising material of a shop may tell us more about the promotion strategy of its owner, William Mossom, than the reality of the shop, how the shop was promoted is important information. There are also limitations of newspapers, such as the subjective perspectives of specific journalists. Therefore, this study was complemented by extensive research at the Darlington city archive, which has provided further detail and an alternative view of the fundraising event.[11]

This chapter first offers a brief overview of the charity bazaar as a typical Victorian event, the British fascination with Japan during the late 19th century, and the economic and cultural relationship between Japan and the North East of England. Then it turns to the Mikado Festival as a contact zone between Japanese and British culture. The global and the local connotations of this cultural encounter are further explored by discussing William Mossom's opening of a Japanese shop. This study demonstrates that in a provincial town such as Darlington, the idea of Japan became a commodified, transcultural concept.

The charity bazaar and the fascination with Japan in late 19th-century Britain

The charity bazaar was a temporary fundraising event which relied mainly on voluntary work and became popular in Britain in the early 19th century.[12] Bazaars supported a designated cause, such as a hospital, school, missionary society or religious institution. They drew heavily on entertainment, including musicians, dancers and actors, to attract visitors and supporters. Decorations and entertainment followed an overarching theme. Foreign locations were among the most common. Attending a charity bazaar represented a chance for many Victorians to have a first contact with objects from an exogenous culture, not dissimilar to what took place during world's fairs.[13]

Charity bazaars became popular in the 1820s, as they adapted features from newly developed commercial bazaars, a permanent premises 'in which counter space was let for the sale of non-food goods'.[14] John Trotter opened the first commercial bazaar in London in 1816, which offered a controlled and respectable environment and accessibility to a wide range of stallholders, who could take advantage of the daily average of around 2,500 visitors.[15] Following Trotter, many other bazaars of this kind were opened all over England; however, their commercial success waned from the early 1840s and most of them closed by the 1850s.[16] Features from the commercial bazaar were almost immediately transposed into its charity counterpart. For example, in a commercial bazaar the organization of each counter space was left to whoever was renting the space; in the charity bazaar this model was further developed, and volunteers provided and sold the objects at their stall in almost complete autonomy. However, crucial differences helped charity bazaars avoid the decline which commercial bazaars faced in the second half of the 19th century. While a commercial bazaar was permanent, a charity bazaar lasted just a couple of days and could therefore be promoted as an entertaining spectacle such as a fancy fair or a festival.[17] In addition, as posited by Sarah Roddy, Julie-Marie Strange and Bertrand Taithe, even if 'charitable fundraising could entail the consumption of goods in commercial contexts ... this was frequently reframed by consumers' desire to express their compassion while consuming'.[18] The charity bazaar's ephemeral nature and philanthropic vocation created a social activity that was simultaneously attractive and respectable for a wide range of Victorian people.

The popularity of Japan-themed bazaars and retailing practices which sold Japanese imported goods needs to be understood in the context of world's fairs, and more generally with the widespread enthusiasm that Japanese objects stirred among Victorian consumers after the reopening of Japan to the West in 1854. Scholars recognize the London International Exposition (1862) as the turning point.[19] On that occasion, Japanese decorative art was exhibited in an individual pavilion that attracted the attention of artists, critics and collectors. Elizabeth Aslin outlined the growing popularization of Japanese objects throughout British society. In the 1860s, Japanese articles were mainly appreciated as artistic objects in circles of artists, collectors and critics. By the 1870s, Japanese art began to be associated with the Aesthetic Movement and appreciated among a wider, but still select, audience. It was only in the 1880s that Japan mania fully took hold in British popular culture.[20]

This was an important decade, even if the complex array of motivations related to the acquisition and display of Japanese decorative objects defies strict periodization.[21] For example, in 1885 two pivotal events occurred in London that played a crucial role in popularizing the British fascination with Japan: the Japanese Native Village and the premiere of the operetta *The Mikado; or, The Town of Titipu*. The former was an exhibition built to resemble a traditional Japanese village, featuring Japanese artisans and entertainers recruited directly in Japan by the mastermind behind the event, Tannaker Buhicrosan. As scholars have suggested, the Japanese Native Village introduced 'ordinary British people to a variety of aspects of Japanese popular culture in a more effective way than could have been gleaned from the books about Japan that were available in England at the time'.[22] It also reinforced the commodified idea of Japanese culture in late Victorian Britain, exemplified by the alienation inflicted by Tannaker on the Japanese workers.[23]

Similarly, the critical and commercial success of William Gilbert and Arthur Sullivan's operetta *The Mikado* both confirmed that the British fascination with an idealized image of Japan had become an established part of Victorian popular culture and reinforced it. The musical operetta, by Gilbert and Sullivan, premiered in London in March 1885 and in Newcastle seven months later.[24] The breadth of its influence can be seen in the reviews in regional newspapers that praised almost every aspect of the production, which was described as 'bright and sparkling, witty and paradoxical, redolent of pungent satire, and laughter-provoking comicalities'.[25] During the following years, the word 'Mikado' began to be used to promote Japan-themed events and shop departments.[26]

Japan and the North East of England

The popular image of Japan in the North East was influenced by cultural encounters, such as public lectures and entertaining spectacles, where Japanese artefacts played a crucial role in attracting the public. From the 1860s, there were numerous public lectures on Japan in major towns such as Newcastle or Durham and also in Humshaugh, a small village near Hexham.[27] For instance, Christopher Dresser (1834–1904), one of the main promoters of Japanese art in Britain at that time, came to Newcastle in 1863 to deliver a series of lectures entitled 'Ornamental Art', in which he showed his collection of Chinese and Japanese articles purchased at the Great London Exposition in 1862.[28] In addition, various troupes of Japanese acrobats arrived in the North East from the 1860s.[29] Tannaker Buhicrosan, famous for having organized the Japanese Native Village in London in 1885, was the manager of the Royal Tycoon Troupe, whose tour reached various towns in the North East from 1869 to 1883.[30] From 1877 Tannaker advertised the giveaway of a Japanese curiosity to all attendees who purchased a ticket, testifying to the popular appeal of decorative objects manufactured in Japan.[31]

In the North East in the 1880s, Japan-themed bazaars were a frequent occurrence, in line with the national trends in late Victorian Japan mania. Various religious institutions organized Japan-themed charity bazaars, in which it was possible to admire Japanese decorations as well as purchase Japanese articles. Among the total of 17 Japan-themed bazaars organized in the second half of the 19th century, 14 were held between 1882 and 1889.[32] The popularity of these philanthropic events further demonstrates that the enthusiasm for Japanese culture was inextricably tied with the consumption of Japanese decorative goods, promoting a commodified, idealized and stereotypical representation of Japan which was disconnected from the real country. At the same time, the local economy in the North East of England was intertwined with modernizing process embraced by the Asian country. As Marie Conte-Helm observes, Japan looked to the North East as a model of industrialization and became a significant client of the heavy industries based in the British region.[33] In the 1880s and 1890s, the Japanese Imperial Navy ordered the warships that were to be important in the military victories of Japan over China (1894–1895) and Russia (1904–1905) from Newcastle shipyards.[34] Moreover, the Japanese government and Japanese private companies started to buy a large amount of pig iron from Middlesbrough furnaces.[35] For this reason, in 1896 Nippon Yusen Kaisha, a semi-governmental shipping company, decided to establish a new European route, with Middlesbrough as the main loading port in Britain.[36] A few years later, Middlesbrough was chosen to host an honorary Japanese consul.[37] However, as this chapter unearths, these economic and industrial relations had no great bearing on the presence of Japanese objects and Japanese-style decoration in local charity bazaars and shops.

Mikado Festival and Feast of Lanterns

The Mikado Festival in Darlington was opened on 19 October 1887 and lasted three days. The name was a direct reference to the Emperor of Japan, also known as the Mikado, as well as an allusion to the musical. Songs from *The Mikado* were performed during the charity bazaar in Darlington by a group of musicians named the Japanese Minstrels.[38] It was building on, rather than introducing, popular ideas of Japan in Britain. The people of Darlington who attended could have engaged with previous events presenting Japanese culture. For instance, Tannaker and his troupe of acrobats performed at least three shows in Darlington between 1875 and 1883.[39] The first Japan-themed charity bazaar in the region was organized in Darlington in 1882 and, two years later, a public lecture entitled 'The Physical Features of Japan' was delivered by W.M. Angus.[40]

Invited to speak by the Reverend Irving, Joseph Whitwell Pease first underlined the importance and the urgency of a new Sunday School in Darlington, then praised the arrangement of the bazaar and the articles on sale.[41] Although no photographs of the Mikado Festival survive, it is possible to imagine the way in which the bazaar was arranged thanks to the official guide and articles in newspapers. Produced by a local publisher and lithographer named William Dresser, the guide of the bazaar includes a detailed description of the arrangement:

> The bazaar represents a Japanese village during the feast of lanterns. … The stalls are arranged in the form of Japanese houses or cottages of varied construction, most elaborately decorated, and include many quaint drawings for which Japan is famous. Overhead a canopy of lanterns, novel in shape and profuse with colour, which adds materially to the scenic effects. At the top of the room stands the temple, with its immense pagoda, 40 ft. high, and is surrounded on either side with enchanting scenery of the Land of the rising Sun. The front of the pagoda is bright with gold while the supporting columns give the building a substantial and magnificent appearance. In the centre of the hall is a correct representation of the Sacred Bridge of Kumkismi Gardens, all bright with colour and emblazoned with lanterns of diversified shape and beauty.[42]

Most of the stalls were named after Japanese towns or regions. The enthusiastic tone of the article in the *Northern Echo* suggests the illusion captivated and convinced contemporary audiences: '[I]t was at first difficult to conceive that it was the Central Hall, so completely had it been transformed to resemble a Japanese village.'[43]

Virtual travelling

The secret of the Mikado Festival's success was its representation of Japanese style according to British popular perception of the East Asian country. This kind of spectacle had been popular since the previous decade in Britain and many people from the local community were familiar with such a display. The idea of a Japanese Village on display began in the Japan Pavilion at the International Exhibition held in Vienna (1873), in which the Japanese government built a model of the five-storey pagoda and recreated a traditional garden with a Shinto shrine.[44] Christopher Dresser purchased the structures of the Japanese garden at the end of the international exposition. In 1875, he re-erected his purchase in London at the Alexandra Park, bringing over also an 'entire Japanese colony' from Vienna.[45] Named 'Japanese Village', the arrangement appealed to the British thirst for the curious and exotic, and, as suggested by Anna Jackson, Dresser's spectacle addressed the 'escapist longing by those coming to terms with the complexities of life in the industrialised West'.[46]

In the North East, the first Japanese Village bazaar was probably arranged in Darlington in 1882 by a company of decorators from Leeds named Womersley. They fitted up the local Central Hall with 'the representations of Japanese architecture', described in the local press as 'perfect and ... tasteful'.[47] The same company was called back to Darlington for the Mikado Festival in 1887, suggesting that the local community appreciated their work. Taking into consideration that Womersley affirmed in an advertisement published in 1881 that they were able to arrange a Japanese Village,[48] it is more than plausible that both bazaars in Darlington were fitted up with the intention to resemble the prototype Dresser arranged at Alexandra Park, which consisted of a couple of Japanese-style buildings and a bridge.

The *Northern Echo* reported that at the Mikado Festival in Darlington, the 'ornamentation of the front of the temple is very chaste, and being in golden hue, it presents a most brilliant a finished appearance. Grapes cluster in profusion around the front. This is a characteristic feature in Japanese architecture, [so] as to hide the otherwise bare aspect of the buildings'.[49] The *York Herald* confirmed the impression, praising the decorators for having 'fitted up the bazaar in truly Japanese style'.[50] The sensation of being in Japan was the result of the decorators' ability to arrange a display that would appear authentic to individuals such as newspaper reporters and visitors, who had limited familiarity with the country at that time, but were acquainted with an idealized image of Japan.

The illustrations that decorated the official guide reveal the way Japan was intended to be represented. There was a profusion of decorative elements traditionally associated with an idealized Japan throughout the entire publication. The cover itself was the best example: along with an egret with retracted neck, and stylized bamboo leaves, there was a generic monster from Japanese folklore that provided a fairy tale atmosphere.[51] This dream-like vision of Japan strongly contrasted with the country that, at the end of the 1880s, was embracing a successful modernizing process. Following the Meiji Restoration in 1869, Japan began to adopt Western political, social and economic organization and this transformation was perceived as a threat to the 'elf-land' so appreciated in Britain from the early 1870s.[52] As suggested by Anna Jackson, this stereotyped Old Japan began to be idealized in order to keep images of East Asian country as similar as possible to the pre-modern vision corresponding to Victorian desires.[53] This attitude is demonstrated with the Mikado Festival; there was no reference to the trade relationship between the North East and Japan in the official guide or newspaper articles. In other words, despite the first-hand experience with modern Japan in the other parts of the North East of England, the orientalist attitude towards

Japanese culture and the representation of Japan as an exotic Other was not subverted in Darlington.[54]

When people in the North East felt themselves transported to Japan upon entering the Darlington Central Hall, that Japan was the pre-modern image which satisfied their exotic desire of escapism. This way of looking at a foreign country resembles John Urry's concept of tourist gaze, which:

> is directed to features of landscape and townscape which separate them off from everyday experience. Such aspects are viewed because they are taken to be in some sense out of the ordinary. … People linger over such gaze which is then normally visually objectified or captured through photographs, postcards, films, models and so on. These enable the gaze to be endlessly reproduced and recaptured.[55]

In the example of the Mikado Festival, the gaze was captured through a constellation of elements related to the British fascination with Japan. Womersley connected with this fascination by displaying Japanese decorative objects such as lanterns and incorporating Japanese traditional houses and a pagoda. Urry argued that 'places are chosen to be gazed upon … through daydreaming and fantasy', helping to explain why such an arrangement was considered authentic even though it contrasted with the image of the country which at that time was purchasing warships and pig iron from the North East.[56] As discussed by Emile de Bruijn, in his study of the meaning of Chinese wallpapers in country homes, this kind of virtual travel had a long tradition in Britain.[57] Initially, virtual travelling was exclusive to the elite families. From the second half of the 19th century, however, this privilege was extended to the rising middle class, who achieved a disposable income that enabled them to buy exotic goods to decorate their homes or attend public events such as the Mikado Festival in Darlington.

Cross dressing

At the Mikado Festival, Womersley provided a full set of Japanese costumes which stallholders could wear.[58] Local newspapers emphasized this feature, writing that 'the lady attendants are attired in Japanese, and their costumes add greatly to an otherwise attractive scene'.[59] The practice of cultural cross dressing was one of the many ways European and American people embraced the orientalized vision of Japan in the second half of the 19th century. Christine Guth suggested that cultural cross dressing more generally was fundamentally a 'strategy of self-presentation … that simultaneously reinforced and subverted dominant colonial ideologies'.[60] Guth also affirmed that such phenomenon partly naturalized Asian Otherness in the West, echoing David Bate, who posited that 'by incorporating the Orient into his or her self-image, the European also acknowledges that the East has entered into the West'.[61] As Elizabeth Kramer concluded, the assimilation of Japanese traditional costumes into British fashion and visual culture 'resonated not only with Victorian yearning to preserve Old Japan, but also with the desire to recapture a time before Britain's own industrialisation'.[62]

As stated in a *York Herald* article, the role of the ladies and gentlemen in cross-cultural attire was to 'personate by their costumes some of the notabilities of Japan'.[63] This was part of providing an engaging spectacle to the visitors. As Yuko Matsukawa has pointed out, the practice of cross dressing as Japanese 'substitute[d] white bodies for Japanese ones' as 'any woman with the right accessories … could become "Japanese"'.[64] The disappearance of Asian bodies allowed for what Josephine Lee termed *decorative orientalism*: 'the fantasy of a particularly close and intimate relationship with Asian objects that were easily acquired and just as easily disposed of'.[65] In other words, cross dressing in Japanese attire turned Western people into 'powerful agents in the production of Orientalism', as suggested by Yoshihara Mari.[66]

Simultaneously, the experience of the people who wore Japanese costumes also functioned as a potential transcultural dialogue motivated by an aesthetic appreciation. Since the early contacts, British people had favourable impressions of Japanese traditional dress, which epitomized the main characteristics of the Japanese style: beauty, decorativeness and simplicity. By wearing Japanese traditional costumes, stallholders attempted to embrace part of the artistic connotation attributed to a Japanese aesthetic, making a statement with regard to their status within the Darlington community. Emma Ferry argued that at the Loan Exhibition of Women's Industries, held in Bristol in 1885, the ladies involved in the organization were not only supporting working-class women displaying their works, they were also shaping an environment in which to promote their philanthropic values, and their active role as middle-class women.[67] Ferry defined this phenomenon as double display, which might be extended to the stallholders who presided at the Mikado Bazaar. As well as displaying works, they were also enhancing their public persona by embracing part of the refinement associated with Japan. Following the ideas suggested by Guth and Kramer, this cross-cultural phenomenon epitomized not only the unequal power relationship between the dominant British Empire and subaltern Meiji Japan in terms of *decorative orientalism*, but also the necessity for Victorians to incorporate Japanese elements to highlight and support their artistic aspirations.

Local community

While virtual travel and cross dressing emphasized the global connotations of the Mikado Festival, the purpose of the fundraising event exemplified the local character. The event was organized to clear the debts of the Paradise Chapel of Darlington and to collect funds to build the new Sunday School. The Darlington community knew that the very local purpose of the charity bazaar was completely unrelated to the Japan-themed setting. This contrasts with missionary bazaars, in which the exotic setting was often connected to the foreign country or countries where missionary activities were in progress.[68] The choice of a Japan-themed event was an attempt to take advantage of the British fascination with Japan as a novelty in the late Victorian period. As discussed by Roddy et al, providing novelty was 'one vital element of fundraising success'.[69] Addressing enthusiasm for everything Japanese was a profitable strategy both for provincial bazaar organizers and for companies of decorators that specialized in charity bazaars.[70]

The prominent and active role played by local volunteers in the Mikado Festival demonstrated its local connections. The official guide stated the event was 'supported by various Ladies and Gentlemen of the Town and District'.[71] Members of local Methodist families such as Kipling and Horsley, and Quaker families such as the Peases, offered their help as volunteers.[72] Local industrial magnates, bankers and political figures attended the opening ceremony and were individually mentioned in newspaper articles.[73] The entrance fee was one shilling, with a child discount, so middle-class families were probably the main target of the organizers, although working-class audiences were incentivized by a special ticket costing six pence on the last day.[74]

Although the decorative scheme was in Japanese style, the origin of the articles on sale was mainly local, with a few exceptions. The goods displayed at each stall consisted of works made by local volunteers – mainly ladies – and other objects donated or bought for the occasion.[75] On the Nagasaki and Yokohama stalls, for example, specimens of embroidery works were the main articles on sale, and in both cases, the guide underlined how they were the result of hard labour from local ladies.[76] Indian trays and vases, Russian leather cases, and Dresden ceramics provided a glimpse of cosmopolitanism and the few Japanese items on sale were displayed on the Matsmai stall. However, even in the latter booth, other articles such as dolls and 'London Novelties' represented the main attractions, according to the local newspaper.[77]

By displaying British and international goods in a Japan-themed setting, local stallholders took advantage of the popularity of Japan and its aesthetic to attract visitors. As suggested in *The Lady's Bazaar & Fancy Fair Book*, employing Japanese decorative objects such as fans and parasols added an artistic appearance to the stall, which enhanced the goods for sale.[78] In addition to attracting people to the bazaar by offering the chance to visit an idealized representation of a Japanese traditional village, each stallholder also took advantage of the excellence attributed to Japanese artistic and decorative objects to increase sales of non-Japanese products.

Japanese Shop

While this fundraising strategy was built upon the popularity and commercial success of Japanese decorative objects in Britain, it is noteworthy that local charity events also served as mediators of national trends into provincial towns such as Darlington. Commercial enterprises and voluntary organizations did not exist in separate worlds, and it was common to find similarities between fundraising and retailing practices in Victorian times.[79] Two years after the Mikado Festival, William Mossom (1847–1933), a local retailer, decided to name his new retail store the Japanese Shop. Mossom was part of a family of 'housepainters, paperhangers, and art decorators'.[80] The few biographical notes obtained from his obituary suggest he was aware of the major artistic trends in Europe, as he 'travelled extensively and had visited most European countries' in his younger age.[81] Before the opening of the new branch, he managed another shop in town at 82 Bondgate. In 1884, an advert for this shop mentioned the availability of 'a large stock of Japanese and other Eastern pottery ware';[82] while in the following years, it was the turn of generic terms such as 'Japanese goods'[83] and Japanese 'novelties'.[84] Mossom was therefore already selling Japanese items before he opened his Japanese Shop.

The name of the Japanese Shop was not an indication of the articles on sale, but, as with the Mikado Festival, a statement about late Victorian taste. Mossom published advertisements in local newspapers for the Japanese Shop from 1889 to 1893.[85] In those adverts, instead of reinforcing the presence of Japanese articles, he limited the references to Japan to 'British and Oriental art pottery'.[86] Even when he purchased a larger advertising space in a minor newspaper, the details provided with regard to the Japanese objects were quite generic in comparison with British wares. For instance, an advert lists 'British and Oriental art pottery, including Abbotsford, Bretby, Burmantofts and Doulton Wares, Japanese, Chinese, Indian, and other Oriental Pottery'.[87] The presence of a wide selection of British wares in a shop called Japanese confirms that in Darlington the idea of Japan developed into a synonym of aesthetic excellence that was able to enhance objects manufactured in other countries.

Following Appadurai's theory of consumption, it might be advanced that Mossom commodified the local appreciation of Japanese culture in order to provide a vocabulary that his customers could use to send and receive social messages. These messages relied on the transcultural values attributed to the stereotyped vision of Japan, such as beauty, exoticism and novelty. Paraphrasing from Roland Barthes' *Rhetoric of the Image*, the Japan mentioned by Mossom is not the actual country, but it connotes what Barthes would have called *Japanicity*, namely 'the condensed essence of everything that could be' Japanese in the broadest sense, including the idealized image of Japan.[88] In contrast to the charity bazaar, in which the supposed accuracy of the setting was a key component of the advertising strategy to attract visitors and benefactors, Mossom relied on the symbolic message associated with *Japanicity*, which had become part of the body of knowledge within people in Darlington thanks to Japan-themed events such as the Mikado Festival.

Conclusion

As demonstrated by the Mikado Festival and the Japanese Shop, the popularity of Japan in Darlington was so high that both fundraising retailers and commercial retailers considered its idea an effective tool to attract visitors and clients. In addition, the idea of Japan represented not only a link to a global trend, but also an appropriate setting to promote local endeavours such as fundraising campaigns and British manufactured products.

Despite the relevant economic and industrial relationship between Japan and the North East of England, the bazaar organizers overlooked this successful trade, deciding to reproduce an idealized vision of Old Japan: a pre-modern Japanese village that wiped out any reference to the country's successful modernization. In a similar manner to contemporary exotic spectacles in other parts of Britain, the appeal of the Mikado Festival in Darlington lay in its function as a vehicle for virtual travel to an idealized, pre-industrial society, while stallholders wearing Japanese costumes erased the indigenous bodies, objectifying the appreciation of Japan and its culture.

However, reinforcing British imperialist discourse was not the only narrative of the Mikado Festival. The effort to arrange an 'authentic' representation of Japan by the company of professional decorators involved a degree of admiration of Japanese culture, which, according to the Victorian design reformers, did not suffer the same artistic decline due to industrialization.[89] Accordingly, by dressing up in Japanese costumes, stallholders also promoted their public persona in line with the late Victorian cosmopolitan taste and fashion. As well as erasing the physicality of the Japanese, the practice of cross dressing in charity bazaars and fairs also transformed the British body into a contact zone for the sake of a philanthropic cause.

Two years after the Mikado Festival, William Mossom decided to promote his new branch, naming it the Japanese Shop. Instead of focusing on Japanese or East Asian products, he opted to promote decorative objects manufactured in any other country but Japan. This strategy demonstrates that the idea of Japan was so popular that provincial retailers took advantage of it and that the Japanese aesthetic became a transcultural synonym of artistic excellence. The ongoing and unresolved negotiation that characterized the idealized image of Japan in Britain allowed Mossom to take advantage of that image to promote his shop even though most of the goods on sale were not manufactured in Japan. Rather than creating a conflict and reinforcing Japanese *Otherness*, Mossom probably believed that by investing in a new shop and naming it the Japanese Shop, he would gain the support of the Darlington community, demonstrating that even in a provincial town such as Darlington the idea of Japan equated to cosmopolitan beauty and artistic taste. Furthermore, it exemplified that fundraising retail and commercial retail practices were inextricably linked to each other, occasionally serving as mediators of national and global trends into provincial towns such as Darlington.

The transcultural approach employed in this chapter has allowed me to take into consideration the coexistence of the imperialistic and cosmopolitan narratives that ultimately shaped the social recognition of Japan as well as the commodification of Japanese culture in a provincial town such as Darlington. Transculturality as a theoretical framework provided a lens through which to view local events such as Japan-themed charity bazaars and retailing premises advertised as Japanese. While reinforcing an unequal power relationship between the dominant British Empire and foreign countries, the resulting image of the Japan also suggests that transcultural phenomena could become so popular to transform retail spaces into contact zones between British and non-British cultures, going beyond concepts of a homogeneous West or East. Charity retailing and commercial retailing practices both played crucial roles as mediators between local communities and transnational trends such as Japan mania. At the same time, however, they remained resistant to the rapidly modernizing and militarizing Japan, its political relationship with Britain, and its trading connection with the North East.

Notes

[1] *Northern Echo*, 20/10/1887, 8.
[2] A. Orde, *Religion, Business and Society in North-East England: The Pease Family of Darlington in the Nineteenth Century* (Stamford: Shaun Tyas, 2000).
[3] F. Ortiz, *Cuban Counterpoint, Tobacco and Sugar* [originally *Contrapunteo Cubano del Tabaco y el azúcar* (Havana, 1940)] (Durham, NC: Duke University Press, 2003), 32–33.
[4] M. Juneja and C. Kravagna, 'Understanding transculturalism: Monica Juneja and Christian Kravagna in conversation', in Model House Research Group (ed), *Transcultural Modernisms* (Berlin: Sternberg Press, 2013).
[5] M.L. Pratt, *Imperial Eyes: Travel Writing and Transculturation* (London: Routledge, 1992), 4.
[6] L. Gartlan, ' "Bronzed and muscular bodies": jinrikishas, tattooed bodies and Yokohama tourist photography', in J. Codell (ed), *Transculturation in British Art, 1770–1930* (Farnham: Ashgate, 2012), 107.
[7] A. Appadurai, 'Introduction: commodities and the politics of value', in A. Appadurai (ed), *The Social Life of Things* (Cambridge University Press, 1986), 3.
[8] Appadurai, 'Introduction', 31.
[9] For a comprehensive investigation of the transcultural relationship between Japan and the North East of England through a transcultural approach, see M. Papini, 'Transcultural flows from Japan to the north east of England 1862–1913: visual and material culture in relation to the Anglo-Japanese interaction', PhD thesis, Northumbria University, 2021.
[10] *Darlington & Stockton Times; Ripon & Richmond Chronicle; Daily Gazette for Middlesbrough; Durham County Advertiser; Jarrow Express; Newcastle Courant; Newcastle Daily Chronicle; Northern Echo.* The British Newspaper Archive (www.britishnewspaperarchive.co.uk).

For a historical overview of the newspapers published in the North East, see P. Isaac (ed), *Newspapers in the Northeast* (Newcastle: Allenholme, 1999).

[11] Darlington Centre for Local Studies.

[12] F. Prochaska, 'Charity bazaars in nineteenth-century England', *Journal of British Studies*, 16:2 (1977), 62–84.

[13] B. Gordon, *Bazaars and Fair Ladies: The History of the American Fundraising Fair* (Knoxville: University of Tennessee, 1998), 132.

[14] I. Mitchell, 'Innovation in non-food retailing in the early nineteenth century: the curious case of the bazaar', *Business History*, 52:6 (2010), 876.

[15] Prochaska, 'Charity bazaars', 63–64; Mitchell, 'Innovation in non-food retailing', 880.

[16] Mitchell, 'Innovation in non-food retailing', 885.

[17] R. Bowlby, *Back to the Shops* (Oxford University Press, 2022), 170.

[18] S. Roddy, J.-M. Strange and B. Taithe, *The Charity Market and Humanitarianism in Britain, 1870–1912* (London: Bloomsbury Academic, 2018), 4.

[19] O. Checkland, *Japan and Britain after 1859: Creating Cultural Bridges* (London: Routledge, 2002), 187–195. On late Victorian Japonisme, see T. Watanabe, *High Victorian Japonisme* (Bern: P. Lang, 1991); A. Ono, *Japonisme in Britain* (London and New York: Routledge Curzon, 2003).

[20] E. Aslin, *The Aesthetic Movement: Prelude to Art Nouveau* (London: Elek, 1969), 79.

[21] E. Kramer, 'From specimen to scrap: Japanese kimono and textiles in the British Victorian interior, 1875–1900', in J. Potvin and A. Myzelev (eds), *Material Cultures in Britain, 1740–1920* (Farnham: Ashgate, 2009), 129–130.

[22] H. Cortazzi, *Japan in Late Victorian London: The Japanese Native Village in Knightsbridge and 'The Mikado', 1885* (Norwich: Sainsbury Institute, 2009), 73–74.

[23] A. Scholtz, '"Almond-eyed artisans"/"dishonouring the national polity": the Japanese village exhibition in Victorian London', *Japanese Studies*, 27:1 (2007), 80.

[24] M. Conte-Helm, *Japan and the North East of England: From 1862 to the Present Day* (London: Athlone, 1989), 65–66. A Newcastle newspaper reported that the sale of advance booked seating before the first performance was an unprecedent success. *Newcastle Weekly Chronicle*, 10/10/1885, 11.

[25] *Newcastle Courant*, 20/03/1885, 4.

[26] M. Papini, 'A "veritable fairyland": Mikado bazaar in Sunderland and the commodification of Japanese culture in the north east of England, 1861–1900', *History of Retailing and Consumption*, 6:2 (2020), 97–117.

[27] *Newcastle Journal*, 01/04/1862, 4.

[28] W. Halén, *Christopher Dresser: A Pioneer of Modern Design* (London: Phaidon Press, 1993); *Newcastle Journal*, 02/12/1863, 2.

[29] *Newcastle Journal*, 03/10/1867, 2.

[30] *Newcastle Daily Chronicle*, 02/03/1869, 1; *Northern Echo*, 27/06/1883, 1.

[31] *Northern Echo*, 31/05/1877, 1; *Jarrow Express*, 04/081877, 3.

[32] For example, in Darlington, *Newcastle Courant*, 27/10/1882, 5; Durham, *Durham County Advertiser*, 30/05/1884, 8; and Middlesbrough, *Northern Echo*, 30/10/1889, 1.

[33] Conte-Helm, *Japan and the North East of England*, 6–7.

[34] Conte-Helm, *Japan and the North East of England*, 20–51.

[35] *Daily Gazette for Middlesbrough*, 03/09/1886, 4.

[36] W.D. Wray, *Mitsubishi and the N.Y.K., Business Strategy in the Japanese Shipping Industry* (Cambridge, MA: Harvard University Press, 1984), 315–318.

[37] Conte-Helm, *Japan and the North East of England*, 99, 111.

[38] *Northern Eco*, 15/10/1887, 1.

[39] *Northern Echo*, 04/01/1875, 1; *Northern Echo*, 05/051877, 1; *Northern Echo*, 22/06/1883, 1.

[40] *Newcastle Courant*, 27/10/1882, 5; *Northern Echo*, 19/02/1884, 4.

41 *Northern Echo*, 19/02/1884, 4.

42 W. Dresser, *The Mikado Festival and Feast of Lanterns: A Recherche Bazaar, October 19, 20 and 21 1887*, Darlington Centre for Local Studies, U418h56.

43 *Northern Echo*, 20/10/1887, 8.

44 C. Baird, 'British ceramic collections at the Vienna Weltausstellung 1873: some British and American visitors' perspectives with comparative comments on the Japanese ceramic display', *Journal of the History of Collections*, 26:1 (2014), 79–82.

45 Cortazzi, *Japan in Late Victorian London*, 3.

46 A. Jackson, 'Imagining Japan: the Victorian perception and acquisition of Japanese culture', *Journal of Design History*, 5:4 (1992), 250.

47 *Newcastle Courant*, 27/10/1882, 5.

48 *Northern Echo*, 29/10/1881, 1.

49 *Northern Echo*, 20/10/1887, 8.

50 *York Herald*, 22/10/1887, 3.

51 Dresser, *The Mikado Festival*.

52 T. Yokoyama, *Japan in the Victorian Mind: A Study of Stereotyped Images of a Nation, 1850–80* (London: Palgrave Macmillan, 1987), 170–175.

53 Jackson, 'Imagining Japan', 250–252.

54 For the foundational works on orientalism, see E. Said, *Orientalism* (New York: Pantheon Books, 1978) and *Culture and Imperialism* (London: Chatto & Windus, 1993).

55 J. Urry, *The Tourist Gaze*, 2nd edn (London: SAGE, 2002), 3.

56 Urry, *The Tourist Gaze*.

57 E. de Bruijn, 'Virtual travel and virtuous objects: chinoiseries and the country house', in J. Stobart (ed), *Travel and the British Country House: Cultures, Critiques and Consumption in the Long Eighteenth Century* (Manchester University Press, 2017).

58 *Northern Echo*, 29/10/1881, 1.

59 *Northern Echo*, 20/10/1887, 8.

60 C. Guth, *Longfellow's Tattoos, Tourism, Collecting and Japan* (Seattle and London: University of Washington Press, 2004), 607.

61 D. Bate, 'The Occidental tourist: photography and the colonizing vision', *Afterimage*, 20:1 (1992), 12.

62 E. Kramer, '"Not so Japan-easy": the British reception of Japanese dress in the late nineteenth century', *Textile History*, 44:1 (2013), 20.

63 *York Herald*, 22/10/1887, 3.

64 Y. Matsukawa, 'Cross-dressing as whitewashing: the kimono Wednesdays protests and the erasure of Asian/American bodies', *Inter-Asia Cultural Studies*, 20:4 (2019), 591.

65 J. Lee, 'American decorative orientalism from the 19th into the 20th century', in K. Kitayama, M. Kinoshita and Y. Matsukawa (eds), *Orientalism at the Turn into the Twentieth Century: Cultural Representations and Glocal Studies* (Tokyo: Seijo University Center for Glocal Studies, 2015), 18.

66 M. Yoshihara, *Embracing the East: White Women and American Orientalism* (Oxford University Press, 2003), 10.

67 E. Ferry, '"A novelty among exhibitions": the loan exhibition of women's industries, Bristol 1885', in E. Darling and L. Whitworth (eds), *Women and the Making of Built Space in England, 1870–1950* (Aldershot: Ashgate, 2007), 54.

68 S. Cheang, '"Our missionary Wembley": China, local community and the British missionary empire, 1901–1924', *East Asian History*, 32/33 (2007): 177–198.

69 Roddy et al, *The Charity Market*, 1.

70 Roddy et al, *The Charity Market*, 36–37.

71 Dresser, *The Mikado Festival*.

72 *Northern Echo*, 20/10/1887, 8.

73 *Northern Echo*, 20/10/1887, 8.

74 In late Victorian Britain, the admission fee of six pence was probably considered the highest possible price for working-class people, as testified by tickets cost of Music Hall spectacles, which were mainly aiming at lower middle-class and upper working-class audiences. P. Summerfield, 'Patriotism and empire: music-hall entertainment, 1870–1914', in J. MacKenzie (ed), *Imperialism and Popular Culture* (Manchester University Press, 1986), 21–24, 33.

75 Prochaska, 'Charity bazaars', 83.

76 Dresser, *The Mikado Festival*.

77 *Northern Echo*, 20/10/1887, 8. In addition, the *Northern Echo* reporter speaks briefly of a Japanese pottery stall not mentioned in the guide, which allows us to speculate that it was a last-minute addition.

78 *The Lady's Bazaar & Fancy Fair Book* (London: Ward, Lock & Co., 1875), 23.

79 Roddy et al, *The Charity Market*.

80 *Northern Echo*, 01/02/1933, 7.

81 *Northern Echo*, 01/08/1933, 7.

82 *Northern Echo*, 17/12/1884, 1.

83 *Northern Echo*, 02/02/1885, 1; 18/12/1886, 1.

84 *Northern Echo*, 18/12/1886, 1.

85 *Northern Echo*, 01/02/1889, 1; 28/06/1893, 1.

86 *Northern Echo*, 01/02/1889, 1.

87 *Darlington and & Stockton Times*, 28/12/1889, 1.

88 R. Barthes, *Image Music Text*, essays selected and translated by S. Heath (London: Fontana Press, 1977), 48.

89 Y. Kikuchi and T. Watanabe, 'British discovery of Japanese art', in *The History of Anglo-Japanese Relations, 1600–2000*, vol 5 (London: Palgrave Macmillan, 2002), 153.

3

Hall and Spindler, Bespoke Tailors and Outfitters of Leamington Spa, 1878–1895: A Study in Retail Credit, Trust and Loyalty

Nick Gray

Introduction

This chapter explores the social and community relations of Hall and Spindler, a firm of bespoke tailors and outfitters in Leamington Spa, through the lens of the credit that they extended to their customers during an 18-year period at the end of the 19th century. It is a business history that engages with the relationship between retailing and community through economic records by examining the giving and repayment of credit, particularly from a social and cultural perspective. It analyses the firm's response to a rising level of bad (unrecoverable) debt and to an increase in the time taken to repay credit, and identifies customer loyalty as the most important factor in sustaining the firm's trust in its customer base. During a period that has been associated with increasing anonymity in retail processes, personal connections between the firm's partners and their customers emerge as key to its sustainability. Along with Chapter 12, it brings out the social embeddedness of retailing, particularly where credit was concerned.

The firm's business records show how credit was used in practice. The entries in the firm's ledgers follow the principles of double-entry bookkeeping and show the name and place of residence of each customer, the items purchased, the amount of credit given, and details of when credit was repaid including whether a discount was given.[1] The chapter examines a sample of customer accounts extracted from three ledgers that provide a continuous record of the firm's transactions with 113 customers from 1878 to circa 1896.[2] In addition, all the bad (unrecoverable) debts that were recorded in the account books have been analysed, as have claims made by the firm against debtors in Warwickshire County Court.[3]

Historians have debated the role of social factors in credit relations between retailers and their customers, particularly factors to do with class. In her landmark study of credit and debt in English culture during the long 19th century, Margot Finn argued that customers were awarded differential credit terms on the basis of their perceived social status and that this reinforced hierarchical social relations.[4] Jan de Vries challenged her view about the significance of class, arguing that, while credit relations were undoubtedly 'socially charged', they were nevertheless rational commercial agreements.[5] Finn also stressed the importance of retailers' personal knowledge of their customers and sociable behaviour towards them. Drawing on work by anthropologists, she argued that recipients of credit had a sense of having received a gift that placed an obligation on them.[6] This study of Hall and Spindler examines the extent to which the firm's relations were affected by the social status of customers, and it explores the part that social and cultural factors played in their business.

Examining Hall and Spindler begins to fill a gap in knowledge about how credit operated between small-scale retailers and male customers from the middle classes. The forms of late 19th-century retailing that have received most attention from historians have been those that sold mainly to women, such as department stores, co-operatives, corner shops, credit drapers or 'tallymen', and mail order companies.[7] Shops that sold mainly to men have received less attention, as have men as consumers.[8] It is also the case that, while some historians have observed that long credit could be problematic for traders that dealt with middle- and upper-class customers, there are no detailed studies of how it operated in practice to compare with work that has been carried out on working-class credit.[9]

Historians have called for a greater focus on small-scale retailing and this chapter responds to that call. Reviewing the composition of the global retail sector in the 20th century, Heinz-Gerhard Haupt has stressed the persistence of small-scale shops in varying degrees throughout Europe, Japan and China.[10] He has argued that small-scale forms of retailing merit more study, and other historians such as John Benson and Laura Ugolini have made the same point in relation to retailing in England.[11] Haupt has taken the argument a stage further by calling, in particular, for more insight into the cultural aspects of small-scale retailing and on the 'social practices' that were involved.[12]

The study reflects calls from both sides of the Atlantic for work on the acquisition of material goods to be complemented by studies of how they were actually paid for. Lendol Calder has referred to how 'the financial arts' have been overlooked in the history of consumption, and Frank Trentmann has argued that meaning and representation have been emphasized at the expense of saving and spending.[13] Viviana Zelizer argued that finance has been wrongly perceived as an uninteresting force in the social sciences and Calder suggested that it has not received the attention it deserves from historians for the same reason.[14]

The chapter explores the example of Hall and Spindler in the context of Finn and de Vries' differing views about the nature of credit, in particular the part played by social class in the firm's credit relations with its customers. It examines the extent to which personal knowledge of customers and social connections with them were important to the firm, and whether customers may have felt a sense of obligation on account of the credit they received. It contributes to understanding more about credit relations between small-scale retailers and male customers from a mainly middle-class background.

The chapter begins by setting out the context within which Hall and Spindler operated and their approach to retailing. It goes on to examine the composition of the firm's customer base, the credit that customers received, the payment of debts, and how the firm adapted their trading in response to experience. It draws conclusions about the part that social and cultural factors played in their credit relations, and how the partners maintained trust in their customers.

The town and the firm

Spa towns in England declined during the second half of the 19th century and retailers in Leamington Spa operated within a somewhat stagnant local economy that was characterized by a stasis in overall population numbers and out-migration by men of working age.[15] The early decades of the 19th century had seen a rapid increase in the population of the Parish of Leamington Priors with the emergence of the spa town. By mid-century, growth had slowed and during the period that is the focus of this study the population remained almost static at around 25,000.[16] In 1891, the Medical Officer of Health for Leamington Spa commented that the near stasis in population over the previous ten years was not surprising given that, for the most part, the population was elderly, the town was not a centre for manufacturing, and it had no rising industry to cause an influx of workers. He added that economic depression had caused out-migration by artisans, and that the birth rate was low.[17] While the town was no longer a haunt of the fashionable London elite, guidebooks nevertheless continued to promote it on account of its attractive built environment, the availability of a wide range of leisure activities and amenities, and its convenient location for visiting other places of interest.[18]

The retail sector in the town comprised mainly small-scale independent traders. Trade directories and local newspaper advertisements referenced just two multiple branch boot and shoe dealers and a drapery store with a branch in another town.[19] There was one large-scale store, the firm of Burgis and Colborne, which sold mainly household goods and no enterprise that could be classed as a department store.[20] Against that background, bespoke tailoring held its own, with approximately 40 firms trading during the last two decades of the 19th century.[21]

George Hall and John Spindler announced the formation of their partnership in the *Leamington Spa Courier* in April 1878.[22] Their advertisements stated that both partners had been foremen at J. Franklin & Co., a bespoke tailoring firm in the town, and that they were going into business on their own account following Franklin's retirement.[23] During the early years of trading, they set up once a week at a hotel in Coventry and in Banbury to take orders.[24] Franklin had operated in both towns before he retired and the new firm therefore had an existing client base in those locations as well as in Leamington Spa.[25] In 1888, they relocated from Bath Street, which was situated in the old and less fashionable part of the town, to The Parade, one of the streets where premier shops were located.[26] The partnership between them was dissolved on 30 September 1896 'by mutual consent', and Hall continued to trade with his son, Edgar, as 'Hall and Son'.[27]

George Hall was the lead partner in the firm. The 1881 census showed that he and his family lived on the premises and that he was a 'Tailor, employing 12 men'.[28] He continued to live above the shop when the firm relocated to The Parade. In the 1891 census his younger son, Edgar, aged 19, was present in the household and involved in the business as a 'Tailor's assistant'.[29] Against the background of what James B. Jefferys described as decline in the family tradition of retailing and a rise in the number of lock-up shops, Hall's family involvement and residency in his shop suggests that he was a traditional retailer who would have taken a close personal interest in his customers.[30]

Hall appears to have remained private in his personal socializing, but regarded his business as an integral part of the Leamington Spa community. His death notice recorded that he was one of the town's 'oldest and most respected business men ... of a quiet, retiring disposition ... [who] never took part in public life'.[31] The firm did however contribute, in its own name, to civic and sporting enterprises. They made donations to the town cricket club and were subscribers to the agricultural show and to the town improvement association.[32]

The firm's customer account books showed their concern to fulfil customers' individual sartorial requirements. A wide range of woollen fabrics were available, including cheviot wool, and finer types such as cashmere, saxony, beaver and angora. A surviving purchase ledger shows that from 1899, they were sourcing fabrics from merchants such as Holland and Sherry in London, as well as high-quality ready-made items such as shirts and hats from London suppliers.[33] The descriptions of bespoke clothing in the firm's account books are detailed and consistent and they varied little between 1878 and 1895: they specified the material and colour to be used, the style, and whether any additional features were required. The majority of the firm's advertisements stressed the quality of their work with phrases such as 'Every attention [would be] given to style and fit'.[34] They ceased advertising in 1884, showing they could rely on repeat business, referrals from existing customers, their reputation for quality, service and value, and on the credit terms they offered.

Customers and the credit they received

Customers included in the sample were classified according to their social status following the principles used by Alan Armstrong, who attributed social classes to people on the basis of the details about them that were recorded in census enumerators' books.[35] Any such method of classifying customers by social class is to some extent artificial, but Armstrong's approach has achieved a high degree of support, at least as a starting point for analysis.[36] The three social classes that feature in this study are:

- Social Class I: Professional occupations, including lawyers, clergymen, businessmen who employed 25 or more people, those whose income came from the ownership of land or property.
- Social Class II: Intermediate occupations, those who employed at least one person outside of their family but fewer than 25.
- Social Class III: Skilled occupations, skilled workers who were not employers.

The firm's customer base was concentrated around the partners' lower-middle-class social peers, such as the owners of small businesses and small-scale farmers. It also included a significant proportion of customers who were their upper-middle-class social superiors as well as a number of skilled manual workers and clerks. Table 3.1 shows how credit was distributed from the perspective of social class. Approximately half the customers were the partners' social peers, and they obtained 47 per cent of the total credit that the firm gave. The remaining credit was divided almost equally between customers who belonged to Social Class I, and those in Social Class III.

Customers do not seem to have received more or less credit on account of their social class. Those in Social Classes I and II received almost the same amount of credit per head. Customers in Social Class III received less. They also spent almost twice the proportion of the credit they received on cleaning, alterations and repairs compared with their social superiors. It seems most likely that customers from Social Class III obtained less credit because they had less disposable income to spend on new clothes.

Table 3.1: Allocation of credit to customers in the sample, by social class

Social class	Number of customers	Total credit received (nearest £)	Percentage of the total credit given	Credit received per customer (mean average to nearest shilling)
Social Class I	28	582	26	£20 16s
Social Class II	52*	1,066	47	£20 10s
Social Class III	40*	601	27	£15 10s
Totals	120*	2,249	100	

Note: * Seven customers were classified in two social classes (II and III) at different times.

Source: Customers Ledgers, 1878–c1896, Hall and Son, Tailors, Leamington Spa, CR 3446/1–3, WCRO, totals for 1879–1880, 1887–1888, 1894–1895 ('The Sample').

Payment of debts

The credit that the firm gave was informal in the sense that that customers did not sign a contract, as was the case with the retailers featured in Chapter 7. However, the evidence suggests that there were clear expectations on both sides. All customers were able to continue to obtain credit after they had accumulated unpaid debts and they all received the same discount terms: a shilling in the pound on credit repaid within six months of receiving it. From the firm's perspective, Hall and Spindler were prepared to pursue debtors from all walks of life in the courts if they defaulted: they made more use of Warwickshire County Court than any other tailoring firm in the town.[37] The overall sense is that the firm's credit relations with its customers were characterized by equality of treatment, irrespective of the social status of customers.

Compared with the equal treatment that customers received from Hall and Spindler, they varied widely in how they treated the firm. Certain categories of customer stand out as particularly fast or slow payers. In contrast to findings by historians about a general laxity in the payment of debt by middle- and upper-class customers, and in particular debts that were owed to tailors, Hall and Spindler's customers who belonged to Social Class I generally paid their debts much more quickly compared with those in other social classes.[38] Table 3.2 compares the cumulative percentage of the credit received by customers that was repaid. Nearly two-thirds of the credit received by customers that belonged to Social Class I was repaid within three months, compared with a third by customers in Social Class II and less than a third by those in Social Class III.

Two groups of customers stand out as particularly slow payers: farmers, and those who appear in census returns as 'sons' living in a parent's household. If these groups are excluded from the calculation, a different pattern emerges,

Table 3.2: Time taken for credit given to be repaid by customers in the sample: comparison between social classes

Social class	Within three months	Within six months	Within 12 months	Within 18 months
Social Class I	60	77	91	96
Social Class II	34	64	86	93
Social Class III	29	65	84	95

Source: The Sample

Table 3.3: Time taken for credit given to be repaid by customers in the sample: comparison between social classes, excluding farmers and 'sons'

Social class	Up to three months	Up to six months	Up to 12 months	Up to 18 months
Social Class I	60	77	91	96
Social Class II, excluding farmers	42	79	93	100
Social Class III, excluding 'sons'	38	74	91	99

Source: The Sample

as shown in Table 3.3. While customers in Social Class I repaid a higher proportion of the credit they received within three months, there was little difference at the six-month point and beyond. From this perspective, Hall and Spindler's social superiors emerge as marginally faster payers, but class was not a major determinant of repayment rate. Farming as an occupational category, and whether a customer was living in a parent's household, were more significant factors in the matter of paying debts.

Hall and Spindler's credit relations contrast with Margot Finn's view that considerations of social status dominated credit relations between retailers and customers. The firm's customers who were members of the professions, owners of large businesses and of independent means did not receive differential credit terms, in respect of the amounts of credit, the discounts that they received, or how long they were allowed to repay it. This group may have settled their debts relatively quickly simply because they had the means to do so, but there is no sense that they withheld payment because they held the firm in low esteem or for any other reason. Rather than reinforcing the social hierarchy, as Finn suggested may have been the case, Hall and Spindler made common terms available to all their customers.

The firm faced increasing long credit and escalating bad debt and its response suggests the factors that were most important to them in their credit relations. The speed with which debts were paid changed through the period 1878–1895, slowing significantly between the beginning and the middle of the period. Table 3.4 shows a comparison of the overall speed of repayment by customers in all social classes in 1879–1880, 1887–1888 and 1894–1895. Whereas half of the credit given in 1879–1880 was repaid within three months, less than a third was repaid within three months in 1887–1888. By the end of the period, there was little change, suggesting that the firm had gained a measure of control over the problem.

Increasing laxity in the payment of debts during the first half of the period was accompanied by a rise in the level of bad debt. This was followed by a significant fall, suggesting that the firm had significantly reduced their exposure to the risk of bad debt, as well as gaining a measure of control over the use of long credit. Figure 3.1 shows how the level of bad debt changed

Table 3.4: Time taken for the credit given to customers to be repaid

Period	<Three months	<Six months	<12 months	<18 months
1879–1880	49%	80%	95%	98%
1887–1888	31%	60%	83%	99%
1894–1895	33%	61%	80%	90%

Source: The Sample

Figure 3.1: Total bad debt (£) on purchases made in each year (1878–1895)

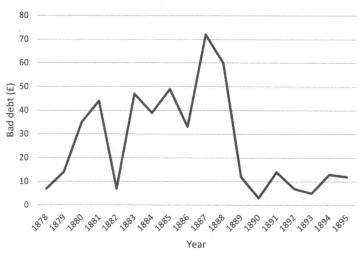

Source: Customers Ledgers 1878–c1896, Hall and Son, Tailors, Leamington Spa, CR 3446/1–3, WCRO: all bad debts recorded in the ledgers.

through the period. Overall, bad debt accounted for only around 1 per cent of the total value of the credit that the firm gave. There was, however, a seven-fold rise in the first half of the period, followed by a sharp fall, after which it remained at a relatively low level. The firm's account books show that a small number of customers were responsible for a high proportion of the total value of the bad debt.

Examination of the accounts of customers who failed to pay their debts, alongside census returns and vital records, show that they were either customers who were relatively mobile (they were not present at the address shown in the firm's account books in a census year – the majority of the firm's customers were), or who lived some distance away from Leamington Spa and had died. The next section will outline how the firm mitigated the risks that arose from long credit and bad debt, and the factors that were most important to them to maintain trust in their customer base.

Trust and loyalty

There were significant changes in the social mix of customers and in the distribution of credit during the period, which are illustrated in Table 3.5. Social Class II was the most prominent group throughout, in terms of both

Table 3.5: Changes in credit received by customers in the sample, by social class over time

	Number of customers who made purchases	Percentage of all customers who made purchases	Percentage of total credit given by the firm	Credit per customer (mean average)
1879–1880				
Social Class I	12	23%	24%	£13 15s
Social Class II	20	38%	46%	£16 5s
Social Class III	20	38%	30%	£10 10s
1887–1888				
Social Class I	12	20%	22%	£14 8s
Social Class II	30	51%	51%	£13 12s
Social Class III	17	29%	27%	£12 11s
1894–1895				
Social Class I	11	24%	32%	£22 2s
Social Class II	24	52%	44%	£13 18s
Social Class III	11	24%	24%	£16 2s

Source: The Sample

the number of customers and the proportion of the total credit received. The proportion of Social Class II customers in the firm's customer base rose from 38 per cent in 1879–1880 to 51 per cent by 1887–1888, and the absolute number increased by 50 per cent. By the end of the period, the number had fallen, but this class still accounted for half the total number of customers, and they received just under half the total credit. The number of customers in Social Class III fell sharply between the middle and the end of the period, but the amount of credit that they received, per head, increased and exceeded that received by customers in Social Class II. The number of customers in Social Class I remained at a constant level throughout the period, however, by 1894–1895 they accounted for a higher proportion of the firm's customers, and the amount of credit that they received, per head, had increased significantly.

Changes in the sample over time suggest that Hall and Spindler increasingly focused their business on those who had been known to them for a relatively long time. Customers in Social Class II, which was the dominant social group throughout the period, generally had much longer trading relationships with the firm compared with those in other social classes. Few of them made a single purchase, and those that made repeat purchases continued to buy from the firm for six years and three months, on average, compared with three years and four months for those in Social Class I, and four years and four months for those in Social Class III.[39] Almost two-thirds of those who made purchases in 1894–1895 had been customers in 1887–1888.

Customers who belonged to Social Class III generally had relatively short trading relationships with the firm, however, of the 11 that made purchases in 1894–1895, seven of them had been customers of the firm for over six years. The evidence suggests that the firm became more selective in giving credit to customers from Social Class III based on how long they had dealt with them, advancing relatively high amounts of credit to a small number.

It also seems that customers who belonged to Social Class I earned Hall and Spindler's trust, as a class, irrespective of the length of their association with the firm. They had the shortest trading relationships with the firm compared with those in other classes: in 1894–1895, only two out of the 11 customers who made purchases had been customers of the firm in 1887–1888. As noted earlier, however, customers from this class were significantly faster payers compared with other social groups, and it seems likely that the firm would have had a high level of trust in them as a class, notwithstanding their relatively brief trading relationships as individuals.

Loyalty, long credit and social connection

Many of Hall and Spindler's customers continued to purchase from the firm over many years even though there was a wide choice of tailors in

Leamington Spa and beyond. The evidence suggests that a social connection with the partners may have played a part in sustaining their loyalty to the firm. A high proportion of Hall and Spindler's social peers lived outside the town, and many of them were closer to other bespoke tailors. There was little difference in the degree of loyalty shown by out of town customers compared with town dwellers, suggesting that out of town customers had particular reasons for continuing to patronize the firm. It seems likely, in the absence of any economic explanation, that the reasons for their exceptionally long association with the firm was to do with the social and cultural aspects of the relationships they had with the partners. It is possible that a social connection with them, possibly based on the common interests of small businessmen, fostered the long-term loyalty of this group. To that extent, the evidence supports Margot Finn's view that sociable behaviour between retailers and customers played an essential part in cultivating trust, in this case through the longevity of the relationships that resulted from it.[40]

Farmers had very long trading relationships with the firm and they also enjoyed some of the longest credit. Farmers continued to purchase from the firm for six years and one month, on average, notwithstanding the fact that many of them had alternative sources of bespoke tailoring in market towns closer to where they lived. Their laxity in paying their debts persisted through the period: in 1894–1895, only 29 per cent of the credit they received was repaid within three months, 46 per cent within six months and 77 per cent within a year. They nevertheless accounted for a larger proportion of the customer base at the end of the period compared with the middle and early years, and the amount of credit that they received per head had increased. In common with other members of their social class, it is possible that social and cultural factors played a part in the degree of loyalty that they showed to the firm, and they may have felt a sense of obligation on account of the exceptionally long credit they received, as suggested by Finn.[41] They would certainly have found long credit attractive given the fluctuating fortunes of farming. From the firm's perspective, the evidence suggests that the risk associated with the long credit that these customers enjoyed was outweighed by the trust that resulted from the length of time over which they had been known to the firm.

Evidence about customers that were recorded in censuses as sons adds weight to the suggestion that granting long credit inspired loyalty in customers, possibly involving a sense of obligation towards the firm. They enjoyed exceptionally long credit: apart from one case that resulted in a bad debt, the remaining 20 sons repaid only 20 per cent of the credit they were given within three months, 55 per cent within six months and 77 per cent within 12 months. Ten per cent of the credit that they were given remained outstanding after 18 months. Sons also had exceptionally long trading relationships with the firm: a median average of seven years and ten months. While those customers who began purchasing from the firm at a young age would have been more likely to have had long trading relationships compared with older customers, sons stand out prominently compared with other members of the social class to which they belonged, for whom the median average trading relationship was four years and four months. Seven customers who first purchased from the firm when they were recorded as sons in the censuses migrated from Social Class III to Social Class II during the course of the period, and they had particularly long trading relationships with the firm: five of them made purchases over a period exceeding 16 years. The correlation between the degree of trust and tolerance that the firm showed towards this group of customers and their exceptional loyalty is striking. It supports the suggestion that the receipt of credit could result in a sense of obligation on the part of the debtor.

Customers, particularly farmers and sons, may have remained loyal to Hall and Spindler over long periods simply because the credit terms that were available were attractive to them. However, long credit was widely available from bespoke tailors and the evidence points to social connections with customers, possibly involving a sense of obligation on their part, as important factors in securing loyalty, and thereby the firm's trust, during a period in which retailing was becoming less socially embedded in communities.

Conclusion

In the case of Hall and Spindler, the evidence supports de Vries' view that credit relations were based on rational economic judgements in which considerations of social status played little part. The firm's customers did not gain more or less credit or different terms on account of the social status they held. Finn's argument that credit relations were dominated by considerations of social status may have applied to retailers that dealt more with the upper classes but, as far as Hall and Spindler's mainly middle-class clientele was concerned, this was not evident. Rather than reinforcing the social hierarchy, as Finn suggests may have been the case, Hall and Spindler offered common credit terms.

The particular significance of the social status of customers in the case of this firm lay in the high degree of loyalty shown by customers who were the partners' lower-middle-class social peers. They were the dominant social group throughout the period 1879–1895 and they generally had significantly longer trading relationships with the firm compared with customers from other social classes. In the absence of any other likely explanation, it seems that a social connection with the partners, possibly born out of shared interests and culture as small businessmen, may have played a part in their loyalty to the firm. The finding supports Finn's view about the importance of social behaviour between retailers and customers. Notwithstanding Hall's apparently quiet and retiring disposition he seems to have regarded sociability towards these customers, as well as contributing to local endeavours in the town, as an important parts of his role as a businessman.

Customer loyalty emerges as key to the firm's sustainability. When the level of bad debt escalated and the time taken for credit to be repaid increased, Hall and Spindler focused their business around a smaller number of customers that had dealt with them for a relatively long time. These included a significant number of farmers and young men who lived in a parent's household despite them being among the slowest payers, further suggesting that customer loyalty was the most important factor for the firm in maintaining trust. The findings support Margot Finn's view that personal knowledge of customers was important in credit relations. The correlation between the degree of trust and tolerance that the firm showed towards farmers and particularly sons, and their exceptional loyalty, supports Finn's view that recipients of credit could feel a sense of obligation. The trust that the firm placed in them was reciprocated by loyal patronage.

Purchasing by middle-class men emerges from the study of Hall and Spindler as fundamentally different from that of their female counterparts, as do the business models operated by the retailers that they patronized. If the department store is taken to be the shopping experience of choice for many middle-class women at the end of the 19th century, the equivalent for men might be seen as a visit to their bespoke tailor, which involved a very different kind of relationship between consumer and retailer. In the case of Hall and Spindler, most of their customers would have been known to them. Without those personal ties, and the trust that resulted from them, the firm's business model would have been unsustainable.

This study of Hall and Spindler's credit relations supports the opinions of historians who have argued that there is much to be gained from studying how goods and services were paid for, as well as those who have stressed the importance of the social and cultural aspects of small-scale retailing. The firm emerges as an integral part of the social fabric of the community that it served, and its sustainability depended on the high degree of embeddedness that it achieved.

Acknowledgements
Nick Gray wishes to express his thanks to staff in the Department of Humanities at the University of Wolverhampton for their encouragement and support in the writing of this chapter.

Notes
[1] B. Brackenbury, *Bookkeeping for Beginners* (London: Longmans, Green & Co., 1908), 12–13; W.G. Day, *Elementary Bookkeeping* (London: Gee & Co., 1901), 12–17.

[2] Customers ledgers, 1878–c1886, 1883–c1897, 1890–c1896, Hall and Son, Tailors, Leamington Spa, 1878–c1896, CR 3446/1–3, Warwickshire County Record Office, Warwick (WCRO).

[3] Plaint and Minute Book A, vol 5 (1896–1897) and vol 9 (1900–1901), Warwickshire County Court, 1847–1901, WCRO, CR 2922/6–7.

[4] M. Finn, *The Character of Credit: Personal Debt in English Culture, 1740–1914* (Cambridge University Press, 2003), 10, 280.

[5] J. de Vries, *The Industrious Revolution: Consumer Behaviour and the Household Economy, 1650 to the Present* (Cambridge University Press, 2008), 175.

[6] Finn, *The Character of Credit*, 19–21, 95, 9–10.

[7] In particular, J.B. Jefferys, *Retail Trading in Britain, 1850–1950: A Study of Trends in Retailing with Special Reference to the Development of Co-operative, Multiple Shop and Department Store Methods of Retailing* (Cambridge University Press, 1954); G. Crossick and S. Jaumain (eds), *Cathedrals of Consumption: The European Department Store, 1850–1939* (Aldershot: Ashgate, 1999); G. Rubin, 'From packmen, tallymen and "perambulating Scotchmen" to credit drapers' associations, c.1840–1914', *Business History*, 28:2 (2006), 210–212; R. Coopey, S. O'Connell and D. Porter, *Mail Order Retailing in Britain: A Business and Social History* (Oxford University Press, 2005).

[8] Notable exceptions are: C. Breward, *The Hidden Consumer: Masculinities, Fashion and City Life, 1860–1914* (Manchester University Press, 1995); L. Ugolini, *Men and Menswear: Sartorial Consumption in Britain, 1880–1914* (Aldershot: Ashgate, 2007).

[9] On long credit see M. Winstanley, *The Shopkeeper's World, 1830–1914* (Manchester University Press, 1983), 55; W.H. Fraser, *The Coming of the Mass Market, 1850–1914*, new edn (Brighton: Edward Everett Root, 2017), 92; Ugolini, *Men and Menswear*, 248, 130–134. No complementary studies have been done that compare with: P. Johnson, *Saving and Spending: The Working-Class Economy in Britain, 1870–1939* (Oxford: Clarendon Press, 1986); A. Taylor, *Working-Class Credit and Community since 1918* (Basingstoke: Palgrave Macmillan, 2002); S. O'Connell, *Credit and Community: Working-Class Debt in the UK since 1880* (Oxford University Press, 2009).

[10] H.-G. Haupt, 'Small shops and department stores', in F. Trentmann (ed), *The Oxford Handbook of the History of Consumption* (Oxford University Press, 2012), 268–269.

[11] Haupt, 'Small shops and department stores', 285; J. Benson and L. Ugolini, 'Introduction: historians and the nation of shopkeepers', in J. Benson and L. Ugolini (eds), *A Nation of Shopkeepers: Five Centuries of British Retailing* (London: Tauris & Co., 2003), 4–5.

[12] Haupt, 'Small shops and department stores', 285.

[13] L. Calder, 'Saving and spending', in F. Trentmann (ed), *The Oxford Handbook of the History of Consumption* (Oxford University Press, 2012), 350–351; F. Trentmann, 'Introduction', in F. Trentmann (ed), *The Oxford Handbook of the History of Consumption* (Oxford University Press, 2012), 14–15.

[14] Calder, 'Saving and spending', 352–353, referring to V.A. Zelizer, *The Social Meaning of Money: Pin Money, Pay Checks, Poor Reliefs and Other Currencies* (Chichester: Princeton University Press, 1997), 4.

[15] J. Walton, 'The history of British spa resorts: an exceptional case in Europe', *Transportes, Servicios y Telecommunicaciones: Journal of History*, 20 (2011), 138–157.

[16] R.B. Pugh (ed), *The Victoria History of the Counties of England, Volume VIII: A History of Warwick* (London: Oxford University Press, for the University of London Institute of Historical Research, 1969), 157.

[17] S. Browne, Medical Officer of Health, *Sanitary Report of the Borough of Royal Leamington Spa for the Year 1891* (Leamington Spa: J. Beck, 1892), 4.

[18] *Black's Guide to Leamington and its Environs including Warwick, Stratford-on-Avon, and Kenilworth* (London: Adam and Charles Black, 1891), 1–15; *A New Pictorial and Descriptive Guide to Leamington and Warwick ie., with Excursions to Kenilworth, Coventry, Stratford-on-Avon, Rugby etc.* (London: Ward Lock and Co., 1897), 2–17; B. Walters, *Illustrated Guide to Leamington Spa, Warwick, Kenilworth and Coventry* (London: Dawbarn and Ward, 1898), 14.

19   *Kelly's Directory of Warwickshire* (London: Kelly and Co., 1896), 326–328, 344; *Leamington Spa Courier*, 1878–1896.

20   *Courier*, 23/10/1897; 04/02/1899, 4; *House of Fraser Archive*, Burgis and Colbourne, https://housefraserarchive.ac.uk/company/?id=c1641 (accessed 15/11/2022).

21   *Kelly's Directory of Warwickshire*, 1880, 1007–1008; 1888, 347–348; 1896, 405–406.

22   *Courier*, 20/04/1878, 5.

23   *Courier*, 20/04/1878, 5.

24   *Coventry Standard and General Advertiser for Coventry and the Midland Counties*, 12/09/1878, 1; *Banbury Guardian*, 24/07/1879, 1; 13/07/1882, 1.

25   *Coventry Standard*, 01/02/1878, 1; *Banbury Guardian*, 18/06/1877, 2.

26   W.V. Gorman, *A Perfect Fit: A Story of Bespoke Tailoring in Leamington Spa, 1877–1998* (Warwick: W.V. Gorman, 1999), 54.

27   *Courier*, 12/09/1896, 5.

28   Enumeration Book (EB), 1881, Census of England and Wales, RG 11/3091, f.145, 22, The National Archives, findmypast.co.uk (accessed 22/11/2022).

29   Gorman, *A Perfect Fit*, 18; EB, 1891, RG12/2471, f.34, 14.

30   Jefferys, *Retail Trading in Britain*, 6–8.

31   *Courier*, 07/01/1916, 4.

32   *Courier*, 25/05/1900, 5.

33   Suppliers ledger, 1889–c1919, Hall and Son, Tailors, Leamington Spa, CR 3446/5, WCRO; Holland and Sherry, 'Our story', https://apparel.hollandandsherry.com/en/ourstory (accessed 30/11/2022); *Grace's Guide to British Industrial History*, 'Christy & Co.', https://www.gracesguide.co.uk/Christy_and_Co (accessed 30/11/2022).

34   For example, *Courier*, 21/10/1882, 2.

35   A. Armstrong, 'The use of information about occupation', in A.E. Wrigley (ed), *Nineteenth-Century Society: Essays in the Use of Quantitative Methods for the Study of Social Data* (Cambridge University Press, 1972), 191–224, referred to in D. Mills and K. Schurer, 'Employment and occupations', in D. Mills and K. Schurer (eds), *Local Communities in the Victorian Census Enumerators' Books* (Oxford: Leopard's Head Press Limited, 1996), 151–156.

36   Mills and Schurer, 'Employment and occupations', 150–159; E. Higgs, *Making Sense of the Census Revisited* (London: University of London School of Advanced Study Institute of Historical Research in conjunction with The National Archives, 2005), 138–140.

37   No records from Warwickshire County Court have survived for the period 1878–1895. However, records from 1896–1897 and 1900–1901 provide an indication of the use of the Court by Hall and Spindler and by other tailors: CR 2922/6–7, WCRO, contain the details of 13 summonses issued by the firm over a period of 27 months.

38   D. Alexander, *Retailing in England during the Industrial Revolution* (University of London, Athlone Press, 1970), 181; Ugolini, *Men and Menswear*, 248.

39   Estimates are based on those customers in the sample who began and ended their trading relationship with the firm within the period covered by the surviving account books.

40   Finn, *The Character of Credit*, 95.

41   Finn, *The Character of Credit*, 9–10.

4

Shopkeeper and Educator: Aspects of the Co-operative Movement in England, 1870–1914

Ian Mitchell

Introduction

In 1914, F.W. Peoples wrote: 'If the members of the Co-operative Societies ever begin to consider shopkeeping and the production of wealth as the sole end and aim of their existence, then their doom is sealed.'[1] For Peoples, the goal was the creation of a new co-operative commonwealth in which the interests of labour prevailed and production met the needs of society as a whole. This utopian vision might have been very well in theory, but the challenge for the co-operative movement was to keep the vision alive while dealing with the everyday issues involved in running retail establishments and being a presence in the local community.

This collection brings together charity, commercial and co-operative retailing and this chapter explores the way that commercial, community and even charitable elements played out within the co-operative movement. Co-op stores were businesses, even if businesses with a difference. The Co-op was not a charity, but it intervened in society by providing education, like many charities did, and individual societies also occasionally engaged in charitable activities.[2] This chapter will open with a discussion of the tensions within these different aspects of the co-operative movement and then explore how these tensions played out in more detail, with a particular focus on the Co-op as a retailer; the Co-op and community; the Co-op and education; and the Co-op and women. A successful Co-op had indeed to be much more than a store. As this chapter will demonstrate, the Co-op was generally successful in balancing these objectives.

There is a substantial literature about consumer co-operatives and their wider implications both for retailing and for the community, ranging from global perspectives to valuable local studies.[3] Retail history has quite properly treated the Co-op as the third major development alongside the growth of multiples and department stores in the late 19th century and early 20th century. Historians have discussed the formative ideas around co-operation and broader issues related to the impact of the movement on consumerism, the labour movement and local communities in Britain.[4] The Co-operative Women's Guild, which was instrumental in providing many working-class women with the skills and confidence to take a more active role in both co-operative and wider public life, as well as offering education on domestic and other topics, has been widely studied.[5] Former Secretary Margaret Llewelyn Davies collected the voices of members describing both the grinding poverty they often experienced and the sense of hope given to them by the Guild.[6]

As well as drawing on the wide-ranging secondary literature, this chapter makes use of two other main sources. First, there are the voluminous, and scattered, archives of individual Co-operative Societies, comprising mainly minute books of members' meetings and committees. Second, many Societies published their own histories, often to mark an anniversary of their establishment. These provide much valuable information, although they are almost always written from a non-critical perspective.

Principles and tensions

The earliest experiments with co-operative trading often had quite a short lifespan and the failure rate of societies based on Rochdale principles in the middle of the 19th century remained high: less than 40 per cent of those founded in the years 1867–1881 were still trading in 1900. Failed societies were usually small. Only when a society had over 200 members was its chance of survival better than even.[7] Although very difficult to quantify, there is good reason to assume that failure rates among more marginal retailers such as market traders, street traders and those having a shop in the front room of their house were similar. Co-operative growth in the last third of the century was rapid and sustained. By 1900, the co-operative movement in Britain accounted for some 7 per cent of all retail sales and 15 per cent of grocery and provisions sales. By 1914, there were over 1,000 separate societies with a total membership of around three million.[8] The larger societies, as in Leeds, had over 50,000 members and annual sales of well over £1 million.[9] Coverage was patchy – the heartlands were North West England (though not Merseyside); West Yorkshire; and the North East. In some of these areas over a fifth of the population were members.[10] The Co-op offered a strong range of groceries and most stores sold drapery goods, boots and shoes, and household items. Co-op stores were less successful in selling meat, fish and greengrocery, though many had managed to do so by the early 20th century. The success of the Co-op inevitably fuelled opposition from established shopkeepers, some of whom believed that they faced unfair competition.[11] Supporters of the movement might have claimed that what they offered was ethical shopping or indeed a gateway to a much wider cultural experience.[12]

The working people who established the Rochdale Equitable Pioneer Society in 1844 set out principles which were recognized as foundational by Co-ops in the second half of the 19th century and the early part of the 20th century.[13] These principles laid down that Co-op Societies should sell pure and unadulterated goods, and trade on cash not credit terms. Any surplus was to be distributed to members according to the amount purchased. Organizationally, each member would have one vote irrespective of the number of shares held. Finally, educational facilities were to be provided for members. It was not always easy to put these principles into practice and hold firm to them. There were potential tensions in the objectives of co-operation and between principles and prices.

It is misleading to treat the Co-op as a cohesive organization. While there was a shared vision and common aims, the co-operative movement comprised autonomous local societies, hopefully committed to the fundamental principles of co-operation, but operating under different circumstances with different members. All had to focus on four potentially conflicting objectives. First, there was the need to run a successful business, generating a surplus which could be distributed among members or used to fund wider objectives. Second, the business had to be ethical, both in terms of the conditions under which staff were employed and the sourcing of the products sold. Third, members, particularly those who sat on the plethora of committees spawned by the organization, had to be kept on side and had to feel that they were gaining benefits from membership. Finally, local societies needed to show that they were doing something connected to the wider objectives of the movement such as providing education or offering leisure facilities.

In his delightful and very accessible history of shopping, *Spend, Spend, Spend!*, Jon Stobart entitled his section on the Co-op, 'Shopping with Principles'.[14] Those principles required both a commitment to selling high-quality unadulterated goods and using some of surplus generated by the retail business to fund programmes of social improvement such as libraries, schools and decent houses for the working classes.[15] This meant that prices were higher than in other competing shops. Shopping at the Co-op was not for everyone. If you were among the poorest of the poor, who used Saturday night markets to purchase foodstuffs, and were not able to care too much about the quality, or indeed freshness, of what you were buying, then the Co-op was not for you. But if you had sufficient surplus income to be able to care about quality, and indeed about the conditions in which goods were produced, then the Co-op was a rational choice. As Peter Gurney comments, 'Although co-operation was not confined to any putative "labour aristocracy", membership of a society was undoubtedly a sign of respectability and was often beyond the reach of the lower echelons of the working class'.[16] Gurney also notes that most of those who shopped at the Co-op were not committed ideologically but could be tempted by bargains elsewhere.[17] In particular, the growing number of chain stores in the late 19th century and early 20th century provided the sort of competition to the Co-op that small neighbourhood or village shops were unable to do. In smaller areas, the Co-op might be the only store in town. In larger areas there was often a choice to be made between shopping with principles (which came with the deferred benefit represented by the dividend) and simply seeking out the cheapest option. The Co-op's primary target was the aspirational working classes and some of the middle classes, particularly those who valued ethics over cheapness.

Four Co-operative Societies

The previous section outlined the competing tensions within the co-operative movement, and the rest of the chapter will explore these tensions in detail, using four contrasting local societies: Bolton, Sheffield, Derby and Braintree. Bolton had a population just under 170,000 in 1901. It was at the heart of the Lancashire cotton industry with its landscape dominated by huge spinning mills. The Bolton Co-operative Society was founded in 1859 and within five years was well established in the town. Out of the four societies discussed in this section, Bolton was probably the one that was most engaged with its local communities. It was also one of the most important shops in the town centre. It was at the heart of the local community both in terms of providing good quality products and promoting education and welfare. In addition, members were made very aware of wider social and political issues, particularly through the activities of the Women's Guild.

Sheffield, a metal working town in South Yorkshire, had a population of around 400,000 in 1901. The co-operative movement emerged later in Sheffield than in many North West towns and was not well established until the last two decades of the 19th century. There were initially two societies in Sheffield (Eccleshall and Sheffield), which merged in 1907. By this stage, a visitor would have got the impression that the Co-op was one of the largest shops in a city where there were already three significant department stores. The local community was an important focus for providing opportunities; the exhibitions organized by the Society promoted and encouraged local arts and crafts. The community of members was equally significant, with a particular emphasis on education and social events. There was perhaps less emphasis on, or engagement with, the wider community of shared interest in progressive political or social action than elsewhere, particularly Bolton.

Derby in the English Midlands had a population of just below 120,000 in 1901. An industrial town, it had significant engineering and railway-related activities and was an administrative and retail centre. Although not usually regarded as Co-op heartlands, Derbyshire was well supplied with Co-ops by the end of the 19th century. The Derby Co-op traced its origins to a small store opened in the 1850s. Initially it grew gradually, but rapidly expanded in the last quarter of the century. The Derby Co-op was in essence a very big shop, competing with other shops in the town centre. Members were offered benefits, particularly housing and education, but there is little evidence of a vibrant community of members participating in a wide range of activities. The focus was on providing the local community with a large department store and a wide range of neighbourhood shops, with some recognition of the community of shared progressive interests, especially around working conditions.

Located in Essex some 60 or so kilometres north east of London, the adjacent towns of Braintree and Bocking were a long way from the traditional Co-op heartlands. These were small towns with a combined population of well under 20,000 in 1901. They had a significant textile industry, as did many towns in the Co-op heartlands of Northern England, although silk rather than wool or cotton was produced in Braintree and Bocking. The first store was opened in 1864 and sold basic provisions such as tea, butter, sugar and soap. It was open on Saturday afternoons and probably staffed by volunteers, though in 1865 a shopman was employed at a wage of 15 shillings a week. By this time the shop was open for five half-days a week and all day Saturday. The Society struggled in its early year. In 1866 closure was proposed, but members agreed that it should continue.[18] The Braintree and Bocking Society was a good example of a relatively small Co-op in which the interests of members were predominant. Their role in the community was limited as the Courtauld family was the major employer in Braintree and Bocking and was responsible for much of the local public provision. A relatively small Co-operative Society was not going to be a major player locally.

Although located in different geographical areas and operating on different scales, these four Co-operative Societies had much in common. Braintree was the smallest society, and the one furthest from the Co-op heartlands of North West England, West Yorkshire and the North East, but the Co-op was still one of the most significant shops in the town centre. The central stores of the other three societies were, at least by the early 20th century, essentially a department store competing with other independently owned department stores. All four sought to engage with their local communities, albeit in slightly different ways.

The Co-op as retailer

Local Co-ops had to succeed in their core business of retailing, carried out in competition with other retailers. Everything else the Co-op did depended on the revenue generated by selling goods and providing services. Undertakings like only selling unadulterated goods made the Co-op very attractive to ordinary customers, but were easier in theory than in practice. Complaints from customers, and store managers, about the quality of provisions like butter, cheese and meat were not uncommon. At Braintree it was said that local traders had little sympathy with the co-operative movement and there was a suspicion that they supplied inferior goods and short weight to the society.[19] Purchasing from the Co-operative Wholesale Society (CWS) became the norm after 1873, though not all goods came from there.[20] Indeed the way forward was for the Co-op to take control of the supply chain. Even then, it was never easy to stop a local manager from seeking to buy cheaper to boost sales or profits.

Keeping in control of credit was a perennial problem for retailers (see Chapters 3, 7 and 12). Credit should not have been an issue for the Co-op as one of the founding principles was to sell for cash only. In reality credit seems to have been commonplace. By 1886, of the 946 Societies in England, 511 offered credit terms. Most of these were probably short-term or limited in some other way, but 87 societies gave unconditional credit.[21] In some cases, customers simply took a long time to settle their bills. The Braintree Society wrote to a Mr Galley in 1881 asking him to discharge the amount owing as the success of the society depended on ready money dealing.[22] More formalized credit seems to have become more common in the early 20th century. For example, in 1902 the Birkenhead (Cheshire) Society decided to allow hire purchase terms for the furniture business; and in 1911 members were offered an official Credit Book which recorded name, address and amount allowed.[23] In this respect, at least, local Co-op shops were not so different from commercial retail.

There was often a slightly uneasy relationship between Co-ops and the trade union movement. In theory, Co-ops supported improved wages and conditions, but in practice, paying a fair wage and reducing working hours could put Co-ops at a disadvantage with local competitors. An easier option was to try to insist that goods sold in Co-op shops were made in accordance with the trade practices recommended by unions. This tended to mean buying from co-operative producers rather than other firms. In 1895, the Derby Co-op passed a resolution to the effect that all purchases of boots and shoes should be from co-operatives and that all arrangements with other boot and shoe manufacturers should be discontinued.[24] Dangerous working conditions could also be a concern. In 1902, for example, the Hebden Bridge branch of the Christian Social Union persuaded the local co-operative store to stock leadless glass ware: lead poisoning was a known risk in the ceramic and related industries.[25] Paying fair wages remained a contentious issue. In 1912, the National Co-operative Congress agreed a minimum wage for female employees; progress but hardly a resounding vote for equal pay.[26] In other respects, Co-op attitudes to staffing reflected the ethos of the age. For example, at Derby in 1902 there was a discussion at the quarterly meeting about whether a Mrs Ford could be retained as manager of the drapery department following her marriage. The almost unanimous view was that she could not be – the Co-op was just as opposed to the employment of married women as was the retail sector as a whole – but this was subsequently challenged by some of the directors. Their more tolerant attitude appears not to have prevailed, though it is perhaps significant that the issue was deemed worthy of discussion.[27]

As already indicated, Co-ops were somewhat bureaucratic in their organization. Management was by committee rather than by directive. The complex organizational structure of most societies with members' meetings, management committees and numerous sub-committees produced inevitable tensions between paid managers and members, each of whom could exercise a vote. So in Derby, for example, monthly meetings of members dealt with many matters of conduct. In 1897, a complaint from a member about the limited assortment of boots that assistants in the boot department showed customers was referred for further investigation.[28] Other and more miscellaneous complaints were also aired at such meetings: for example, in 1903, there were comments about bad eggs, Irish bacon and delays in supplying boots. Committee members kept a careful eye on sales figures. Similarly, at Braintree the Management Committee took a close interest in what was happening in the stores. This included general oversight of purchases and involvement in staffing issues. By the mid-1870s, sub-committees existed for grocery and provisions, the boot shop, the bakehouse, and coal.[29] It must sometimes have been a thankless task to be the manager caught between the need to be efficient and make a profit and having to refer many routine decisions to a committee.

The dividend was a big selling point, but also a cause of some difficulty. Towards the end of the 19th century and in the early 20th century dividends of at least two shillings in the pound (10 per cent) were normal and three shillings (15 per cent) or more not unusual.[30] Such dividends could only be achieved by keeping prices relatively high. The dividend was partly designed to encourage thrift: your reward was deferred and it was hoped you would save not spend it. This was all very well for those with some spare resources; it was less helpful for those on or below the poverty line. High dividends and the commensurate high prices were cited as one reason why the Co-op struggled to gain a foothold in the poorest areas.[31] Even more disturbing was the policy of the Sheffield Co-operative Society in 1894 to reduce wages in order to maintain or enhance the dividend, a striking (though rare) example of a conflict between the membership community and the community of shared progressive interests. Two members of the General Committee resigned in protest, saying that this was 'sweating with a vengeance' and 'truly un-co-operative'.[32] This was an extreme case but illustrates the difficulties of trying to achieve consistently high dividends.

The dividend was discussed in some detail at a Bolton members' meeting in 1898 following a paper on how to reach out to a wider section of the population. Suggestions were: to keep prices low, not paying a large dividend, and recognizing that shops in poor districts needed to prioritize low prices and small dividends.[33] It was not surprising that organized opposition to Co-ops, which emerged in Lancashire at the turn of the century, often targeted the dividend as a bogus inducement to shop at a store where prices were much higher. Despite this, the evidence very strongly suggests that the main appeal of the Co-op was the dividend. In the words of a felt hat worker reflecting on discussions about the Co-op: 'At our work we had many debates over Co-operation, and one thing always struck me; it was the poorest people in the room that were the most loyal. Ideals had nothing to do with it, it was the "divi" that was so useful.'[34] Working-class autobiographies tend to say less about the Co-op than might be expected, but when it is mentioned, it tends to be the dividend that is emphasized. For example, Bessie Wallis of West Melton recalled that most people shopped at the Co-op and that the dividend of four shillings in the pound provided clothes for children.[35]

Despite the opposition some Co-ops faced, the movement as a whole grew rapidly in the late 19th century and early 20th century. By the end of the 19th century the Bolton Society was operating 103 stores in its local area and the town's Central Stores was effectively the town's very substantial department store offering a wide range of provisions, textiles, clothing and house furnishings at a fair price.[36] It was a similar story in Sheffield. By 1913 the society had 17,500 members and an annual turnover of £344,000.[37] It was exploring the possibility of advertising on the curtains of cinemas. The Sheffield Co-op served not just Sheffield, but also its hinterland going out towards the Peak District. This could lead to the sort of problems that were likely to be experienced by any large store. For example, a disgruntled customer complained in 1912 that one delivery per week was not convenient for customers who were likely to desert the Co-op in favour of independent small shops that used handcarts for daily deliveries. He proposed that each shop should employ one or two youths primarily to deliver goods.[38] There was also much discussion in 1911 about buying a three-ton motor lorry to convey goods from the warehouse to branch stores. A light motor van was hired as an experiment. It worked with regard to delivering goods to branches, but not for deliveries to customers.[39] Growth came with its own challenges.

The Central Stores in Derby were located in the very heart of the town and when opened in the 1870s they were described as 'the most inspiring commercial sight in Derby'. With departments for grocery, provisions, drapery, boots and shoes, together with a meat store and a restaurant it was an embryonic department store in all but name. By the end of the century the stores had expanded to include warehouses, a large hall, a lecture room, work-rooms for dressmakers, tailors and milliners, and a furniture department. At that time there were some 13,000 members and annual sales were around £350,000. Like many such major town societies, the Derby Co-op sought to extend its reach both by establishing branches throughout the Derby suburbs, no doubt in competition with existing shops, and taking over adjacent societies such as Ashbourne (south west Derbyshire) and Uttoxeter (Staffordshire).[40] The Braintree Society opened a branch store at Bocking in 1874 and purchased larger premises in Braintree in the following year.[41] The story then is largely of steady if unspectacular growth. A butchery department was opened in 1885 and a new branch store at the nearby village of Shalford in 1892. This was not a great success and closed in 1903. On the other hand, larger central stores were opened in Braintree in 1907, comprising a variety of departments, and a new store was built in Bocking in 1913. A Co-operative Wholesale Society audit in 1914 found some serious shortcomings in record keeping and that the drapery department was holding stock well in excess of total annual sales but that other departments were sound.[42]

In the period studied, the co-operative movement was growing significantly and faced the difficulties of growth, alongside the difficulties of balancing the necessity of being a successful retailer alongside other goals. Co-ops varied significantly. The Co-op might be the village shop in a small mining community; or it might be essentially a department store in competition with similar privately owned stores in a large town. What they had in common is that they had to be a successful retailer for the local conditions, albeit with some very different ethical values than those of their main competitors, in order to thrive and therefore be able to be much more than a store.

The Co-op and community

The concept of community, or indeed communities, provides a bridge between the business side of the movement and its more ideological, didactic or cultural elements. It is possible to identify at least three different communities with which the Co-op engaged. The basic building block of the movement was the local society consisting of paid up members who had provided the initial capital for the society and expected to receive interest on these and a share in the profits, if any. There was an element of risk involved: if a society failed, which was not uncommon, a member could lose the hard-earned savings which they had invested in it.[43] These members formed one community with a vested interest in the economic viability of their society. Each society existed in a local setting where there were already markets, shops and probably other more informal forms of retailing. So the Co-op also had to relate to the local community, both the business community which might complain of unfair competition, and the community of potential shoppers or members, some of whom might prefer cheap prices to a share in the profits. Also, committed co-operators were concerned about wider social and political issues including working conditions and the empowerment of those whose voices often went unheard. So, there was also a community of shared interests which might not necessarily coincide with the immediate concerns of either members or shoppers.

Although there is evidence of some local societies having an awareness of Co-ops existing in other countries, for example a visit to Belgium from Bolton in 1907, there is little to suggest that international links had a high profile. Indeed there was often something quite insular about local Co-ops. On 4 August 1914 the secretary of the Stainland and Holywell Society in Yorkshire wrote to the local Member of Parliament urging him to use his influence to prevent 'our country' from being involved in a European war. One question for co-operators concerned with a community of shared interests was the problem of how to expand into the poorest working-class areas. Many talked about it, but few acted. An exception was Sunderland where the Women's Guild was particularly proactive spreading co-operation to poorer areas. Noting that co-operators in York had successfully established a general store in one of the poorer areas of the city, they opened a store in Coronation Street in 1902. This was the sort of area that the co-operative movement often shunned, fearing, probably rightly, that the need to finance generous dividends by charging high prices would be an obstacle to the retail business succeeding. The Coronation Street store offered cheap and nourishing take-away food such as hot soup and pease pudding, together with cheap bread and meat. There were parties for members and weekly children's meetings. Membership increased rapidly in the earlier months. It was also said that in the first ten days of trading the grocery store had doubled the trade of the old shop. Profits on cooked food boosted the dividend. Even so, within two years the experiment was discontinued.[44] While this may be an example of a conflict between the interests of the members community and the interests of the local community, or at least the poorer parts of this, the issue seems to have been less one of money (the dividend was not at risk) and more that the social aspirations of at least some members were being threatened.

By contrast, the Sheffield Society took a particular, and perhaps unusual, interest in promoting arts and crafts. As well as showcasing goods available in store, the society promoted the work of local artists and craftspeople. The Co-op ran exhibitions in 1908 and 1910. The 1908 exhibition seems to have been quite ambitious. Towards the end of 1907 there was a call for loans of works of art and curios together with a promise that all would be insured. A few months later, the emphasis seemed to have shifted to competitions for crafts such as boot polishing, metal polishing and cake baking. Only if space permitted, were departmental Co-op goods to be exhibited. Possibly the exhibition was more successful in showcasing members' art and crafts than in drawing in major art treasures from a wider area. The exhibition was opened on 16 April 1908 by the Lord Mayor of Sheffield. It was open from 2.00 pm until 10.00 pm daily with an admission charge of 2d for adults and 1d for children. It made a very small profit (£6 16s 6d). The 1910 exhibition seems to have been less ambitious, perhaps because of lessons learned from 1908. It was planned well in advance and focused on prizes for needlework, painting, photography, breadmaking, cakes and handicraft with a separate kindergarten section. The essay competition included categories such as: *Co-operative News*, *The Wheatsheaf*, a review of a book in the Co-operative Free Library, and the Women's Guilds.[45] Targeting a more affluent or aspirational set of customers was no doubt easier and more profitable than trying to reach out to the poorest. It is perhaps more realistic to think of communities rather than community. Local Co-ops had to be responsive to the needs and aspirations of the particular communities which they served. One common factor was a concern for education.

The Co-op and education

Local societies were keen to invest in education, often allocating at least 2.5 per cent of profits to educational activities. For this to happen, the shopkeeping element of the movement had to thrive and generate a surplus. Activities included the provision of reading rooms well stocked with newspapers, the creation of libraries with perhaps an emphasis on more radical publications, programmes of lectures, and organizations like choirs and music clubs which blended education with leisure, as did outings to places of interest and regular tea meetings.

The Braintree Society was neither particularly large nor wealthy, but even so members and others were offered much more than shops. As early as 1873, members agreed that 2.5 per cent of profits should be placed in an education fund. There was also a Women's Guild, although no records of its activities survive. All members had access to a reading room and funds were made available for the purchase of books. Quarterly Reports from 1903 state that the room was well supplied with daily and weekly papers and that the librarian attended on Friday evenings for the exchange of books, but there was a hint of disappointment regarding the number of members using these facilities.[46] Tea meetings, which were held from at least 1874 onwards, festivals and exhibitions may have been more popular. Some 500 tickets were sold for an excursion to Yarmouth in Norfolk in July 1904.

In Sheffield, the Eccleshall Society had had an active Education Committee that organized regular meetings with speakers and entertainment. A choir was formed in 1900. Books added to the library in 1901 included John Ruskin's *Unto this Last*. Much effort was put into organizing an excursion to Manchester with the intention of visiting the CWS head office as well as Belle Vue zoo and amusement park. Speakers could be people of note. In 1903–1904, the society organized a series of lectures by Philip Snowden, the socialist politician and future Chancellor of the Exchequer in the first Labour government some 20 years later.[47] The amount of time and effort many societies put into education is impressive, though it is difficult if not impossible to measure the outcome of this. On the other hand, a very specific initiative, the Women's Co-operative Guild, can reasonably be claimed to have had a significant impact and spread the message of co-operation more widely.

The Co-op and the Women's Co-operative Guild

The Women's Co-operative Guild was founded in 1883 on the belief that women could make much more use of the Co-op: they could learn more about the advantages and basic principles of co-operation and improve the conditions in which they worked and lived. By the end of the decade, the Guild had 51 branches with membership approaching 2,000.[48] The Guild was surprisingly strong in Southern England, given that this was not the Co-op heartlands, though by no means absent in the North and Midlands. Campaigns often focused on the very poorest; the Guild was keen to facilitate the spread of co-operative trading into the poorer areas of cities and towns. As the Guild matured, it focused on the importance of equality between women and men, particularly within marriage, and campaigns for suffrage.

Concern about working conditions was a constant theme, with shop workers a particular focus. Co-op women were particularly interested in reducing working hours, especially very late closing times, sometimes as late as midnight, with an hour of clearing up after closing. Guild members were urged to do their shopping as early in the day as possible. The Guild also tackled the use of phosphorus in matches. In 1898, a resolution denounced the use of yellow phosphorus in match factories because of its implication in causing jaw disease. The Guild asked the General Committee of the Co-op to ensure that shops only sold non-poisonous safety matches (and in a sense to boycott Bryant and May) and to explore selling Salvation Army matches that met health and safety standards.[49] Threats to female employment were also an issue: in 1911 the Guild objected to amendments to the Coal Mines Bill that would have excluded women from some sorts of surface work.[50]

Individual Guild branches tended to create their own key areas of interest; many prioritized social activities over social action. For example, meetings of the Ipswich Guild in the late 19th century were dominated by activities such as needlework and discussions about drapery and home furnishings. Alternative meetings focused on so-called work, meaning such activities as embroidery and garment repair. They also compared prices of groceries at independent shops and the Co-op. Regular teas and entertainments were an important focus.[51] The focus was essentially on the community of members.

By contrast, in the 1910s, the Ilford Guild was much more concerned about the principles of co-operation and divorce law reform. The Guild also expressed its concern about the employment of non-union labour by the adjoining Stratford Society.[52] In the Midlands, the Guild at Kirby in Ashfield, part of the Nottinghamshire coal mining area, was very politically aware. As at Ilford, members supported divorce law reform to ensure equal treatment for men and women, minimum wages, giving the vote to all adult women and men, and believed that women should be represented at the highest levels of Co-operative Society governance.[53] Guilds of this type provide good examples of how local parts of the co-operative movement related in a positive way to the wider community of shared progressive concerns.

The Sheffield Guild was more proactive, with a particular focus on the local community. It conducted an inquiry into the state of the poor in the town and in particular the nature of the retail provision. Small general shops often sold poor quality goods. The larger shops offered better quality but were expensive. Trading and similar clubs tended to tie poorer people to specific shops. Many people bought on credit and paid more than they would have done for cash.[54] Although not stated, the implication was clear: fair trading at a fair price by an organization like the Co-op would have been beneficial if only the Co-op could get over its unease about opening in poorer areas, an unease which probably curtailed the apparently successful Sunderland experiment. The Bolton branch of the Co-operative Women's Guild was founded in 1886 and had over 100 members by the end of the following year. Activities included lectures and discussions as well as instruction in needlework, cookery, dressmaking and laundry. The programme for a typical Guild meeting in 1893 included an address by a member of the Education Committee, dumbbells, a lecture on vegetarianism, songs and readings by members, and a question and answer session.

As these examples indicate, the Guild directly addressed women as homemakers, and at times reinforced the belief that homemaking was women's role, while advocating for equality. Bolton provides an example of the range of different views of women's place and work. Examples of a focus of women as homemakers include 1893 exhibition of members' work in such categories as dresses, crochet and embroidery and the School for Mothers (designed to reduce infant mortality), which was one of its main early 20th-century initiatives. The Guild, however, was about much more than reinforcing the prevailing view of women in a society of 'separate spheres'. Other activities, both educational and practical, demanded access for women to political power and equality. For example, in 1894 members had heard a lecture about the place of women in local government and in 1896 a resolution in favour of there being a larger number of women factory inspectors was passed, though with the proviso that they should have first-hand experience of working in mills (presumably cotton in the case of Bolton). In the same year the Guild unanimously passed a resolution about improved conditions of work (pay and hours) in textile mills. At a well-attended meeting in 1899, members heard a lecture on how to read a balance sheet. A delegation of members visited Belgium in 1907 to investigate the differences between co-operators in their respective countries. Women's suffrage issues were also on the agenda. In 1908 four members of the Guild were to be sent each day to the October Women's Suffrage demonstration in Manchester.[55] As one Lancashire member wrote:

> I attended the Guild Annual Meeting, which was a revelation ... I had longings and aspirations within myself which had never had an opportunity for realisation ... I formerly held the view that my husband could manage my politics – that there was no need for me to have a vote. I heard the question debated at an Annual Meeting, read, and thought the matter out, and came to the conclusion that a human responsibility cannot be taken by another. Each, whether man or woman, must use their own responsibility.[56]

The Guild was organized by women and for women.

Conclusion

The Co-op was both national and local and it is only by paying attention to its role in specific localities that its significance can be properly assessed. First, particularly in its heartlands, the Co-op was often one of the biggest shops in the town centre. It also had an extensive branch network. Whatever the distortions of anti-Co-op campaigns, other retailers had good cause to be concerned that they faced real competition. It also had, or tried to have, a set of values which influenced its approach to trade. Second, it provided opportunities for adult education and leisure activities which might not have been otherwise available. Third, the Women's Co-operative Guild gave a powerful voice to women. These wider activities, which made it much more than a store, depended on successful retailing to generate the funds needed to support them.

The Co-op began as a working-class movement and continued to be viewed with affection in many working-class communities. There was good reason for this, as it gave value for money, particularly when compared with many independent neighbourhood shops. Customers could also have confidence, at least most of the time, in the quality of the goods on offer and feel reasonably confident that they had been made in acceptable working conditions. It was therefore often central to community life, even if mainly used by working-class people, at least in its earlier years. But it struggled to meet the needs of the very poorest and, although some Societies tried to address this, the overall impression is that this was rarely high priority.

The Co-op was very much more than a store even if making a profit from its trading activities was a necessary condition for the delivery of its other community-based objectives. It largely succeeded in achieving the four potentially conflicting objectives referred to in the introduction: running a successful business; doing so with regard to wider ethical issues; keeping members satisfied; and promoting co-operation in its widest sense through education and other activities. However, while committed co-operators might have had a vision of a Co-operative Commonwealth, the Co-op considered as a business was firmly embedded in the market economy. Members were arguably encouraged to work *within* the existing system with a view to improving it rather than inspired to *overthrow and replace* it. But that was probably more realistic option. The Co-op had a vision, but it was a measured and achievable one.

Acknowledgements

This chapter is a much expanded and revised version of a paper presented at a University of Wolverhampton workshop on 'Retailing and the Community' in May 2019. I am very grateful to all those who made helpful comments and suggestions then and subsequently, especially the editors of this collection.

Notes

[1] F.W. Peoples, *History of the Educational Department of the Bolton Co-operative Society 1861–1914* (Manchester: Co-operative Wholesale Society Printing Works, 1914), 2.

[2] For example, National Co-operative Archive, Derby Committee Meetings 1892–1996, MID/1/2/2/2/1/1/8, 19/02/1895; West Yorkshire Archives Service, Bradford, Sheffield and Eccleshall Co-operative Society, Education Committee, 09/04/1902, 58D86/2/232.

[3] E. Furlough and C. Strickwerde (eds), *Consumers against Capitalism? Consumer Cooperation in Europe, North America, and Japan, 1840–1990* (Lanham: Rowman & Littlefield, 1999); B. Lancaster and P. Maguire (eds), *Towards the Co-operative Commonwealth: Essays in the History of Co-operation* (Manchester: Co-op College and History Workshop Trust, 1996). A useful bibliography and summary of the wider literature is to be found in M. Hilson, S. Neunsinger and G. Patmore, 'Co-operative retailing', in J. Stobart and V. Howard (eds), *The Routledge Companion to the History of Retailing* (London: Routledge, 2019), 301–318.

[4] P. Backstrom, *Christian Socialism and Co-operation in Victorian England: Edward Vansittart Neale and the Co-operative Movement* (London: Croom Helm, 1974); R. Black and N. Robertson (eds), *Consumerism and the Co-operative Movement in Modern British History* (Manchester University Press, 2009) and N. Robertson, *The Co-operative Movement and Communities in Britain 1960* (Farnham: Ashgate, 2010).

[5] The basic story can be found in C. Webb, *The Woman with the Basket: The History of the Women's Co-operative Guild, 1883–1927* (London: Women's Co-operative Guild, 1927); J. Gaffin and D. Thoms, *Caring and Sharing: The Centenary History of the Co-operative Women's Guild*, 2nd edn (Manchester: Holyoake Books, 1993); G. Scott, *Feminism and the Politics of Working Women: The Women's Co-operative Guild, 1880s to the Second World War* (London: Routledge, 1998).

[6] M. Llewelyn Davies (ed), *Life as We Have Known It by Co-operative Working Women* (New York: Norton & Co. edition, 1975).

[7] M. Purvis, 'Nineteenth century co-operative retailing in England and Wales: a geographical approach', DPhil thesis, University of Oxford, 1987, 122, 205.

[8] J. Stobart, *Spend, Spend, Spend!* (Stroud: Tempus, 2008), 134–137, 174.

[9] G.J. Holyoake, *The Jubilee History of the Leeds Industrial Co-operative Society Limited* (Manchester: Central Co-Operative Offices, 1897), 190–191.

[10] The most comprehensive account of the geographical coverage of the Co-op remains: Purvis, 'Nineteenth century co-operative retailing in England and Wales'.

[11] M. Winstanley, *The Shopkeeper's World 1880–1914* (Manchester University Press, 1983), 83–89.

[12] P. Gurney, *The Making of Consumer Culture in Modern Britain* (London: Bloomsbury, 2017), 109–116. See also P. Gurney, *Co-operative Culture and the Politics of Consumption in England, 1870–1930* (Manchester University Press, 1996).

[13] J.F. Wilson, A. Webster and R. Vorberg-Rugh, *Building Co-operation* (Oxford University Press, 2013), 37–40.

[14] Stobart, *Spend, Spend, Spend!*, 133–137.

[15] Stobart, *Spend, Spend Spend!*, 133–135.

[16] Gurney, *The Making of Consumer Culture in Modern Britain*, 114.

[17] Gurney, *The Making of Consumer Culture in Modern Britain*, 114.

[18] B.S. Wood, *Historical Sketch of the Braintree and West Essex Co-operative Society Limited* (Manchester: Co-operative Wholesale Society's Printing Works, 1914), 19.

[19] Wood, *Historical Sketch*, 23.

[20] Wood, *Historical Sketch*, 23.

[21] J.C. Gray, *The System of Credit as Practised by Co-operative Societies* (Manchester: Central Co-operative Board, 1891), 5–12.

[22] Braintree Co-operative Society, Management Committee Minutes, 1881–1882, A11977, Box 15, Essex Record Office (ERO).

[23] Birkenhead Co-operative General Committee Minutes, 1901–1904, YBC1/2, 56; 1911–1914, YBC1/5, 1. Wirral Archives.

[24] Derby Committee Meetings Minutes, 04/11/1895, MID/1/2/2/2/1/1/8, National Co-operative Archive.

[25] I. Mitchell, 'Ethical shopping in late Victorian and Edwardian Britain', *Journal of Historical Research in Marketing*, 7 (2015), 323.

[26] Derby Co-operative Society, Monthly Meetings, 1897–1925, MID/1/2/2/2/1/1/5, 15/04/1912.

[27] Derby Co-operative Society, Quarterly Meetings 1899–1911, MID/1/2/2/2/1/2/1, 10/02/1902; 22/12/1902.

[28] Derby, Monthly Meetings, 1897–1925, MID/1/2/2/2/1/1/5, 05/04/1897.

[29] Braintree Co-operative Society, Report for Quarter Ending 6 June 1903, A11977, Box 19 (ERO).

30 For example, Halifax Co-op paid three shillings in 1899 as did Preston in 1903. M. Blatchford, *The History of the Halifax Industrial Society* (Halifax: Halifax Industrial Society, 1901), 207; Preston Industrial Co-operative Society, Quarterly Reports, 1903, DDX1853/1/1, Lancashire Archives.

31 For example, *Bolton Co-operative Record*, 9 (February 1898), 10.

32 Bradford, Sheffield and Eccleshall Co-operative Societies, General Committee Minute Book, 02/10/1894, 58D86/2/1 West Yorkshire Archives Service (WYAS).

33 *Bolton Co-operative Record*, 9 (February 1898), 10.

34 Gurney, *Co-operative Culture*, 91.

35 J. Burnett (ed), *Destiny Obscure: Autobiographies of Childhood, Education and Family from the 1820s to the 1920s* (New York: Routledge, 1982), 325.

36 Peoples, *History of the Educational Department of the Bolton Co-operative Society*, 375–380.

37 *Bradford, Sheffield and Eccleshall Co-operative Society Limited: A Brief History of the Society and Thirty-Nine Year Progress from 1870 to 1913* (nd), np, WYAS.

38 Bradford, Sheffield and Eccleshall Co-operative Society, Special Committee 1907–1912, 58D86/2/131 (loose paper), WYAS,

39 Bradford, Sheffield and Eccleshall Co-operative Society, Special Committee 1907–1912, Minutes 12/12/1911, 10/05/12, 58D86/2/131, WYAS.

40 L. Unsworth, *Seventy-Five Years Co-operation: A Historical Outline of the Birth, Growth and Development of the Derby Co-operative Provident Society Ltd 1850–1925* (Manchester: Co-operative Wholesale Society Limited, 1927).

41 Unsworth, *Seventy-Five Years Co-operation*, 25.

42 As well as Wood, *Historical Sketch*, information about Braintree is drawn from *Braintree Co-operative Management Committee Minutes, 1865–1916*, A11977, Boxes 15 and 16, 11 volumes (ERO).

43 Mrs Layton lost £12 when the Child's Hill Society failed (Llewelyn Davies, *Life as We Have Known It*, 38).

44 Co-operative Women's Guild, vol 2, Misc 268, London School of Economics Library.

45 Arts and Crafts Exhibition Committee, 1907–1910, 58D86/2/234. Also loose papers in / 232, Co-operative Women's Guild, vol 2, Misc 268, London School of Economics Library.

46 Braintree Co-operative Society, Report for Quarter Ending 6 June 1903, A11977, Box 19 (ERO), 3.

47 Bradford, Eccleshall Co-operative Society Education Committee Minutes 1899–1904, 31/08/1904, 58D86/2/232, WYAS.

48 C. Webb, *The Woman with the Basket: The History of the Women's Co-operative Guild, 1883–1927* (London: Women's Co-operative Guild, 1927), 17–30.

49 Women's Co-operative Guild, Minutes, 1896–1900, FCO3/1/2, 26/05/1898, 13/10/1898, Bolton Archives. See Chapter 5 by Marjorie Gerhardt in this volume for an account of the Salvation Army's match factory.

50 Women's Co-operative Guild, Minutes, 1911–1913, FCO3/1/6, 28/09/1911, Bolton Archives.

51 Ipswich Industrial Co-operative Society Ltd, Women's Co-operative Guild, Minutes, 1888–1891, GF2/1/1/1, Suffolk Archives, Ipswich.

52 Women's Co-operative Guild, Ilford, Minutes, 1913–1915, WCG 8/52/1, Bishopsgate Library.

53 Women's Co-operative Guild, Kirkby in Ashfield, Minutes, 1909–1915, WCG/8/57/1, Bishopsgate Library.

54 Co-operative Women's Guild, vol 6, Misc 268, London School of Economics Library.

55 Bolton Co-operative Women's Guild Minute Books, 1891–1913, FCO3/1/1–6, Bolton Archives.

56 Llewelyn Davies, *Life as We Have Known It*, 132.

5

'By the Army, for the Army': The Salvation Army's Early Retail Activities, Criticisms and Responses in the Late 19th and Early 20th Centuries

Marjorie Gehrhardt

Introduction

In a 1906 essay, John Manson claimed that 'the [Salvation] Army thinks itself entitled to compete with the ordinary trader in almost any article, and to take advantage of its peculiar position and of the subsidies given it by the public for religious purposes in the competition'.[1] The Salvation Army was not the first charity involved in retail activities, but it 'pioneered a new kind of purchase-triggered charitable donation and an expanded, distinctly new, material culture of philanthropy'.[2] This chapter examines some of the external tensions between the Salvation Army, lay competitors and the wider public within the UK retail market. It also explores some of the Army's responses to criticisms such as Manson's, in particular how it framed the purchase and consumption of Salvation Army-made goods by Salvationists as a material embodiment of their belonging to the spiritual and social community of the Salvation Army. This chapter provides useful background to Chapter 6, Ruth Macdonald's analysis of women's rescue work, which highlights the originality of rescue retail activities and draws out the internal competition between the rescue work and the trade department's activities. It highlights the role of retail in embedding the Salvation Army within local communities and fostering members' sense of belonging.

This chapter uncovers the wide range of goods and services the Salvation Army traded in and argues that while financial aims were key pre-1890s, the advent of the Darkest England scheme (1890) saw retail activities become more diversified in their nature and in their purpose. This case study showcases the ways in which retail schemes were embedded within its core missions as well as fundraising activities. The Salvation Army was officially launched in 1878 by former Methodist preachers Catherine and William Booth (1829–1912). From its initial focus on evangelism in East London it soon expanded its activities and geographical reach, based on a vision for a united organization with international reach. The deployment and redeployment of officers throughout the territories in which the Salvation Army was present, the organization of international congresses, and the publication of local *War Cry* newspapers contributed to, and reflected, this vision, as highlighted in Chapter 6 on the Army's rescue work.

The international dimension was also reflected in the Salvation Army's trade activities, with the importation and exportation of products across territories, and with territorial trade departments being set up throughout the world. For example, US operations have received scholarly attention and, according to Diane Winston, an American Trade Department existed and was even complemented by a for-profit company, the Reliance Trading Company, which however only operated from 1902 until 1911.[3] In contrast, UK-based retail operations were not established as a for-profit scheme, and although they attracted criticisms, as will be discussed in this chapter, they apparently successfully adapted their products and target clientele in response. This chapter focuses on the United Kingdom, with London appearing in contemporary publications as the centre of the Army's retail operations for the United Kingdom but also overseas: 'Each Territory has its own Trade Department, but [the London-based] International Headquarters, besides acting as the Trade Centre for the United Kingdom, buys and manufactures largely for over-sea Territories.'[4] In addition, despite the existence of territorial trade departments, 'foreign matters' – from orders to customer complaints – were largely dealt with by a London-based officer in the 1890s and 1900s.[5] While this chapter's focus is primarily on UK trading operations, the occasional appeal to patriotic feelings and the responses the Army's retail schemes triggered within the UK retail market, links with overseas Army activities will be considered insofar as they affected UK-based trade operations.

Historical publications by the Salvation Army, especially the weekly newspaper *The War Cry* (often shortened to *War Cry*) are the primary source base for this chapter. These are used to explore how the Army articulated, justified and advertised its retail activities to readers. Reviews of, and responses to, the Salvation Army's activities published in non-Salvationist publications are also examined in this chapter to assess contemporary reactions.

This chapter will start with an overview of the Salvation Army's wide range of retail activities, highlighting the evolving and diverse range of products made and sold. The second section will focus on criticisms and concerns, from within the Army, and among contemporary observers. The last section will argue that the Salvation Army's responses to criticisms showcased the embeddedness of retail activities within its social and spiritual objectives.

A diverse range of retail activities

In the first decade of operation, the Salvation Army set up financially viable trading activities. While the 1880s are not the main focus of this chapter, an analysis of its trading activities during that period helps contextualize the changes (and continuities) that occurred from 1890 onwards.[6] Success led to an increasing understanding of the possibilities associated with trading, as well as to a diversification in the range of items sold:

> Having found, therefore, that no curse but a great blessing, attended this mercantile operation, we have not feared to add it to others; in the first place of a character specially connected with our work, such as musical instruments, watches specially designed to remind the soldier of his God and his duty, mottoes and other articles for home use, all contrived with the same end in view; and now last of all tea.[7]

The items for sale included many publications to support Salvationists in their spiritual growth and evangelism but also an increasing number of everyday objects – some of which bore the Army's logo or mottoes – such as quilts, cutlery, soap, boots, shoes and teas.[8] The Army's early retail ventures were largely inscribed within its fundraising activities. An 1883 report outlining the profits drawn from the sale of publications and items such as uniforms, badges and instruments presents these profits as covering staff and office expenditure, thus releasing funds otherwise donated to be used to further the Army's spiritual mission.[9] The diversification in the range of items sold reflects the understanding of these sales as a fundraising tool, as indicated in 1884: 'other things which cannot, except by means of covers or marks, have so direct a bearing on the propagation of the truth, *but which will at least answer another great purpose which experience has taught us we may safely aim at, the raising of funds by trade profits*'.[10] Despite this success, in 1886, General Booth announced, in his birthday letter, that the organization's trade activities would be 'confined to Literature and Uniform'.[11] A clearance sale followed, lasting until at least the start of 1888, and included watches, drapery and hosiery, cutlery, boots and shoes, and alarm clocks, among other items.[12] The Salvation Army's initial foray into retailing provides context to retail's return to the fore in the 1890s and 1900s, the focus of this chapter.

In 1890, William Booth published *In Darkest England and the Way Out*, which examined the condition of the 'Submerged Tenth' and proposed a social scheme aimed at elevating this category of the UK population.[13] Booth's vision for the Salvation Army to deliver this scheme and his appeal for funds gave rise to heated debates that divided the charitable world and the general public.[14] Letters published in *The Times* in 1890–1891 testify to the controversy caused by Booth's ideas. Nevertheless, by December 1890, 125,000 copies of the book had been sold and £90,000 had been gifted or pledged to the scheme.[15]

Booth's social scheme was motivated by widespread calls for social reforms in late 19th-century England, and the army's early success.[16] This social turn impacted the army's funding as Booth turned to secular sources for financial support, and in doing so drew widespread attention to the scheme among the general public. The Darkest England scheme had three main components: the City Colony, the Farm Colony and the Colony-over-sea. The City Colonies were embedded within local communities in urban areas and often offered food, shelter, basic goods and employment. From there, those in need could be referred to the Farm Colony, located in Essex, where it was hoped that the rural setting and the sense of community would further help spiritual and material rehabilitation. Colonies over-sea were due to welcome British workers who struggled to find employment at home and were willing to emigrate and farm the land abroad, although this part of the scheme did not come to fruition. Booth claimed that his scheme, which emphasized work and self-help, would not only offer basic necessities, training and employment opportunities to the submerged tenth, but it would also enable them to regain their self-esteem. The production and sale of goods featured prominently in the City and Farm colonies; in particular, those in need who could not afford to pay for food and shelter in the City colonies would be allowed to work in the Army's industrial workshops to cover these costs.

Retail had three key roles to play in Booth's Darkest England scheme. The sale of new or upcycled goods, constituted what historians Sarah Roddy, Julie-Marie Strange and Bertrand Taithe describe as an early form of purchase-triggered donations in their essay on charitable fundraising at the turn of the 20th century.[17] In contrast, the sale of cheap food and goods gave those in need access to essential supplies, and the collection and manufacture of goods for sale was intended to give the unemployed work. The operation of food depots, Old Clothes Shops and salvage stores selling cheap essential goods fitted within traditional charitable practices and helped the Army meet the needs of local communities.

In 1890, the Salvation Army was already collecting and selling old clothes and other necessities.[18] The Darkest England scheme greatly increased this activity and led to the opening of Elevator salvage stores that sold a range of items at low prices and were located in the poorest neighbourhoods.[19] The provision of cheap food and goods formed part of the Army's attempt to 'elevate' the submerged tenth. Supplying clothes, for example, was viewed as a way to help beneficiaries find employment, for '[t]he wearing of dilapidated, or even shabby, clothing often forms an impassable bar to the obtaining of employment'.[20] At the same time, it could foster a 'warm-glow' feeling among donors as they knew their used garments would not go to waste, and would instead help others: 'Many people are glad to relieve themselves of left-off clothing, especially when they know it will in some small way help the distressed.'[21]

The Leeds Salvage Store described in a 1908 *War Cry* article offered a range of items including hats, clothes, umbrellas, used linoleum, Wellington boots, perambulators, bassinettes and cradles.[22] In 1910, Rider Haggard stressed the diversity of the items for sale at the Spa Road Elevator salvage store, including 'enormous quantities of old clothes, and boots; also a great collection of furniture, including a Turkish bath cabinet, all of which articles had been given to the Army by charitable folk'.[23]

Beyond providing material comforts, retail activities were presented as furthering the spiritual salvation of those in need. Thus, an April 1890 sale at the women's shelter, Hanbury Street, was followed by a hot meal and a salvation meeting. 'Assurance teas' launched in 1902 were an attempt to use the sale of tea to provide people who might not otherwise have taken out an insurance policy, with the benefits of a life assurance: 'Everybody drinks tea – many do not assure owing to procrastination, or the small immediate outlay required. Our Scheme provides for a Good Cup of Tea and the Means of Assuring your Life without any expense beyond the ordinary and current price of the Tea.'[24] The bank, fire insurance and the life assurance schemes operated by the Army were described as encouraging those in need to save and to plan – part of spiritual salvation.

Gift sales, in contrast, appealed to customers beyond the submerged tenth. These, like the charity bazaars discussed in Chapter 2, were popular fundraising methods at this time.[25] The Salvation Army was a late adopter of ventures and the first large-scale gift sales organized by the Salvation Army only took place in 1894, the jubilee anniversary of Booth starting his missionary work. The kind of donations expected from supporters and local businesses included 'tin ware, crockery ware, remnants or other drapery, boots and shoes, groceries, confectionery, articles of furniture, flowers'.[26] Both perishable and non-perishable goods were thus sought, and organizers were encouraged to set up a dedicated stall for the sale of items made in Salvation Army's Social Wing workshops and factories.

The 1894 Jubilee gift sales were initially envisaged as fundraising tools, but other benefits more closely aligned with the Army's goals were also articulated. Thus, the *War Cry* noted that gift sales provided an opportunity for Salvationists to honour God and follow in the tradition of biblical role models through giving their labour.[27] Importantly, gift sales were also presented as a way to foster a greater sense of belonging and unity. Published regulations insisted on gift sales not interfering with regular Salvation Army activities, and on these events being run in a distinctive, Army-like and evangelistically minded way: 'The Army's Gift-Sales will differ as much from the ordinary "Church Bazaar" as The Army's methods differ from the ecclesiastical forms of the country.'[28] Gift sales instructions stipulated that 'Gift-Sales must *always* be combined with definite Salvation meetings, in which efforts shall be made for the conversion of the ungodly and the consecration and holiness both of our own people and others who may be present'.[29] Spiritual salvation and growth were thus highlighted as an important function of gift sales, thus mitigating concerns that these activities detracted from the army's core missions.

Adverts in *War Cry* and other publications invited readers to purchase the goods made in workshops and factories. Products advertised from the Hadleigh Farm Colony included bricks, eggs, jams and preserves.[30] The Salvation Army also opened a bakery in East London in 1890, and invited purchases from 'readers, officers, soldiers, comrades and sympathisers'.[31] While this activity was sometimes presented as a means to raise funds for the social scheme, other selling points were put forward to try and entice customers, including the excellent hygiene conditions at the bakery and the quality of the bread.[32] City and Farm colonies also produced or upcycled a range of items including furniture, mats, shoes and boots. The international reach of the Army was presented as an asset in this context: it could for instance sell tea to Salvation Army officers in Belgium (where tea was expensive) at moderate rates and import cheap wool from Belgium to the United Kingdom.[33]

Similarly, the short-lived production and sale of Kaffy, which was baked at the Clerkenwell Elevator and packed in tins made out of recycled material by salvage wharf workers, was presented as combining several functions, as detailed in this imaginary conversation between a Kaffy-drinker and a friend published in June 1892:

> What shall we drink? Why, Kaffy, to be sure! It possesses a threefold stimulation. First, it stimulates, without weakening the nerves. Secondly, it stimulates English trade. Thirdly, it stimulates conversation even more than tea. ... It's something new, home-made, not a bit of foreign manufacture in its growth and composition.[34]

This advert stresses the health benefits of this new beverage, contrasting it with standard coffee and water, while also appealing to potential customers' sense of patriotism and evangelistic mindset. Indeed, the advert goes on to encourage readers to use Kaffy as a conversation starter to explain the social work of the Army to their friends, and to enquire about their own spiritual salvation. The production and sale of Kaffy thus contributed to giving employment to the submerged, funding the social scheme, and providing outreach opportunities and a chance of expressing their Salvationist identity to members.

Offering employment opportunities was one of the main selling points of social goods made by men in the Elevators. Furniture items and mats made in the Elevators were frequently advertised in the *War Cry*, including in longer pieces that featured interviews with supervisors and testimonies of the men who were helped, thereby highlighting the primary social function of the production of goods. An 1890 article suggested that finding outlets was almost an afterthought:

> Winter is coming, and with its chilly blasts will come an increased crowd of workless ones. It is one thing to find them work; it is another to find a market for the results of their labor. Carpenters, mat-makers, shoemakers, wood-choppers, etc. are at work, and our stocks are daily rising. Here, too, our friends can help us. Will they do so by sending an order for anything they require in the above lines? ... The pressing needs of our kith and kin, the best promptings of our common humanity plead our cause.[35]

The evocation of the forthcoming bleak winter conditions and of the great numbers of people in need gave this appeal a desperate tone, and made the call for help addressed to readers all the more pressing. The emphasis put on shared humanity and brotherhood further demonstrated that the purchase of goods was envisaged as a way to help the 'submerged', rather than to raise funds.

The purchase of Darkest England safety matches was also articulated as an ethical choice, which indirectly helped the destitute working in the Army's factory and beyond. The match factory opened in 1891. Advertisements for Darkest England Safeties stressed the employees' better working conditions, especially the absence of toxic phosphorus in the production process, and higher wages than in the rest of the industry in England and abroad.[36] While Jayne Krisjanous described the sale of Army matches as 'sluggish', she presented the Army's initiative as 'an influential factor in the eventual safer working conditions for match makers and betterment of a segment of Victorian industrial society'.[37] This ethical dimension was frequently underlined in adverts, some of which targeted women specifically: 'Mothers and Daughters! Help the poor sweated Match Girls to healthier and happier conditions of life and labor, by using only Salvation Army improved safety matches. Burn like Wax, Anti-Sweating, Health Preservers, Best, therefore the Cheapest.'[38]

Criticisms levelled against the Salvation Army's retail activities: spiritual, social and economic dimensions

Despite the success of these retail activities, criticism abounded, both from within the Salvationist community, and from outside its ranks. The Salvation Army's first venture into retail in the 1880s outlined the shape of debates to come. An 1884 article addressed the concerns raised by members about the Trade Department expanding its offer to include uniforms, watches, towels and tea.[39] These concerns included the risk that trading may detract from spiritual matters, and the possibility that trading to raise funds showed a lack of faith in God's provision and that retailing may damage other businesses. In response, the positive impact of this income in terms of freeing up Officers' time to focus on evangelism, and the Army's willingness to collaborate with other businesses whenever possible, are stated. Importantly, trading is articulated as an initiative blessed by God:

> We believe the raising of money by means of the Trade Department to be a God sent plan, and it is a very remarkable fact that, from the time our Trade Department has assumed any large proportions, the amount of money received from other sources has been greater than ever.[40]

Despite this defence, the General's 1886 announcement that trading activities would focus on literature and uniforms mentioned ongoing criticism against trading. The General reaffirmed his belief that the Army's trade principles were sound, but the end of his letter suggested that this move was aimed at removing a potential source of disagreement and disunity among Salvationists.[41] A review of the Salvation Army's first 21 years, published in the same year, explained the choice to refocus efforts away from trading as a way to release members to focus on other work and as a result of the lack of capital to invest.[42]

In contrast, criticism from members of the public, especially after the launch of the Darkest England scheme, focused on production methods and competition with other businesses. The wages paid to employees were denounced as being too low, exposing the Army to accusations of sweating. The Darkest England scheme expanded rapidly from 1890, and by 1894, a total of 9,531 men had worked in a Salvation Army establishment.[43] The Salvation Army's match factory and the Hanbury Street Elevator were the main focus of accusations, even though Booth originally presented them as 'anti-sweating experiments'.[44] The Army unambiguously denounced and indeed campaigned against sweating practices, yet it was accused of exploiting men. An 1891 article compared the author's stays at the Salvation Army's Hanbury Street Elevator and at the Church Army's labour home in Crawford Street. The comparison highlighted the more hygienic conditions at the

Church Army's labour home, as well as the latter's better pay for workers. While the author does not explicitly accuse the Elevator leaders of sweating practices, the depiction of living and working conditions at the Hanbury Street Elevator is consistently negative, the author claiming to be writing to draw Salvation Army leaders' – who were described as hard to get hold of – attention to practices of which they may not be aware.[45] In 1905, the Social Democratic Federation condemned the practices of the Salvation Army as a 'gigantic system of sweating carried on under the pretence of charity and religion'.[46]

In 1907, the Trade Union Congress focused on accusations against the Salvation Army's Hanbury Street joinery workshop and requested that the products made there 'may not be put on the market at prices to compete unfairly with the general building firms'.[47] While the author acknowledged the useful work carried out, he claimed that this particular area of trade 'was undermining not only the conditions of trade unionists and other conditions of labour, but was doing really harmful work even to the men they attempted to regenerate'.[48] Other delegates expressed their support for this motion, one of them stating that he had been collating evidence of sweating practices in the Salvation Army's joinery workshop for the previous seven years, thereby suggesting that tensions had been building up since the turn of the century. Support for the motion was unanimous.

A further meeting of the London branch of the Amalgamated Society of Carpenters and Joiners was held in May 1908, resulting in a resolution that condemned the Salvation Army's Hanbury Street works' 'threefold system of sweating, truck-payment and underselling'.[49] The resolution called for a protest and a public inquiry. A demonstration organized by the United Workers Anti-Sweating Committee took place in Trafalgar Square in September 1908.[50] At the September 1908 Trade Union Congress, a delegate described the situation at the Hanbury workshop as 'one of the most gigantic successful frauds ever carried out under the cloak of religion'.[51] They also urged the Congress to 'emphatically brand The Salvation Army as sweaters, aggravated by disguise under the cloak of philanthropic and rescue work'. Unlike in previous meetings, the tone was emphatically critical and the redemptive dimension of the Army's work that had previously been acknowledged was no longer present. The Salvation Army was accused of hypocrisy and deceit, and of being 'the agents of the capitalist class'.[52] A further meeting organized by the United Workers' Anti-Sweating committee in February 1909 condemned the agreement signed by the Hanbury Street Elevator's workers.[53]

Further demonstrations in Trafalgar Square took place in March, April and August 1909; the criticism of the Hanbury Street workshop very strong, one speaker stating that it was 'diabolical'.[54] The duration and increasingly critical tone show the strong feelings that arose from the debate around the

Hanbury Street Elevator's joinery and carpentry workshop, as well as the committee's discontent at the absence of a public enquiry. The September 1909 Trade Union Congress, however, mentioned discussions with General Booth in which a compromise was being discussed.[55] An agreement was found by the time the Congress met again, in September 1910: Salvation Army carpenters would focus on producing items for the exclusive use of the Salvation Army, rather than the general public.[56] Although this only covered one aspect of the retail operations of the Salvation Army, this decision reflected, and perhaps accounted for, a broader change in target audience.

Concerns over sweating were closely linked to accusations of underselling and unfair competition. As early as 1892–1893, the Salvation Army was accused of underselling the product of its wood-chopping business, an accusation relayed by the Church Army, another organization also engaged in spiritual and social rehabilitation.[57] The public enquiry carried out in 1892 considered claims of underselling firewood but only issued a suggestion 'that every care should be taken when disposing of the articles produced in the institutions under the control of the Social Wing, that the prices charged should not be lower than those which may fairly be demanded by ordinary tradesmen or workmen'.[58] Unfair competition was also one of the key arguments used by John Manson in his 1906 essay quoted in the introduction to this chapter.[59] Manson also noted that:

> The trading activities of the Army are very extensive, and the articles traded in are supplied not only to members of the Army. 'The Trade Department,' says an advertisement in the War Cry, 'is at the service of any and every person who contemplates purchasing any such goods as are mentioned'.

Manson identified a range of factors that he argued led to the Army's unfair competition. These included the conditions of production, which he described as subsidized by donations diverted from their original purpose and also referenced sweating accusations, but also the range of items on offer and the customers targeted. Criticisms of the range of items on offer and of the customers targeted reflected – or led to – evolutions within the Army's retail schemes.

Responses: the multifaceted benefits of the Salvation Army's retail schemes

The Salvation Army emphasized the embedding of retail activities within its social rehabilitation scheme in response to sweating accusations. In a letter to the editor of the *Times* in September 1908, the Army challenged some of the evidence used by critics at the Trade Union Congress, citing the example of a former employee who had been offered money to speak about the workshop in negative terms.[60] The Salvation Army also held a series of demonstrations in September 1908, where it presented Hanbury Street workers, items they had made, and samples of the food they received as exhibits.[61] Through these, and through the release of pamphlets such as *The Truth about the so-called Sweating Charges: Official denials* (1908) and *A Calumny Exposed: Reply to the unfounded charges of Sweating brought against the Hanbury Street Labour Home* (1909), the Army argued that the wages paid reflected the men's often diminished abilities due to illness, old age or addictions.[62] A change in rhetoric began as early as 1907, with the Hanbury Street workshop being increasingly referred to as a 'social derelicts' industrial hospital'.[63] Inmates were referred to as patients in the press and in Army publications, emphasizing the men's altered physical and psychological state and the therapeutic function of these institutions, distancing them from common factories and workshops. The Salvation Army argued that men staying and working in Hanbury Street would in all likelihood not find another position or be eligible for help from the trade union, further emphasizing their helplessness.[64]

Accusations of underselling and unfair competition were also rebutted on multiple occasions. For example, the Army stated in 1894 that 'prices are often higher than competitors'.[65] A 1905 appeal for donations of old clothing, shoes, furniture, books and newspapers published in *The Times* stressed that 'WE ARE NOT DISPLACING OTHER WORKMEN, but utilising London's Waste in providing employment for some of London's Waste Labour'.[66] In 1908, they emphasized that not all quotes were successful, the Hanbury Street Elevator was run at a loss and the prices used as evidence by critics were incorrect.[67]

The Salvation Army sometimes contradicted its denial of any interference with existing trades and businesses. As the Army expanded its operations in the late 1890s and early 1900s, it occasionally acknowledged a competitive dimension. In an 1898 interview, outgoing International Trade operations director Colonel Lamb was asked if the Salvation Army could compete with other firms and stated: 'Decidedly, *and we do it!* … We can compete in quality and price with any of them.'[68] The emphasis, in adverts, on the high quality of items on offer suggested that customers beyond Army supporters were encouraged to purchase and take advantage of the good value for money offered. The *Darkest England Gazette* journalist visited the Hanbury Street carpentry workshop in 1893, and reported: 'Nor is the workmanship of the men of a cheap, common or nasty character. "Here", remarked our genial guide, "is a splendid suite of drawing-room furniture in walnut, covered in crimson plush," the chair-backs being elegantly carved in a May-blossom design.'[69] The sophistication of the objects was highlighted, and the patronage of respectable people was mentioned, which would encourage readers to follow their example: '[J]ust before we arrived at the Elevator a suite of bedroom furniture had been dispatched to the order of a well-known M.D., as a wedding present to his daughter.'[70]

In time, the Salvation Army increasingly made a distinction between social goods, and other items for sale:

> In a great undertaking such as ours, we must necessarily have many departments that are run on purely commercial lines. ...
>
> Take, for instance, our Joinery and General Works Department, which employs carpenters. That pays its hands according to the Trade Union rate. The same applies to our Printing, Publishing, Book-binding, Instrument-making and other Departments that we need not name here.
>
> The vital difference between these branches and the Hanbury Street, is that the former have no connection with our Social Work. The employees are not submerged, whereas the men employed in Hanbury Street are largely of the class already enumerated.[71]

After the crisis of 1907–1908, a shift was observed from targeting the general public to Salvationists almost exclusively.[72] The amount of space devoted to adverts in the *War Cry* expanded significantly from the mid-1890s until the early 1910s, with close to a full page (sometimes even more) reserved for the International Trade Headquarters to promote their products, reflecting the growing importance of trade activities. Adverts increasingly focused on products made by Salvation Army soldiers or sourced from other suppliers, rather than made by beneficiaries, although these never completely disappeared, especially in connection with the women's rescue work and the furniture department.[73] After the compromise reached with trade unions in 1909–1910, the focus on Salvation Army members as customers became even clearer. A 1913 advert stated:

> Everything for Salvationists' wear and use.
>
> We specialize in the requirements of Salvationists; and from long experience and close association we have become peculiarly conversant with their tastes and needs. We are always on the look-out for dependable goods that will best serve their interests, giving the best value in every line.[74]

While not all of the goods on offer were specific to the usage of Salvationists, advertising targeted soldiers and officers. For example, owning a reliable bicycle was linked to spreading the gospel: 'The Cycle will be in the future a means of reaching the outlying villages and districts with the Salvation message of "Peace on Earth, Goodwill towards Men".'[75] As the organization itself was expanding and responding to criticisms, it focused on winning Salvationists' custom.

Building on the growth of the Salvation Army as an organization, the International Trade Headquarters increasingly advertised goods as an opportunity for customers to publicly display their affiliation. Alongside uniforms – which *War Cry* readers were urged to wear more and more frequently – the Army also sold a range of branded products, such as 'Darkest England' matches, clocks bearing the Salvation Army crest, Triumph Tea and Triumph soap. The Army also registered trademarks, for example: Arc bicycles, Sanis underwear, a portable platform for open-air meetings and Silmer cloth.[76] The Trade pages praised the quality and value for money of the products on offer, and sought to educate Salvationists in a better approach to shopping. Under the heading 'Why the Best is Cheapest', an 1897 advert suggested that buying a cheap garment would ultimately result in higher costs, as it would have to be replaced sooner, than a more expensive, better quality item.[77] Advertising often reflected wider Salvation Army culture; historians have noted the large role that General Booth and his family played in the organization, and they were frequently used to advertise products.[78] *The War Cry* often used a statement by General Booth's daughter-in-law Florence Booth: 'The use of Good materials is the Truest Economy.'[79] Adverts also included endorsements by Booth family members, for example, Mrs Booth for Sanis underwear: 'I consider the "SANIS" Underclothing very satisfactory indeed, and have been very pleased with the wear of that which we have used at home. I should certainly recommend all our Officers to purchase it.'[80]

Adverts repeatedly stressed that purchasing all of their goods from the Army was the only logical choice for Salvationists: 'The equipment of Officers and Soldiers differs in so many points from the requirements of others that it is essential that those who supply these needs should know, and be fully in sympathy with, the principles of The Army.'[81] As noted by Diane Winston, Army products had 'added value; the tea wasn't just tea, it was a salvation blend'.[82] The Trade Headquarters emphasized this unique selling point in their slogan 'Established <u>by</u> the Army, <u>for</u> the Army' and in their messages: 'You cannot do better than purchase from the trade headquarters' and 'The Trade Headquarters exists to help save the world. Its profits are entirely devoted to that purpose'.[83]

In order to further incentivize Salvationists to shop with the Trade Headquarters, rewards were introduced, such as money towards travel costs to London events featuring an Army trade stall (for example, to Trade showroom visitors in 1894), free tea to buyers who recruited new customers for the Missionary Tea League, free goods for people spending a certain amount (for example, a Special Christmas tea blend in 1898), and later on a profit-sharing scheme (1913).[84] All these decisions moved Salvation Army retailing to focus on Salvationists and also brought retailing further into the culture and practice of the Salvation Army. The retail activities of the Salvation Army were increasingly framed as an opportunity for the Army to support its members in all of their needs, be they spiritual or material, and for members to express their commitment to the organization and its missions. Focusing on a Salvationist clientele helped the Army mitigate criticisms from other businesses and unions, and to some extent limit competition with rescue work items, as shown in Chapter 6.

Conclusion

As this chapter has shown, the Army's production and sale of goods was very diverse in its nature and aims, and target customers varied depending on the items and the period of time. The scope evolved, partly as a result of criticisms and concerns raised by Salvationists and outside observers. The target customers and the producers of the items sold by the Salvation Army were also complex: in addition to the inmates of the industrial workshops, the Salvation Army also employed qualified tradesmen to make musical instruments, uniforms, or blend tea. In terms of customers, while salvage stores were aimed at providing essential goods to poorer people at a low price, the Salvation Army also sought to appeal to the general public, emphasizing the quality of the items made, their good value and the ethical dimension of purchasing from the Army. While Salvation Army soldiers were almost a captive market for certain goods (for example, uniforms, regulation caps and bonnets, music books), the Army also urged its members to shop with the Army for other everyday goods and gifts. The selling points put forward in International Trade Headquarters advertisements included ethical, spiritual and financial considerations, highlighting the quality and value of the items sold, but also the reinvestment of profits in the Army's core spiritual mission. Beyond this, for Salvation Army soldiers, shopping with the organization's trade departments became viewed as a material embodiment of belonging to the Army. Retail activities were thus a means to fulfil the Army's spiritual and social missions, as well as a fundraising method and a community-building tool. Like present-day retail initiatives run by charities, the Salvation Army faced criticisms focusing mainly on the conditions in which items were produced, on trade being a 'distraction' from its core missions and on grounds of unfair competition. Clearly embedding the production and sale of goods within the Army's spiritual and social salvation project post-1890, however, helped alleviate some of these concerns.

Acknowledgements
I am grateful to the Salvation Army International Heritage Centre team and to the editorial team for their helpful comments and suggestions.

Notes

[1] J. Manson, *The Salvation Army and the Public: A Religious, Social and Financial Study* (London: Routledge, 1906).

[2] S. Roddy, J.M. Strange and B. Taithe, *The Charity Market and Humanitarianism in Britain, 1870–1912* (London: Bloomsbury, 2018), 41.

[3] On the American Trade Department, see D. Winston, *Red-Hot and Righteous: The Urban Religion of the Salvation Army* (Cambridge, MA: Harvard University Press, 2000), 137–140.

[4] 1907 *Salvation Army Year Book*, 47, Salvation Army Archives.

[5] 1914 International Congress brochure, *Inside the Trade Headquarters*, 124–125, Salvation Army Archives; *All the World*, March 1892, 199.

[6] *The Salvation War*, 1882, 171; *The Salvation War*, 1883, 123.

[7] *The Salvation War*, 1884, 117.

[8] *Salvation Soldiers' Pocket Book*, 1885, 77–79.

[9] *The Salvation War*, 1883, 123.

[10] *The Salvation War*, 1884, 117 (my emphasis).

[11] W. Booth, 'Birthday letter', *War Cry*, 17/04/1886.

[12] 'Clearance sale', *War Cry*, 27/11/1886, 16; 'Clearance sale', 31/12/1887, 16; 'Clearance sale', 04/02/1888, 16.

[13] W. Booth, *In Darkest England and the Way Out* (London: International Headquarters of the Salvation Army, 1890).

[14] H. Ausubel, 'General Booth's scheme of social salvation', *The American Historical Review*, 56:3 (1951), 519–525; D. Owen, *English Philanthropy: 1660–1960* (London: Oxford University Press, 1965), 243.

[15] London Correspondent, *The Times*, 27/12/1890, 5.

[16] N. Murdoch, *Origins of the Salvation Army* (Knoxville: University of Tennessee Press, 1994), 169.

[17] Roddy et al, *The Charity Market*.

[18] J. Short, *The Christian Mission Magazine*, London, April 1870, quoted in J. Fairbank, *Booth's Boots: Social Service Beginnings in The Salvation Army* (London: Salvationist Publishing, 1983), 2.

[19] M.W., 'Elevator salvage store: waste turned to good account', *The War Cry*, 08/02/1908, 3.

[20] D. Lyall, *Pictures of Joy and Sorrow, The Salvation Army Social Work 1913–14* (London: Salvation Army, 1914), 88.

[21] Lyall, *Pictures of Joy and Sorrow*, 35.

[22] Lyall, *Pictures of Joy and Sorrow*, 35.

[23] H. Rider Haggard, *Regeneration Being an Account of the Social Work of the Salvation Army in Great Britain* (London: Longmans, Green & Co., 1910), 30.

[24] *War Cry*, 14/06/1902, 15.

[25] See, for example, F. Prochaska, 'Charity bazaars in nineteenth-century England', *Journal of British Studies*, 16:2 (1977), 62–84.

[26] *The Officer*, 05/05/1894, 146.

[27] *War Cry*, 14/04/1894, 9.

[28] *War Cry*, 26/05/1894, 3.

[29] *War Cry*, 26/05/1894, 3 (emphasis in original).

[30] *War Cry*, 04/06/1892, 15.

[31] *War Cry*, 26/09/1891, 11.

[32] *Darkest England Gazette*, 09/12/1893, 11.

[33] *War Cry*, 03/11/1894, 4.

[34] *War Cry*, 03/11/1894, 4.

[35] *War Cry*, 11/10/1890, 5.

36 *War Cry*, 16/05/1891, 6.

37 J. Krisjanous, 'Examining the historical roots of social marketing through the lights in darkest England campaign', *Journal of Macromarketing*, 34:4 (2014), 448.

38 *War Cry*, 04/03/1893, 15.

39 *War Cry*, 31/12/1884, 4.

40 *War Cry*, 31/12/1884, 4.

41 Booth, 'Birthday letter'.

42 Salvation Army, *Twenty-One Years of Salvation Army, 1886*, 198, Salvation Army International Heritage Centre.

43 *War Cry*, 29/12/1894, 7.

44 Booth, *Darkest England*, 81.

45 ' "General" Booth's "Elevator" and the Church Army's labour-home', *The Times*, 28/08/1891, 8.

46 'Social democratic federation', *The Times*, 24/04/1905, 4.

47 'Trade Union Congress', *The Times*, 6/09/1907, 5.

48 'Trade Union Congress', *The Times*, 6/09/1907, 5.

49 'Alleged "sweating" by the Salvation Army', *The Times*, 28/05/1908, 12.

50 'Trade Union Congress', *The Times*, 09/09/1908, 12; 'Trade Union Congress', *Daily Telegraph*, 09/09/1908, 8; *War Cry*, 19/09/1908, 9.

51 'Trade Union Congress', *The Times*, 09/09/1908, 12; 'Trade Union Congress', *Daily Telegraph*, 09/09/1908, 8; *War Cry*, 19/09/1908, 9.

52 'Trade Union Congress', *The Times*, 09/09/1908, 12.

53 'The Salvation Army and sweating', *The Times*, 05/02/1909, 7.

54 *The Times*, 08/03/1909, 10; 26/04/1909, 7; 30/08/1909, 2.

55 *The Times*, 07/09/1909, 6.

56 'Trade Union Congress', *The Times*, 14/09/1910, 8.

57 E. Cadman, 'The Salvation Army and wood-chopping', *The Times*, 04/01/1893, 4.

58 *In Darkest England and the Way Out: Report of the Committee* (London: Harrison & Sons, 1892), 15–16, 39.

59 J. Manson, *The Salvation Army and the Public: A Religious, Social and Financial Study* (London: Routledge, 1906).

60 A. Nicol, 'The Salvation Army and charges of sweating', *The Times*, 12/09/1908, 2.

61 Anon, 'The Salvation Army and "sweated" labour', *The Times*, 22/09/1908.

62 Commissioner Sturgess and Colonel Jacobs, *The Truth about the so-called Sweating Charges: Official Denials* (1908), Salvation Army International Heritage Centre PAM/R.10; Commissioner Sturgess and Colonel Jacobs, *A Calumny Exposed: Reply to the Unfounded Charges of Sweating Brought Against the Hanbury Street Labour Home* (London: The Salvation Army, 1909).

63 *The Times*, 07/09/1907, 7; *War Cry*, 21/09/1907, 1; Sturgess and Jacobs, *The Truth about the so-called Sweating Charges*, 4, 19.

64 W. Booth, Letter, 22/07/1908, cited in Sturgess and Jacobs, *A Calumny Exposed*, 5–7.

65 *War Cry*, 23/06/1894, 4.

66 'The Salvation Army', *The Times*, 11/12/1905, 13 (emphasis in original).

67 Sturgess and Jacobs, *The Truth about the so-called Sweating Charges*, 4–6.

68 *War Cry*, 12/11/1898, 5 (emphasis in original); see also *War Cry*, 18/04/1903, 15; 27/01/1906, 3; 07/11/1907, 9.

69 *Darkest England Gazette*, 22/07/1893, 8.

70 *Darkest England Gazette*, 22/07/1893, 8.

71 Sturgess and Jacobs, *A Calumny Exposed*, 18.

72 Miscellaneous, *The Times*, 04/05/1908, 1.

73 *War Cry*, 12/01/1895, 15.

74 *War Cry*, 24/05/1913, 14.
75 *War Cry*, 28/03/1896, 14.
76 *War Cry*, 28/03/1896, 14; 17/08/1895, 12; 03/10/1903, 11; 25/05/1907, 15; 21/03/1908, 15.
77 *War Cry*, 6/02/1897, 14.
78 Roddy et al, *The Charity Market*; Ausubel, 'General Booth's scheme of social salvation'; Krisjanous, 'Examining the historical roots of social marketing'.
79 *War Cry*, 03/04/1897, 12.
80 *War Cry*, 26/10/1895, 14; 18/01/1902, 15.
81 *War Cry*, 29/12/1913, 16.
82 D. Winston, 'Living in the material world: Salvation Army lassies and urban commercial culture, 1880–1918', in J. Giggie and D. Winston (eds), *Faith in the Market* (New Brunswick: Rutgers University Press, 2002), 16.
83 *War Cry*, 16/04//1910, 14; 26/08/1911, 14; 29/12/1894, 16 (emphasis in original).
84 *War Cry*, 15/12/1894, 15; 30/10/1897, 15; 03/12/1898, 15; 04/01/1913, 9; *The Times*, 26/12/1912, 9.

6

A Labour of Love: The Role of Retail in Salvation Army Rescue Work for Women

Ruth Macdonald

Introduction

In July 1902, a full-page cartoon in the Salvation Army's monthly rescue work magazine, *The Deliverer*, posed the question 'Is Love's Labour Lost?'. It comprised three rows of seven frames. The first graphically depicted a woman's pitiable descent into poverty, alcoholism, crime, prostitution and homelessness followed in the second by her subsequent rescue by Salvation Army officers and restoration to health, home, work, leisure and a state of moral and spiritual respectability. It would appear all was not lost, but for the third row. Headed 'What you can do', it made the answer conditional upon the reader who was prompted to 'Purchase our girls' work'. The closing text revealed the true purpose of the cartoon by giving an address for orders of needlework and knitted goods: it was a retail advert.[1]

As Chapter 5 showed, by the turn of the century, retail had permeated nearly every branch of Salvation Army work. Over the course of the 1880s and 1890s, the Salvation Army's London Trade Headquarters became the central powerhouse of almost all its retail activity in the United Kingdom and internationally, including selling the products of its British men's social work industries. However, a separate retail subculture developed within the Salvation Army's British women's rescue work wing and was allowed to continue operating independently and in parallel with the Salvation Army's main trading activities. Surviving records do not make explicit why the retail activities of the women's social wing remained independent. However, in this chapter, I will argue that retail came to occupy an indispensable place in the operational model of the women's wing because of the opportunities it offered to further the wing's aims beyond raising funds. These aims were best served by forms of retail that favoured personal social interactions and community building.

Recent scholarship has explored the Salvation Army's participation in late 19th-century consumer capitalist culture and examined how the Salvation Army embraced entrepreneurial methods and used innovative marketing strategies to expand its donor markets and make ethical consumption accessible.[2] My chapter builds on this recent research and earlier writings that explored how rescue work allowed women in Victorian Britain to expand their agency in the public sphere.[3] Frank Prochaska addressed rescue work and charity retail separately, but the close union of retail and rescue work that was cultivated by the Salvation Army has yet to be examined in any depth.[4] This chapter examines that connection, drawing on Winston's US-focused work connecting the spiritual expansionism of the Salvation Army and the economic expansionism of the time. The Salvation Army's rescue work in Britain contributed to and was envisioned as part of an international project. The early Salvation Army began expanding outside Great Britain in 1880 and, as it spread internationally, it exported not only its people and worship practices, but its rescue work model and the attitudes which supported it too. Rescue work retail also developed in other national contexts but there is not scope here to explore these. For the British rescue wing, the Salvation Army's growing international field steadily widened the consumer markets it could access through its retail operations. Winston argued that both the Salvation Army and industrial capitalism shared 'a vision of individual transformation that would lead to a corporate utopia'.[5] Existing studies of Salvation Army retail in other contexts have foregrounded its transformative effects on the individual, and thereby wider society, through the roles of producer and consumer. This case study of rescue work retail will focus instead on how the act of selling was seen to contribute to both individual and corporate transformation.

Carrying out this research while working as an archivist at the Salvation Army's International Heritage Centre in London, I have drawn on surviving archival records from the Salvation Army's women's social work wing. However, while the archives detailing the case histories of rescue home residents are extensive, there are fewer covering the homes' retail activities, so published primary sources have also been used to understand this branch of work. Its aims were most widely articulated in the Salvation Army's own press and publicity literature, particularly the rescue wing's *Deliverer* magazine, but also the weekly *War Cry* newspaper, and annual reports and reviews. In this chapter, these Salvation Army-produced sources are not treated as straightforward accounts of actions or events. Rather, they are recognized as a constitutive part of the developing system of rescue work and retail that is under consideration. As such, the sources reveal the concerns, intentions, aspirations and abortive efforts of rescue workers as much as their accomplishments and serve as a window into the apparatus and mindset of rescue work. The power dynamics intrinsic in the surviving records, which were almost exclusively created by official representatives of the Salvation Army, make it difficult to know how far rescued women felt part of a community, or how they felt about being used to exemplify the need for and success of rescue work. Published sources like *The War Cry* tend to present a one-sided view of them engaging enthusiastically with the rescue work and the wider Salvation Army community long beyond their stay in a home, but unpublished archival sources reveal a range of more varied and nuanced responses including ambivalence, evasion, resistance and waning interest over time.[6] It is because of their largely one-sided nature that these sources offer an excellent opportunity to 'move away from treating the archives as an *extractive* exercise to an ethnographic one'.[7]

Rescue work and the development of industries in Salvation Army rescue homes

Rescue work was a practical expression of the moral reform and social purity movements of the mid-to-late Victorian period. Undertaken by numerous religious philanthropic groups and individuals, predominantly middle- and upper-class women, its goal was the rehabilitation of women whose behaviour transgressed societal expectations, most commonly young working-class women. Founded on a moral code that viewed only marital sex as acceptable for women, and a climate of fear over the effects of contagious diseases on society, rescue work had strong associations with prostitution and the control of female sexuality. There was often also a preventive element which sought to reach women perceived to be at risk, as well as concern for other behaviours such as alcohol consumption.[8] Although the language surrounding rescue work was overwhelmingly moral in its tone, practitioners sometimes recognized the role of precarity in the situations and behaviours they sought to remedy. Leading social purity campaigner and rescue worker Josephine Butler, whose connections with the Salvation Army shaped its early rescue work, asserted that 'economics lie at the very root of practical morality'.[9] As a result, most rescue homes provided training for future employment, usually in domestic service, and placed residents in employment once their rehabilitation was considered complete. This model was adopted by the Salvation Army when it started opening rescue homes in 1883, but Salvation Army homes soon began to incorporate economics into their moral reform programme in a more fundamental way. Their residents undertook not just training but *work* while in the homes. This work was intended as a form of therapy that would simultaneously contribute towards residents' rehabilitation, ensure they were kept suitably occupied and under supervision, and subsidize the running costs of the home.

The first Salvation Army rescue home opened in Glasgow on 25 May 1883 and a second opened a year later in the Whitechapel area of London.[10] By the end of the decade there were 11 across Britain. Run by female officers, these homes provided a short- to medium-term residence for women, intended as a refuge from bad influences and habits.[11] Salvation Army rescue work proliferated fastest in London where one home became three within two years and five by the end of the decade. The London homes first developed the concept of work therapy into a system of small-scale industrial production reliant on retail for its income. Initially there had been no organized system and rescue home residents contributed income by undertaking odd jobs inside and outside the homes. Announcing the recent launch of rescue work in London in 1884, *The War Cry* reported that 'the young women are busily employed in various ways, sewing, machining, washing, etc.'.[12] An income and expenditure book from the first London home records that jobs carried out included embroidering Salvation Army mottos and crests on jerseys worn as part of members' uniforms and scrubbing the local Salvation Army hall.[13] In Glasgow it was reported that 'sewing and knitting are ... undertaken, under a competent overseer; and, wherever suitable opportunity offers, the girls go out charing and scrubbing'.[14]

Officers refined their approach to work as they gained experience. Jobs undertaken outside the homes, like charing, were rejected in favour of in-house manual production, a decision with both moral and economic motives. In 1887, the leader of Salvation Army rescue work, Florence Booth, was quoted in the *Pall Mall Gazette* as saying:

> [N]eedlework is good for giving the mind constant employment; and then it is so much better than laundry work, which is the usual resort, because it gives more opportunities for getting to know and influence the women; and then washing work is so hard, it goes on, on, on; and we try to make the Homes really homelike to the women.[15]

Salvation Army rescue officers believed that personal influence, a homely environment and industrious use of time were crucial in bringing about their goal of moral reform, so they made needlework, which could be performed inside the home under their supervision, the default source of income. The Salvation Army press abounds with descriptions of communal singing, reading and praying contributing to the restorative moral environment of the rescue home workrooms.[16] This policy also served to limit and control the communities women could engage with and form while resident in the homes. Rescue workers were wary of women associating with friends and acquaintances from their former lives for fear of the regressive influence this might have. They also sought to carefully supervise and manage residents' interaction with one another for similar reasons.[17] Keeping work in-house aided their efforts to restrict the opportunities women had for communicating their life histories (viewed as potentially scandalous and shameful) to one another and the wider community.[18]

Yet although the rescue homes existed to address a perceived moral problem, they were nonetheless part of the 'remarkable fundraising machine' that the Salvation Army was becoming.[19] Enterprise and innovation were encouraged in every branch of its work, and rescue officers did not allow the economic potential of their homes to be limited by a narrow view of needlework: by 1887, rescue home residents were practising needlecrafts as diverse as sewing, knitting, crochet, embroidery, straw weaving and bookbinding.[20] Officers were alert to opportunities for improving the productivity of their workrooms and thereby their income, borrowing techniques from industrial mass production including mechanization, specialization and the division of labour. This began when the Salvation Army received several knitting machines as gifts in 1886 and 1887 which led to the workroom of the first London rescue home being given over entirely to knitwear production. As new homes opened each was assigned an industry. By the fourth anniversary of London rescue work in June 1888, *The War Cry* reported: 'We [have] two branches – [knitting] machine work, making jerseys, stockings &c., and bookbinding. Already the girls [are] earning a large sum of money, something like £200 in the last six months.'[21]

Around the same time, another London home began exclusively manufacturing washing texts, washable wall hangings decorated with machine-embroidered religious mottos, bringing the number of homes with a specialised product line to three.[22] Specializing brought the homes closer to self-sufficiency, with the knitting home leading the way.[23] The rescue work balance sheet for 1888 shows how substantial the income from machine knitted goods had become in little over a year, comfortably covering production costs and allowing £125 of profit to be paid to the home.[24] The running costs of the home for that year amounted to £323 so this £125 contribution was significant. By 1889, ten of the 11 Salvation Army rescue homes had a nominated industry or industries, the exception being the maternity home where childcare was given priority.

Selling and marketing the products of industry

The decision to focus on manufacturing as the preferred form of work in the rescue homes required finding ways of selling the goods that were being produced. Initially, rescue officers looked inwards, aiming to sell the homes' products to Salvationists. During the 1880s, the Salvation Army held numerous major celebrations at large venues in London, bringing together its local, national and international membership. Stalls selling rescue work products were always present at these mass gatherings, and rescue officers made use of spectacle to draw attention to the homes' wares. On one occasion they suspended enormous washing texts with eye-catching messages like 'Where will you spend eternity?' from the side galleries of the Exeter Hall; on another they sold needlework from a pony trap doing circuits of the grounds of Alexandra Palace.[25] Rescue home residents were brought to some of these events to participate in selling their wares, an action which simultaneously positioned them as members of the expanding Salvation Army community while also making them objects of display of Salvationist rescue work.[26]

It soon became convention for rescue officers to carry out the work of selling rescue home goods. In 1888, a staff member at rescue work headquarters was assigned the role of commercial traveller. She visited Army corps (churches) around London by horse and cart bringing with her 'articles made by our lasses'.[27] Although the internal target markets accessible at corps and mass events had the advantage of being predisposed to sympathize with the cause (and there was also a degree to which peer pressure could be exerted), most of the Salvation Army's core working-class membership had little disposable income. The product lines offered by the rescue homes mitigated this problem to an extent because they were either cheap, everyday necessities (socks, vests, shirts and children's clothes), or items that were marketed as an essential part of Salvation Army evangelical work (washing texts for the walls of Salvation Army halls, or pamphlets spreading the organization's message). Nonetheless, marketing principally to an internal customer base, albeit a sizeable and growing one, was economically limiting, particularly as rescue work was not the only branch of the Salvation Army soliciting purchases from members; the Trade Department also tugged insistently at their purse strings. The internal competition between the two sections is most apparent when looking at another form of retail used by the rescue wing: mail order.

Mail order and the developing Salvation Army press

In mid-1886, notices requesting orders for needlework began to appear in *The War Cry* and in 1887 these were replaced by more formal adverts listing specific products and prices. As the Salvation Army's main organ of communication, *The War Cry* aimed to serve several purposes at once: it communicated internal news to members and officers of the Salvation Army, news of progress to supporters and benefactors, and the good news of the gospel to potential converts to whom it was sold in pubs, brothels and streets. Its weekly circulation at this time was in the hundreds of thousands and because readership did not strictly correspond to membership, mail order advertising through the newspaper gave access to a large and diverse customer base.[28]

However, within the pages of *The War Cry*, the rescue homes' adverts sat alongside other, larger and more eye-catching ones from the Trade Department, which also sold by mail order and frequently stocked similar products for cheaper prices. Slight differences between the products on offer made the competition between trade and rescue less direct than it first appears. The goods sold by the Trade Department usually bore visible signs of affiliation with the Salvation Army, such as a crest, shield or likeness of General Booth, and so were the domain of members. Conversely, rescue work products, which, barring washing texts, carried no overt signs of religious affiliation, had the potential to appeal not only to members but to quiet sympathizers and benefactors, including those whose sympathies lay only with the organization's rescue work. Yet, despite the intent to reach multiple audiences through *The War Cry*, the preponderance of evangelical content in the newspaper hampered the chances of rescue adverts being seen by those primarily interested in social work.

The launch of *The Deliverer* in 1889 remedied this. *The Deliverer* was a monthly magazine dedicated to news of the Salvation Army's rescue work. Although, like *The War Cry*, it contained content for both internal and external audiences, its declared aim was to 'find fresh channels among those who know nothing of Army work'.[29] Through it, rescue homes' products could be marketed to an audience outside the Salvation Army's own ranks for the first time. It also created a clearer demarcation between support for the organization's rescue work and support for its exuberant evangelical methods which frequently affronted respectable sensibilities.[30] This significant departure set the tone for other outward-looking shifts in retail practices used by the rescue wing in the course of the following decade.

In the early years of the magazine, adverts for rescue homes' products often occupied the back page of *The Deliverer*. They were generally the most visually captivating content, besides the cover. The frequency of adverts ebbed and flowed as the years passed but they continued to be striking, emotive and inventive. *The Deliverer* was a magazine produced by women for women, and its illustrations, photographs, articles, adverts and testimonies almost exclusively depicted the sellers and customers of rescue homes' products as women. So, as well as signalling a new focus on outside custom, *The Deliverer* was instrumental in developing a gendered retail culture.

The impact of *In Darkest England, and the Way Out*

The two interlinked trajectories that have been traced so far – increasing productivity on the one hand and expansion into non-Salvation Army markets on the other – led to a bifurcation in Salvation Army rescue work that lasted the duration of the 1890s. The move coincided with the launch of William Booth's highly publicized Darkest England scheme, which thrust the Salvation Army's social work into the public eye to be met with a mixed reception.[31] The scheme received sufficient public backing to provide the finance and impetus for the rapid expansion of Salvation Army social work but, as Chapter 5 showed, with that came significant criticism. However, the scheme's visibility gave the Salvation Army a platform to build on the foundations it had laid in its rescue home workrooms of providing morally and physically healthful working environments. Promoting good working conditions became an integral part of the scheme, the best-known example being the match factory discussed in Chapter 5.[32]

The two most remunerative rescue work industries, knitting and bookbinding, were removed from rescue home settings where they benefited from the unpaid labour of women on the rescue programme. Instead, they began to be run as commercial factories providing paid employment for women out of work or who had successfully passed out of the rescue homes. Essentially operating as early forms of social enterprise, the factories were designed to promote model working conditions and offer work to women in precarious circumstances.[33] At the same time they sought to achieve a measure of commercial success. The factories did not always turn a profit, but when they did, a proportion of it was paid over as a grant towards the rescue homes.[34] New premises on Clapton High Road were acquired for the knitting factory with 'a very attractive shop-front, displaying a Certificate of Honor for goods recently shewn at the Aberdeen Woodside Exhibition'.[35] That goods were sent from the London knitting factory for display at such a distant industrial exhibition reveals the scope of rescue leaders' ambition for their business.[36]

In the rescue homes, needlework, in its more conventional sense of sewing and embroidery, continued as the main form of work therapy throughout the 1890s. Income from the sale of needlework was treated as residents' contribution towards their own maintenance during their stay, which was free of any direct charge. The proceeds from needlework rarely came close to covering the running costs of the homes, which left most homes reliant on grants and donations. A small measure of financial independence was achieved by some homes towards the end of the decade, when there was a renewed push to reach self-sufficiency. *The Deliverer* reported Florence Booth's announcement that:

> many of the branches had come within near realization of the goal – self-support. She mentioned two Homes as examples: Clock House, the maintenance of which cost £480. Of this, £357 had been made by sale of the girls' work, etc. and £123 subscribed; the gross cost of the Amhurst Road Home was £490, of this, £439 had been realized by work, chiefly text-making, which left only £51 to be raised by subscription.[37]

The following year it was reported that 'Amhurst Road Rescue Home was entirely supported by the girls' work'.[38]

Although the Salvation Army's rescue homes and factories of the 1890s differed in their approaches and their economic models, they were united by a common use of industry and shared retail methods and outlets. Despite the mixed fortunes of both the factories and the homes, the rescue wing's commitment to keeping a central place for industry and retail in its work remained unshaken, indicating that the value retail had for the Salvation Army rescue wing was more than purely financial. The other forms of value can be understood by examining what those involved in Salvation Army rescue work wrote and said about the retail methods they used, both publicly and privately. The remainder of this chapter will explore what surviving archival records and published sources reveal about the face-to-face sales methods that were used by the rescue wing in the 1890s and beyond. What did these methods mean to their practitioners, both as individual saleswomen and as members of the Salvation Army community?

'Salvation peddling: one of the least known wonders of The Salvation Army'

The rescue wing began to use commercial travellers more extensively from 1896, with at least one attached to each rescue home.[39] Known as pedlars until around 1928 and thereafter called Sales Officers, these were female rescue officers, cadets in training, or volunteers. Most homes had their own pedlars attached, but from 1903 to 1910 there was also a central group of pedlars called the Lollards headquartered at 52 Thistlewaite Road in Clapton. As well as managing the postal orders received by the Women's Social Work, Lollards sold stock for 'those London Homes having no Pedlars or making more work than they can sell'.[40] Pedlars travelled further and further afield as their aim shifted from selling at Salvation Army corps towards selling to unaffiliated individuals, predominantly women, in private homes. They initially travelled by foot, public transport or in some cases horse (or donkey) and cart, but by 1930, there were five Trojan motor vans dedicated to the purpose.[41]

Rescue homes relied heavily on the pedlars to sell their stock. In 1901, it was reported that 'last year these women-pedlars sold goods to all classes of the community, amounting in value to £4,000'.[42] When interviewed for *The Deliverer* about her success in making Amhurst Road home self-sufficient in 1898, the officer-in-charge stated:

At present a large proportion of our goods are sold by our pedlars. They are faithful and enthusiastic workers, and show a beautiful spirit as they trudge about day after day in all sorts of weather. Yesterday, one, with not an especially interesting parcel of goods, sold three pounds' worth, and got two people saved.[43]

The potential for spiritual influence was an important added value of peddling for the Salvation Army. By entering the homes of people not affiliated with the Salvation Army, the pedlar had an opportunity to be of service, pray with them and possibly also convert them. The rescue wing's retail became a more subtle and socially acceptable extension of the Salvation Army's evangelistic work, particularly between women. As such, there was a good deal of co-operation between rescue and 'field' (evangelical) officers when it came to peddling. The pedlars from the Amhurst Road rescue home organized fortnightly tours in other parts of the country, when they found that their near neighbourhood 'ceased to be a wide enough field'.[44] By the 20th century, there were over 20 rescue homes and peddling grounds had to be mapped out to ensure there was no overlap.[45]

The pedlars' own accounts of their work tend to give equal weight to spiritual and financial rewards as incentives:

'Sometimes, when I have felt the most weary, I have gone to ladies and found the Lord had just prepared them by His Spirit, and when they have bought the goods, they have asked me to pray with them.'

'Often the doors are closed in my face, and I am driven away like a beggar, and if it were not for prayer … I should have to give up.'

'Then I get into their parlours, and they let me pray. After a few visits they become regular customers. They open their hearts, and tell me of prodigal boys, and my own faith has been strengthened as I have promised to join them in prayer that their wandering children might be brought back to God.'[46]

Léa Leboitissier has noted that by the late 19th century peddling 'was regularly criticized … as it was believed to promote outdated or dangerous trading techniques and consumption patterns, based on emotions, credit and interpersonal relations rather than reason and anonymity'.[47] There is no evidence that Salvation Army pedlars offered credit, but the maligned emotional and interpersonal dynamics were an important part of peddling's appeal and usefulness to rescue officers. Even as the wider Salvation Army was pioneering 'a new kind of purchase-triggered charitable donation' by developing the multifaceted commercial retail practices described in the previous chapter, rescue work embraced an outdated retail method reliant on local personal networks and continued to find spiritual and financial value in it well into the 20th century.[48] As late as October 1948, *The Deliverer* printed the story of Major Brewer of

Tor maternity home in Edinburgh, 'one of the few remaining Sales Officers, who ... has sold her wares in crofter's cottage and millionaire's mansion'.[49]

Statements on the aims and methods of Salvation Army pedlars tend, like this late example, to foreground the female and class-crossing nature of the networks it fostered. Peddling was framed as a practical incarnation of the vision of Christian Feminism put forward by women like Josephine Butler: 'its aim and purpose is the emancipation of our fallen sisters from the vilest form of slavery'.[50] It was claimed 'the golden thread of woman's sympathy [ran] through the entire enterprise' which was 'a truly glorious work, and essentially a woman's'.[51] This claim is noteworthy when counterposed to the wider landscape of peddling and contemporary preconceptions about itinerant trade. Leboitissier points out that criticisms of peddling were often based on stereotypes about women consumers such as greed and ignorance, but pedlars themselves were commonly men, often from immigrant communities.[52] The Salvation Army's characterization of rescue work peddling tacitly overturns these norms, reframing female consumers as sympathetic rather than greedy, peddling as worthy, and pedlars as women rather than men. It is possible to view this appropriation of peddling as another facet of several more widespread tactics used in the Salvation Army's evangelistic work: its support of women working in fields traditionally reserved for men, its appropriation of elements of secular, working-class culture for religious ends, and its placement of women as figures of influence in disreputable spaces.[53] However, it also raises questions, which are beyond the scope of this chapter, about how the rescue work pedlars fitted into the wider landscape of itinerant trade in the United Kingdom and what the nature of their relationship was to true commercial travellers who relied on the trade for their income rather than charity fundraising.

The pedlar was the crucial link in the realization of the Salvation Army's imagined cross-class spiritual sisterhood. For several years, Clock House rescue home in London used an 'auxiliary pedlar', Miss Bott. In an interview with *The Deliverer*, she described how, for her, peddling was an avenue of 'love-service to God' without having to don a Salvation Army uniform.[54] Indeed, she reported that not wearing uniform 'is an advantage to me, as I get into many houses because of this; and talking, as a lady to a lady can, often overcomes prejudices that have simply sprung from entirely false or erroneous reports'.[55]

Using unaffiliated volunteers like Miss Bott, from a higher social class than most rescue officers, multiplied the benefits and opportunities that peddling could offer. Like rescue officers, the devout Miss Bott was able to connect with customers spiritually, but she could do other things that might not have been possible for rescue officers, like discussing servant problems with the mistress of the house on level terms to secure future situations for rescue home residents.[56] The pedlar's role as intermediary was intended to work in the other direction as well: '[O]n the termination of a round, worker and pedlar meet together and tell their experiences – the one as to how a garment was made, and the other how it was sold – the work itself is thereby raised to a high and sacred level.'[57] For most rescue home residents, these conversations would have been their only means of involvement in the sale of their products and their connection to the customers who supported them and wished them well. So, the emotional and interpersonal form of retail the pedlar practised was designed to effect positive personal transformation in customers, producers and the seller herself.

Shops, 'mammoth Bazaars' and sales of work

Dedicated shops became a short-lived feature of the Salvation Army's rescue work retailing operations in the late 1920s. In October 1926, the first of three shops opened in Cardiff. Two more opened in London in 1927 but all three had closed by the end of 1931.[58] Their brief existence is little documented but the interpersonal dynamics that peddling embodied for the Salvation Army also came to the fore in the few accounts of shop life that survive. *The Deliverer* honed in on the shops' multifarious opportunities for community service, even more than for sales:

> Ready all day long to direct inquirers to the right department of The Army, the Staff-Captain gets a variety of requests. … One wants to sell work. Another wants a baby minded. A third wants a free meal. Many ladies want maids. A father brings a girl he can't manage. Foreigners ask their way to places written on paper. All depart cheered by ready help or at least by a kind smile.[59]

The imperative for spiritual justification remained ever present but by the 1920s the rescue wing's retail had become a touchpoint for the expanding community of people who used Salvation Army services more widely. This position developed during the preceding decades through another sales method: the use of special events for commercial trade.

The Salvation Army was not immune to the exhibition fever of the late 19th century. In the 1890s, it held two great international exhibitions of its own: the Salvation Army Exhibitions at the Royal Agricultural Hall in Islington in 1896 and 1899. These were important retail opportunities for both the rescue and trade wings, with the rescue work receiving generous allocations of floor space at both events. The *Official Guide* to the 1896 exhibition introduced the rescue section as 'a species of mammoth Bazaar'.[60] This was a clear indication that the Salvation Army had overcome its reluctance towards bazaar-style sales described in Chapter 5 and become open to combining retail and spectacle as a means of attracting more traditional philanthropic audiences from the wealthier classes. The exhibitions appear to have achieved this aim: across ten days in 1896, 100,000 people passed through the turnstiles, with the takings from rescue work stalls approaching £440, an amount deemed satisfactory in a departmental post-mortem of the event.[61] At the 1899 exhibition, which lasted 18 days, the rescue work takings were in excess of £680.[62]

Exhibitions were a rare opportunity for rescue home residents and factory workers to see their craft being appreciated by customers first hand and to actively participate in promoting and selling the fruits of their labour. Residents acted as living pictures at the exhibition: they demonstrated and promoted their work in elaborate model workrooms and factories set up near the rescue work stalls. At the 1899 exhibition, the entire staff and machinery of the knitting factory were moved to the Agricultural Hall for the duration of the event. These were opportunities for the Salvation Army to counter the criticism of its Darkest England scheme discussed in Chapter 5 by showing off exemplary working conditions and the 'smiling, well-conditioned appearance of the girls and women employed both in the ... Book-binding, and Knitting Factory'.[63] The exhibition served as advertisement for their campaign to improve working conditions more widely as well as an incentive to support the rescue work by buying their products.

The 1896 *Official Guide* positioned the exhibition as playing its part in the reform of work-shy rescue cases through the sense of purpose and self-worth it supplied: '[G]irls whom no police magistrate could tame nor prison cells coerce, have pleaded for "just five minutes more at this apron, Captain," to finish it thoroughly well for the Exhibition.'[64] Reviewing the 1896 exhibition for *The Deliverer* after the fact, Florence Booth emphasized this:

> The Exhibition of last month was undoubtedly a great encouragement to our Rescue girls, and has wonderfully helped them to work. The interest they took in preparing the goods for sale went a long way towards helping to conquer what, in some of them, is their besetting sin – they have not wanted to be idle.[65]

Statements like this show how closely intertwined morality, economics and retail had become in the eyes of Salvation Army rescue workers, with retail having an important role to play in the moral reform of their charges by creating habits that would help guarantee their future economic security.

Despite the advantages such grand exhibitions were seen to have, the high costs and labour associated with holding them limited their frequency. Sales, usually held at Christmas, winter or harvest time, became increasingly common for the rescue wing in the 1890s.[66] An internal record book was kept to document the strategies and layouts employed at sales and reflect privately on their successes and failings. The sales were initially held in hired venues but soon moved to Salvation Army halls which had the advantages of reducing costs and allowing greater flexibility. Most importantly, it made sales occasions for bringing in members of local communities from across the social spectrum. The record book describes the tactics used to attract different classes of customer, from personalized invite cards for wealthier supporters to sandwich boards, handbills and posters for steering in ordinary passers-by from the streets.[67] By the early 20th century, civic dignitaries and minor nobles routinely opened sales alongside Salvation Army leaders. Mildly religious programmes of music, addresses, services and prayers were intended to ensure that 'everybody – and that includes donor, purchaser, and seller – was satisfied that really good Salvation business was done' but their compatibility with Christian principles was still doubted by some.[68]

The financial importance of sales of work never equalled that of pedlars, but their continuation well into the 20th century shows that their social function had other value.[69] The turn towards more conventional sales of this kind was part of a significant shift in the Salvation Army's status as it shed its early reputation as 'vulgar, sensationalist, and crude'.[70] By the late 1890s it was well along the road to establishment respectability, thanks in part to the outward-looking marketing and sales strategies of the rescue work, and this trajectory continued in the next century. The Salvation Army was also becoming embedded in local communities as an established religious denomination and a known and trusted provider of charitable and community services.

Conclusion

The rescue work's retail reflected the special status that rescue work occupied among the Salvation Army's activities: from a Salvation Army perspective, rescue work was indivisible from the overall spiritual mission of the organization but from an external point of view, it appeared quite distinct from the boisterous street evangelism that made the Salvation Army deeply unpalatable to many respectable, monied observers. The negotiation of internal points of friction, like competition with the Trade Department, helped shape the Salvation Army's rescue work retail into something more than just a fundraising mechanism: they forced the rescue wing to consider and articulate how retail fitted into its combined spiritual, moral and social mission and develop its practices accordingly.

These practices were equally influenced by the rescue wing's engagement with and participation in wider movements and trends: the social purity movement, industrial mass production, labour campaigns, mail order shopping and exhibition fever. This wider engagement allowed the rescue wing's niche brand of retail to reach well beyond the Salvation Army community. The rescue wing found the expansionism of commercial capitalism to be entirely compatible with the Salvation Army's evangelical ambitions, the clearest illustration of this being its use of pedlars to reach and extend the market for its goods while also spreading its religious message. It endeavoured to find methods of production and distribution that befitted its Christian ethos and its goals of moral and social reform, while also acting as a counterpoint and alternative to the problematic aspects of wider commercial capitalism. Consequently, it devised a form of retail that made all parties – producer, saleswoman and consumer – co-workers towards the same vision of corporate utopia effected through many small individual transformations. For them, the labour of retail became an active expression of Christian love.

Acknowledgements

Many thanks to all my colleagues and friends at the Salvation Army International Heritage Centre for their support while researching and writing this chapter, particularly to Steven Spencer and Dr Flore Janssen who read and provided valuable feedback on various drafts.

Notes

1   'Is love's labour lost? Seven stages of women', *The Deliverer*, July 1902, 15.
2   F. Janssen, ' "Buy cheap, buy dear!": selling consumer activism in the Salvation Army c. 1885–1905', *Journal of Victorian Culture* 27:4 (2022), 670–685; J. Krisjanous, 'Examining the historical roots of social marketing through the lights in darkest England campaign', *Journal of Macromarketing* 34:4 (2014), 1–17; J. Rappoport, *Giving Women: Alliance and Exchange in Victorian Culture* (New York: Oxford University Press, 2012); S. Roddy, J.-M. Strange and B. Taithe, *The Charity Market and Humanitarianism in Britain, 1870–1912* (London: Bloomsbury Academic, 2019); J. Roddy and S. Roddy, 'Banking for Jesus: financial services, charity, and an ethical economy in late Victorian and Edwardian Britain', *Capitalism: A Journal of History and Economics*, 3:1 (2022), 106–135; D. Winston, 'Living in the material world: Salvation Army lassies and urban commercial culture, 1880–1918', in J. Giggie and D. Winston (eds), *Faith in the Market: Religion and the Rise of Urban Commercial Culture* (New Brunswick: Rutgers University Press, 2002), 13–36.
3   J. Walkowitz, *Prostitution and Victorian Society: Women, Class and the State* (Cambridge University Press, 1980); F.K. Prochaska, *Women and Philanthropy in Nineteenth-Century England* (Oxford University Press, 1980).
4   Prochaska, *Women and Philanthropy*, 47–72, 182–221.
5   Winston, 'Living in the material world', 17.
6   Case books, known as 'History Books', that detail each resident's case history have survived from the Knitting Home from 1901–1916 (Records of Lanark House and the Knitting Home, ref.: LNK/2, The Salvation Army International Heritage Centre). Although these books do not offer direct access to the voices of 'rescued' women, they do offer opportunities to read alternative stories from their recorded actions. Several recent unpublished studies have sought to recover alternative, unofficial versions of 'rescued' women's life histories by juxtaposing various archival and published sources in the Salvation Army's archives. These include M.C. David, ' "Unpacking meanings": Competing narratives or versions of the same story in the Salvation Army Archive and how they affect interpretation', unpublished essay, Birkbeck, University of London, 2015; E. Stubbings, 'Spirituality, selfhood and self-representation: a study of two Salvationist women in England, 1884–1935', undergraduate thesis, University of Oxford, Faculty of History, 2015; C. Taylor, 'The maiden tribute of modern Babylon: a re-examination of the role of the Salvation Army', unpublished essay, Birkbeck, University of London, 2014; C. Taylor,

'Women, alcohol and the male response: a case study of Grove House Female Inebriates Home, 1896–1901, master's thesis, Birkbeck, University of London, 2014.

[7] A.L. Stoler, *Along the Archival Grain: Epistemic Anxieties and Colonial Common Sense* (Princeton University Press, 2009), 47 (emphasis in original).

[8] On the preventive side of rescue work in a Salvation Army context see G. Ball, 'Practical religion: a study of the Salvation Army's social services for women 1884–1914', PhD thesis, University of Leicester, 1987.

[9] Testimony before the Royal Commission on the Contagious Diseases Acts, 1871; quoted in R. Strachey, *The Cause: A Short History of the Women's Movement in Great Britain* (London: Virago, 1978), 202.

[10] Annual report of the Salvation Army in Scotland, August 1882–August 1883, Papers of the Salvation Army Scotland Command, ref.: ST/1/1/1: 9, The Salvation Army International Heritage Centre; *The Salvation War 1884. Under the Generalship of William Booth* (London: Salvation Army Book Depot, [1884]), 143.

[11] For detailed information on the running of Salvation Army rescue homes, see *Orders and Regulations for Rescue Homes* (London: The Salvation Army, 1892), ref.: Pam/R.24, The Salvation Army International Heritage Centre; W. Booth, *Orders and Regulations for the Social Officers of the Salvation Army* (London: The Salvation Army International Headquarters, 1898).

[12] 'Rescue work: a new undertaking', *War Cry*, 09/08/1884, 3.

[13] Rescue Work Account Book, July 1884–October 1885, Papers of Hanbury Street and Navarino Road Refuge, ref.: HSNR/2, The Salvation Army International Heritage Centre.

[14] *The Advance of the Salvation Army in Scotland*, Fifth Year, August 1886, Papers of the Salvation Army Scotland Command, ref.: ST/1/1/1: 12, The Salvation Army International Heritage Centre.

[15] Extract from *Pall Mall Gazette* quoted in 'The rescue officers at the palace', *War Cry*, 30/07/1887, 7.

[16] See, for instance, 'In the workroom: an afternoon at Clock House', *The Deliverer*, November 1896, 265–266.

[17] See *Orders and Regulations for Rescue Homes*, 20, 23–25.

[18] See *Orders and Regulations for Rescue Homes*, 24.

[19] Roddy et al, *The Charity Market*, 10.

[20] See 'Rescue work. Important', *War Cry*, 18/09/1886, 11; 'The rescue officers at the palace', 30/07/1887, 7; 'Triennial report of the rescue work', 03/03/1888, 9.

[21] 'Salvation Army rescue work fourth anniversary', *War Cry*, 23/06/1888, 8.

[22] For more on the washing text industry, see R. Macdonald, 'An industry that does not compete with any outside our corner of the world: Salvation Army washing texts', *Retail History*, December 2019, https://retailhistory.wordpress.com/2019/12/16/texts/ (accessed 29/09/2020).

[23] *Harvest Sheaves* (annual report of The Salvation Army Women's Rescue Work for 1888–1889), Papers of the Salvation Army Women's Social Services in Great Britain and Ireland, ref.: WSW/10/1: 16, The Salvation Army International Heritage Centre.

[24] *Harvest Sheaves*, 51.

[25] 'Our May meeting in Exeter Hall', *War Cry*, 12/05/1888, 9; 'The rescue stall', 21/07/1888, 4; 'With Mrs Bramwell Booth and the rescue officers in the theatre', 21/07/1888, 6.

[26] 'With Mrs Bramwell Booth'.

[27] 'Rescue facts', *War Cry*, 27/10/1888, 2.

[28] Its weekly circulation by 1890 was around 300,000 copies ('Ten thousand a year–and more', *All the World*, August 1890, 414).

[29] F. Booth, 'Personal notes', *The Deliverer*, 15/08/1889, 18.

30 Winston writes 'For nearly a decade, many opinion-makers characterized the group as vulgar, sensationalist, and crude. Its noisy spectacles appeared antithetical to Christianity; its preaching women and boisterous parades were deemed scandalous' ('Living in the material world', 18).

31 See V. Bailey, '"In Darkest England and the Way Out": the Salvation Army, social reform and the labour movement, 1885–1910', *International Review of Social History*, 29:2 (1984): 133–171.

32 See also Bailey, 'In Darkest England'; Janssen, 'Buy cheap, buy dear'; and Krisjanous, 'Examining the historical roots'.

33 For more on late-Victorian charities, including the Salvation Army, as social enterprises see Roddy et al, *The Charity Market*, 11.

34 Accounts survive for only seven years of the decade. Of those seven, the bookbinding factory made a profit in five, the knitting factory in three. On only three occasions during the decade was the Women's Industrial Section, comprising the knitting and bookbinding factories and a laundry, in a position to pay over grants towards the maintenance of the rescue homes. See Annual reviews of the Darkest England Social Scheme, 1891–1901; Finance Departments, ref.no. IFD/2/2/2: files i and ii, The Salvation Army International Heritage Centre.

35 Booth, 'Personal notes', 18; 'Salvation Army Knitting Factory' (illustration) and 'Three outside industries', *The Deliverer*, December 1891, 88–89.

36 'Woodside Industrial Exhibition. Opening ceremony', *The Aberdeen Journal*, 06/07/1891, 6; 'Woodside Exhibition. The awards', 28/07/1891, 5.

37 'Mrs Booth's annual with her social officers', *The Deliverer*, March 1898, 134.

38 'Text-making in the Amhurst Road Rescue Home', *The Deliverer*, February 1899, 122.

39 The title of this section is taken from 'Salvation peddling', *War Cry*, 12/01/1901, 1.

40 'Ensign Anna Smith', *The Deliverer*, January 1910, 6; 'A Lollard's tea party', December 1903, 93.

41 'In the workroom', 265; 'Selling the needlework and why', *The Deliverer*, August 1930, 89.

42 'Salvation peddling', 5.

43 'Text-making', 121.

44 'Text-making', 121.

45 'Adventures and opportunities of a Salvation pedlar', *The Deliverer*, January 1923, 2.

46 'Our "pedlars" on their self-denying rounds', *The Deliverer*, March 1898, 131.

47 Léa Leboitissier, '"A system of licencing vagrancy"? The Pedlars Acts 1871 and the monitoring of commercial mobility in late nineteenth century Britain (1860s–1900s)', *Retail History*, 15/03/2021, https://retailhistory.wordpress.com/2021/03/15/pedlars/ (accessed 27/07/2021).

48 Roddy et al, *The Charity Market*, 41. Another branch of Salvation Army retail work which relied on personal networks created by travelling agents was its Assurance Society. For more on this see Strange and Roddy, 'Banking for Jesus'.

49 '"Ashes for repentance, poplars for hope" at "Tor," Edinburgh's new maternity home', *The Deliverer*, October–November 1948, 177.

50 See A. Milbank, 'Josephine Butler: Christianity, feminism and social action', in J. Obelkevich, L. Roper and R. Samuel (eds), *Disciplines of Faith: Studies in Religion, Politics and Patriarchy* (Oxford: Routledge, 2013); 'Salvation peddling', 5.

51 'Salvation peddling', 5.

52 Leboitissier, 'A system of licencing vagrancy?'.

53 On these subjects see A.M. Eason, *Women in God's Army: Gender and Equality in the Early Salvation Army* (Waterloo: Wilfrid Laurier University Press for the Canadian Corporation for Studies in Religion, 2003) and P.J. Walker, *Pulling the Devil's Kingdom Down: The Salvation Army in Victorian Britain* (Berkeley: University of California Press, 2001).

54 'A chat with our auxiliary pedlar', *The Deliverer*, October 1898, 58.

55 'A chat with our auxiliary pedlar', 58.

56 'A chat with our auxiliary pedlar', 58.

57 'Salvation Peddling', 5.

58 Women's Social Homes and Hostels Books, Papers of the Salvation Army Women's Social Services in Great Britain and Ireland, ref.: WSW/11/4, The Salvation Army International Heritage Centre.

59 'The first London women's social sales depot', *The Deliverer*, May 1928, 23.

60 *Fully Illustrated Official Guide to the Salvation Army Exhibition, August 1–10, Agricultural Hall, London*, 1896, Papers of The Salvation Army Special Events Unit, ref.no. SE/1/1/1: 17, The Salvation Army International Heritage Centre.

61 Unpublished typescript 'The First Salvation Army Exhibition (Congress) 1896', Papers of The Salvation Army Special Events Unit, ref.: SE/1/1/1, The Salvation Army International Heritage Centre; Special Efforts book, 1891–1906, Papers of the Salvation Army Women's Social Services in Great Britain and Ireland, ref.: WSW/9/0, The Salvation Army International Heritage Centre, 73.

62 Special Efforts book, 78.

63 C.F.O., 'Women's social and rescue work at the Agricultural Hall', *The Deliverer*, September 1896, 234.

64 *Fully Illustrated Official Guide*, 18.

65 F. Booth, 'Personal notes', *The Deliverer*, September 1896, 229.

66 Special Efforts book, 83–95.

67 Special Efforts book, 87, 88 and 93.

68 'Sale of work for Ivy Home', 127; see, for instance, 'Desecration by sales of work', *The Officer*, February 1926, 112–113.

69 'A royal contribution of encouragement', *The Deliverer*, January 1937, 3.

70 *Faith in the Market*, 18.

7

Much More than a Gossip Shop: Black Country Independent Womenswear Retail, Family and Community

Nadia Awal and Jenny Gilbert

Introduction

This chapter draws upon museology and social-historical perspectives on clothing, women and retailing to explore how independent, family-owned women's clothing retailers were at the heart of working-class communities in early 20th-century Britain. It will do so through the lens of living history, considering the stories of two such retailers: E.A. and F.S. Hodson General and Fancy Drapers ('the Hodson Shop') and E. Minett's ('Minett's') and their representations at Black Country Living Museum (BCLM).

The Hodson Shop and Minett's were two female-operated and family-owned clothing retail businesses that are partially recreated at BCLM. The Hodson Shop operated in the front of a multigenerational family home, and Minett's started in the family home before opening a permanent shop. Both shops sold womenswear, haberdashery items and more. These two businesses demonstrate the important community functions served by local independent retailers and they present opportunities to tell more inclusive stories of working-class women's everyday lives. The presence of these businesses within a museum context and the wider use of living history interpretation have potential to disrupt and challenge dominant elite and patriarchal narratives of traditional museums and their collections.

This chapter will introduce the two businesses in greater detail. Then three themes are discussed: community relationships, credit and gossip. In each case, both the history of the two shops and the potential of using living history to represent that history is explored. Finally, the chapter considers how the stories of Minett's and the Hodson Shop can be used as starting points for critical reflection and inclusive interpretations of women's history in the 21st-century living history museum, a space where visitors can discuss challenging histories, nostalgia and critically engage with contemporary issues.

The chapter brings together two research projects. Jenny Gilbert completed a doctoral dissertation on the Hodson Shop in 2016 and this chapter draws on the literature review, archival sources, secondary research and historiography of that project. Nadia Awal and colleagues at BCLM conducted oral history interviews, archival research and interpretative work related to the museum's recreation of Minett's. This chapter arose from Gilbert and Awal's ongoing professional dialogue around the potential of women's clothing retailers as sites for engaging, relevant and challenging interpretation of women's lives, work and wardrobes.

The Black Country, Black Country Living Museum and living history interpretation

The Black Country region of England consists of the four West Midlands boroughs of Dudley, Wolverhampton, Walsall and Sandwell. Historically, these boroughs were renowned for their role in heavy industry and mining. As the US Consul to Birmingham, Elihu Burritt, wrote in 1868: the area was 'black by day, red by night'.[1] The region has seen both stratospheric economic successes followed by sharp downturn and deindustrialization.

BCLM is a living history museum of reconstructed shops, houses and industry, set across a 26-acre site in Dudley. It tells the story of the Black Country, one of the first industrialized landscapes of Britain, through immersive experiences and environments. The BCLM site is populated by costumed historic characters and demonstrators who engage directly with visitors and enact historical scenarios and activities. From chain making to retail, historic characters bring the Black Country story to life against a backdrop of red brick chimneys and billowing smoke. Interpretation at BCLM is based on a policy of 'Real Lives, Real Stories', meaning that the stories told on site are rooted in rigorous research into the real lives of Black Country people and places throughout history.[2]

Freeman Tilden authored the first comprehensive texts on heritage interpretation. One of his key principles for interpretation was: 'interpretation that does not somehow relate to what is on display or being described to enhance the visitor experience will be sterile'.[3] While Tilden was referring to interpretation in its broadest sense, living history museums are intrinsically aligned to this principle, as visitors are immersed in an environment which is akin to stepping back in time, surrounded by historic characters explaining the context in which they find themselves and thus ensuring that interactions are anything but sterile.

Museums have long been monopolized by the middle and upper classes. David Fleming, former director of National Museums Liverpool, has commented that British museums have typically 'failed the working class'; Serena Iervolino and Domenico Sergi stated that in recent decades very few museum displays and public programmes have focused on working-class experiences.[4] BCLM is well placed to counter this position. At the core of its narrative are the domestic, working, social and cultural experiences of the working classes. This narrative could be seen to influence the museum's audience demographic. BCLM's Audience Finder data (2021–2022) demonstrates that the museum has a higher than average proportion of working-class visitors compared to other museums and heritage attractions in both the West Midlands region and nationally.[5] While the data does not identify why individuals in these categories elect to visit BCLM, it is pertinent to consider this data in relation to BCLM's non-traditional interpretation methods and its focus on working-class experiences.

Living history is a powerful tool for telling inclusive stories, otherwise ignored or marginalized within traditional museum spaces; a powerful means of redressing the imbalance in museums and their collections that prioritizes the 'interests and worldviews of the white ruling elite'.[6] Jay Anderson defined living history as 'an attempt by people to simulate life in another time'.[7] David Allison expanded Anderson's definition to the built environment: recreations 'of villages, cityscapes, or farms of the past populated by costumed staff members who often take on the role of historical characters from the time periods represented'.[8] Alevtina Naumova highlighted the unique tactile and phenomenological nature of the living history museum; they are a place where visitors can actively touch history.[9] Living history museums are 'purveyors of folklife and the stories of the "common man"', with potential to advocate for 'social and cultural change'.[10] The origins of these museums are entwined with the study of European and American folk history and lore, often with a regional focus and emphasis upon ordinary people and their everyday lives.[11]

This chapter will show how BCLM is providing insight into the everyday lives of working-class women and their communities through living history. Everyday retailing is a key part of the museum, with a number of shops faithfully recreated on the site. Some shops, such as the tailor's and sweet shop, operate as present-day retail outlets, selling period appropriate goods and allowing visitors to experience first-hand how people shopped in the past. Other shops are locations for living history interpretation but do not sell any goods – an example being the pawnbroker's shop, where customers are introduced to the role and risks of pawnbrokers in working-class communities during the early 20th century. Doo's Chemist, set in 1929, also highlights the local pharmacist as a key community figure: providing medical care within poor communities before the foundation of the National Health Service (NHS).

Since 2016, BCLM has been undergoing a major capital development project, *BCLM: Forging Ahead*, bringing the museum into a period of living memory, to tell stories of life in the Black Country in the 1940s–1960s. This includes the construction of an entire mid-20th-century Black Country town. Buildings have been either recreated or translocated to tell the story of the area. The period was transformative for the region: mass immigration, the birth of the NHS and the arrival of rock 'n' roll. There are stories from this period which it would be remiss for the museum to overlook, such as the Dudley Race Riots of 1962, and the racist rhetoric of the notorious MP for Wolverhampton South, Enoch Powell and the Smethwick Conservatives in the 1960s.[12] Changes in Black Country cultures, attitudes and communities will be interpreted in a range of domestic and business buildings by historic characters created specifically to inhabit this town. The two women's clothing retailers considered in this chapter are represented at the museum: the Hodson Shop set in the 1920s–1930s, and Minett's which is set in the heart of the *Forging Ahead* era, in 1959.

E.A. and F.S. Hodson: general and fancy drapers

The Hodson Shop opened at 54 New Road, Willenhall in 1920. Edith Hodson ('Edith H.') opened the shop in the front room of the multigenerational Hodson family home. She was supported by her mother, Sarah, in running the business and was joined by her younger sister, Flora, in 1927. The business traded until around 1971.[13] The shop sold a wide range of clothing, predominantly womenswear, alongside domestic textiles, haberdashery and toiletries. Much of the stock was sourced from local wholesale warehouses.[14] The clothing sold by the shop was every day and non-elite dress.[15]

The town of Willenhall was renowned, both locally and nationally, for its lock-making industry. The Hodson family were an integral part of the lock-making business and community. In addition to being the family home and location of the draper's shop, 54 New Road was also the base for the Hodson family's successful lock-making business. The workshop was located in the small courtyard at the rear of the property and was run by Edith H.'s father, John and brother, Edgar. Life and space within 54 New Road was not necessarily demarcated as domestic or work, family or business. Of the four Hodson children: Edith H., Ida, Edgar and Flora, only Ida married and left the family home. Edith H., Flora and Edgar remained living and working together until their deaths. It is unclear whether this arrangement was by choice or necessity.[16]

A partial recreation of the Hodson Shop is housed within a satellite site of BCLM, the Locksmith's House, located around five miles away from the main museum in Willenhall. This was the original location of the shop, 1920–1971. There is a constant small display of clothing within a recreation of the shop space, but the house only opens to the public on select days throughout the year for special events. At the time of writing no living history interpretation is used within this space. While the museum cares for the building that once housed this shop, the shop stock collection and accompanying archive are held by Walsall Leather Museum. Sources relating to the shop include the unsold stock – over 5,000 items – business archive, oral histories and secondary literature by dress historians dating back to the 1980s.

E. Minett's

Minett's was based in the Black Country town of Wednesbury, and operated for 99 years. Edith Dabbs Minett ('Edith M.') started the business in 1907 in the front room of the family home in Pound Road, before moving to 83 Walsall Street in the 1920s. Like the Hodsons, the Minetts were connected to local industry. Wednesbury was prominent in tube manufacture, and the Minett family had owned a tube works in the town. Minett's was a family-run business. Following the birth of their daughter, Mollie Brenda (known to all as 'Brenda'), Edith M.'s husband, William, managed the shop's accounts and helped with general maintenance. Brenda started working at the shop as a young girl, earning three pence a week by dusting boxes and assisting with other day-to-day tasks. She started working at Minett's full time when she left school. By the 1950s Brenda's husband, John, started to assist in the business. Brenda took on more responsibility, and eventually took over as Edith M.'s health deteriorated. The shop was run by Brenda and the family, with the help of various shop assistants, until it ceased trading in 2006.[17]

Like the Hodson Shop, Minett's bought clothes on mail order from trade catalogues or from trips to wholesalers in Birmingham. Minett's also used non-local suppliers and sales agents who would come to the shop in a van and invite Brenda to browse through the rails of clothes in the back. Minett's catered to the needs and desires of the area and established trust-based relationships with their clientele. Brenda prided herself on buying garments for particular customers, whom she knew would buy them as soon as they saw what she had chosen. She would allow trusted customers to try items for a period, to see if they liked them, before formally purchasing them, as described by Brenda's son Nick:

> Wednesbury, as I remember it, was a very forward thinking, very outward going town. The people were very hard working, they were very loyal, very honest. You know my nan and my mother used to give people stuff on appro because they trusted people, and the people

would always bring stuff back, either they bought it or returned it in equally good condition.[18]

Minett's will be recreated and interpreted as part of *Forging Ahead*. The shop will be set in 1959, allowing for comparisons between postwar austerity and the later rise of consumer affluence. The shop also allows for the representation of female entrepreneurship, the postwar revolution in female fashion, the changing role of women in society and the role and presence of female-owned retail in mid-20th-century working-class communities. The museum will recreate Minett's through various research methods: oral histories, archival records, object biographies and secondary literature.

Representing retail and community relationships

James B. Jefferys discussed the role of localized, personalized and flexible customer service within the changing retail landscape of the early to mid-20th century.[19] He adopted a nuanced view, stating that some customers actively preferred the distance and efficiency of chains while others enjoyed the individual attention of the independent retailer.[20] Both Minett's and the Hodson Shop were deeply connected to their local communities. They were located within small industrial towns, surrounded by a mixture of residential, industrial and similar small-scale retail businesses. They were family owned, independent retailers, operating at a time when chain stores were beginning to dominate high streets and consumer consciousness.[21] This gave Edith M., Brenda and the Hodsons knowledge of their predominantly female customers and opportunities to deliver a more responsive and personalized customer service that was hard for chain stores to replicate. In the case of Minett's, Brenda was known for her personalized and intimate customer service:

> When my mother was older, she would ring Brenda up and she would send clothes down for her to choose from. Not everyone would do that … John delivered the clothes. Left them there for mother to try on and then he would come back to collect what she didn't want, and she would pay him.[22]

Brenda knew her customer's tastes well. Additionally, there was a bond of mutual trust: Barbara's mother trusted Brenda's knowledge and taste while Brenda was happy to provide goods in advance of payment, safe in the knowledge that unwanted goods would be returned in pristine condition. Brenda's son, Nick, considers this quality of service as typical to Black Country retailers: '[Minett's was] typical of a lot of shops in the Black Country. Where you could get good quality stuff for sensible prices and you could get good customer service and you would *be* served.'[23] Quality, price and service are presented here as distinctly Black Country traits, demonstrating how local retail shaped community identity.

Likewise, the Hodson Shop offered a form of personal shopping. Joyce Hammond, historian of the Hodson Shop, described Edith ordering items on behalf of customers.[24] Customers could browse through wholesale catalogues in store and select items; Edith H. would collect the items during her weekly visits to the Birmingham wholesale houses. In an oral history recorded in 1998, former customer, Nora, stated that Edith H. would 'get you anything as you wanted in clothes'.[25] Hosgood noted that the success of the small shopkeeper demanded an investment in the social life of its community. Shops were a meeting place for women, and a space for structuring female working-class culture. Shopkeepers were aware that the success of their businesses were linked to this culture, and in particular to their regular customers in an 'exchange of loyalties … shopkeepers translated their public role into an ideal service to the community'.[26] In this instance, ideal service required businesses like the Hodson Shop and Minett's knowing their customers' tastes and needs intimately and getting them what they wanted.

Edith M. (and Brenda, consequently) worked very hard to build a successful business, which relied on the relationship they had with their local community. The shop owners helped their customers during challenging times. For instance, in the case of Edith M.: 'I know my nan [Edith M.], in the Depression, used to help people out, cook and things and help people because people just didn't have any money. I think that went a long way with customers.'[27] This suggests that the Minetts cared about their customers, but were also aware of their relatively privileged position. They had both a humane, caring desire and a business need to maintain and develop their relationships with customers. This echoes Avram Taylor's description of Tyneside shopkeepers' need to balance their place within the community with their own financial needs and security.[28]

The wider relationships the Hodson sisters and the Minett family enjoyed within their community were likely an asset to their businesses. The Hodson sisters enjoyed a relatively privileged position within their local community. They lived on an affluent street and their family had a well-established and successful lock-making business. This enabled them to undertake leisure activities, such as theatre, music and charitable work in their local community, which was perhaps as much to do with ideas of feminine respectability as it was altruism. Hammond noted that the sisters were members of the Royal British Legion ladies' section. Flora supported the Royal British Legion Poppy Appeal until well into her old age. A summary of Hammond's 1998 oral history project described local people recalling Flora 'always out with her collecting box wearing her famous fur coat'. She clearly took this role very seriously, in 1974 she wrote in her diary: 'Poppy Day receipts – £90.68 the most I have ever collected.' Edith H. and Flora supported servicemen during the Second World War, supporting the *Express & Star* Comforts Fund and the mobile canteen service.[29]

The strong community connection they had fostered was fundamentally important to the survival and growth of their businesses because they did not pay for advertising.[30] The shops had to ensure that their customers were walking advertisements of their quality brand. Word of mouth was key; their customers' clothing and opinion of the service they received had to convince others to seek out their establishments. In the case of Minett's: 'It was all locally bought, it was well resourced stuff, it was good quality. My mother or my grandmother wouldn't have sold anything that was rubbish. You know, it was all built on reputation and word of mouth. I don't think she ever advertised anywhere.'[31]

Community connections can be explored and portrayed effectively through living history interpretation – women's fashion retailers did not exist in isolation; they were community hubs and support systems as well as places where women went to buy clothes. Historic characters at BCLM can pass from domestic, retail and business spaces, giving them the ability to depict interconnected scenarios. Business reputations can be made or broken through chat over garden fences or in the chip shop queue, a community can be galvanized into action to support a struggling family thanks to a conversation while buying some new stockings.

There is also an opportunity for museum interpretation and storytelling that challenges modern museum audiences' ideas about shopping and community. Shopping in the Black Country, much as the rest of the United Kingdom, has shifted to online retailers, chain stores and out-of-town retail parks, with much of the localized and personalized service being lost in this transition. Living history interpretation in Minett's could be used to show the knowledge the shopkeepers possessed of both their community and customers and how this knowledge could be applied to deliver better service and serve the community in times of need, something discussed further in Chapter 12. *Forging Ahead* will also include a recreation of the Halesowen and Hasbury Co-op self-service supermarket. In 1949, it will show changing practices in food retailing and how Black Country people responded to these, in particular the move from counter service to self-service. Together these shops can provoke audiences to question the present, by showing changes in the past; they could be used to provoke thought and discussion around shopping locally and at independent retailers.

Consumer credit

Both the Hodson Shop and Minett's offered consumer credit in the form of payment clubs. However, archival and interview evidence indicate that both Minett's and Hodson's credit schemes were viewed positively by those who used them. If a customer of Minett's wanted something but could not afford it, they could buy it on credit. According to Jefferys, clothing clubs 'flourished in the periods of heavy unemployment and provided many families their only means of affording new clothes'.[32] Taylor cited a 1938 Pilgrim Trust report which stated that a majority of unemployed families relied on clothing clubs, especially for items such as children's shoes.[33] The shops' consumer credit systems were part of their localized service model, existing to support local people and based primarily on a feeling of trust between customer and retailer. As with the rather different credit practices described in Chapter 3, this approach exemplifies a socially charged approach to determining creditworthiness, linked to what Jan de Vries described as 'face-to-face, personal relations'. Though, as de Vries emphasizes, these transactions remained 'rational commercial agreements'.[34]

Minett's operated a 20 Week Club which allowed customers to pay a 10 per cent deposit for items, reserve them and pay the remainder over a 20-week period, without incurring interest. An oral history with Pauline highlights how Minett's clothing club helped the family afford respectable clothing when money was in short supply: '[O]ur best clothes and mom's clothes were bought from Minett's. Because money wasn't very free at that time, and they had a weekly savings club. She could save and buy clothes that she couldn't have afforded to buy straight out for cash.'[35] The shop kept a ledger to record each customer's name and the amount they owed. Account holders had small blue cards that told them how much they had paid and how much was owing. Most regular customers would have an account with the clothing club. In this way customers could amass credit at the shop which would allow them to purchase clothes whenever they needed them, without having to worry about saving up the amount they needed and, most notably, they would not incur interest. The Hodson's Shop also offered credit. An oral history recorded by Hammond with Malcolm Lister in 1998 states:

> We used to have an account, little book, I presume today you would call it an account, where me mother used to pay a few shillings a week ... if me mother owed anything it would gradually work down until it was clear, and on it used to go like that – oh it went on like that for years.[36]

Archival evidence suggests that the Hodson's Shop operated a more ad hoc and informal approach to extending credit, with records of purchases and payments hastily scribbled onto dockets, often running to multiple sheets and sides and throughout many months.[37] Oral history evidence for both shops indicates that the clubs enabled families to buy better quality and harder wearing goods.

There were instances when customers made purchases that they could not afford and consequently failed to make payments. In July 1921 Mrs Griffiths failed to pay for a coat and alterations purchased on credit. Edith H. wrote to the customer's husband threatening legal action.[38] Some of the Hodson Shop's accounts are long running, with payments being made over the course of two or three years. One customer, a Mrs Ely, had a long overdue account outstanding for the purchase of corsets on 19 June 1933, and Edith H. made a firm request for payment on 10 July 1935.[39]

As highlighted by the threat of court action, Edith H. wielded power over her customers – especially those who were unable to pay for their goods. Pamela Horn argued that female shopkeepers could use this ability to gain 'dominance over the lives of their neighbours by their power to give or withhold "tick"'.[40] However, while 'interest free' the schemes came with unspoken social terms and customers were at the mercy of the shopkeeper as to whether credit was extended. There were also consequences – reputational or financial – for failure to pay for goods purchased through these clothing clubs.

The clothing club concept lends itself to living history scenarios that provoke thought and debate around the ethics of credit within communities. Much like the pawnbroker, the role of credit is ambivalent – a lifeline or a road to ruin? A vital community service or a community scourge? Were the shopkeepers wielding power or offering kindly support? Were credit decisions rational and business focused or socially and community driven? The controversy around buy now, pay later payment models for clothing has taken on clear contemporary relevance in the 2020s, with the rise of online payment platforms such as Klarna and Clearpay.[41] There is potential to weave these questions into stories and historic character interactions across BCLM, with contemporary resonance and comparison to present-day debates around financial technology.

Women's clothing retail and the social role of gossip

The proprietors of both businesses developed friendly conversational relationships with their customers and chatted about daily life as well as the products on sale. Brenda would even offer a cup of tea to Minett's customers with whom she was particularly friendly when they visited.[42] While small, the Hodson Shop served as a social destination for the women of Willenhall. Edith H. was known for her love of talking to her customers. Hammond described how customer visits were often lengthy due to chatting over the counter.[43] While this helped to enhance the personalized service of the shop, it was not universally popular. Neighbour Margaret did not use the shop, preferring to buy clothes from larger and more expensive stores in nearby Walsall. Her family considered the Hodson Shop to be a gossip shop due to Edith H.'s propensity to talk.[44]

Gossip was a positive business strategy and central to the vital community functions of the shops. Gossip can be defined as 'information exchanged with acquaintances about other people who are known mutually'.[45] The role of gossip in these shops was an important one; a useful tool for the individual, the community and the business. In derogatively dismissing the Hodson Shop as a gossip shop, Margaret's remarks can be considered a clear illustration of how 'women's talk has traditionally been disparaged as an inferior form of conversation'.[46] However, since the mid-1990s historians have provided positive and empowering interpretations of the role of women's gossip and its role within creating cohesive and supportive communities. Melanie Tebbutt argued that disparaging views of gossip were rooted in misogynistic and classist modes of thinking, intended to ideologically undermine working-class women and their daily lives.[47] Shops and shopkeepers were vital conduits for valuable information: '[S]hopkeepers were frequently at the apex of the communication networks which permeated working-class neighbourhoods since their close relationship with customers meant they were privy to much of the gossip which took place in the public domain.'[48]

The role of gossip between shopkeeper and customer was reciprocal, providing relief from social isolation and an exchange of potentially valuable information.[49] The shopkeeper could glean details of the economic circumstances of people within the community which would enable them to make decisions regarding credit. Yet the value of gossip went beyond economic decision making, with information sometimes being used to support and help those in times of need.

Minett's offered their predominantly female customers advice to help them look after and care for their items and homes. Advice ranged from green furnishings fading slower, to holding up a piece of washing in front of a mirror – if it was still damp, it would steam up the mirror.[50] Such pieces of wisdom have stayed with the customers of Minett's, such as Barbara: 'The drawers of clothes you know they were so meticulously kept ... it taught me, and I still do it today ... every row of clothes would have a sheeting over the top, to keep the dust off, and I've done that ever since.'[51]

The Hodson Shop also stocked menstrual hygiene products, sold from beneath the counter and in discrete unmarked packaging.[52] The shop was an important space for women, at once a part of, yet distinct from, the soot, smoke and noise of the lock trade. Perhaps gossip contributed to the shop becoming such a space or, conversely, the availability of such products is what made it a place where some women felt comfortable in sharing stories, knowledge and concerns.

Menstrual items and stories are generally not present within mainstream museums, with notable exceptions such as the Vagina Museum in East London and the Science Museum's developing obstetrics, gynaecology and contraception collection.[53] The presence of period care products, stories and scenarios within a living history context, be it in a retail setting like Minett's or a medical setting like the Infant Welfare Centre, can be a starting point for breaking down taboos around the historical everyday reality for those who menstruate. A scenario in which a customer requests sanitary towels from 'below the counter' while sharing stories with the shopkeeper would at once be a relatively radical and challenging act of living history interpretation, while also locating menstruation as an everyday and mundane reality of life.

The Hodson Shop, Minett's and the 21st-century museum

The Hodson Shop and Minett's have a key role to play at BCLM as spaces where visitors can be prompted to discuss challenging histories and nostalgia. The idea of critically engaging with the present through consideration of the past is at the heart of *Forging Ahead*, as demonstrated by its Interpretation Plan: 'BCLM does not wallow in false nostalgia. Uncomfortable and controversial issues are presented, engaging audiences by provoking thought and debate.'[54] Challenging histories are not just about the past, museums can harness nostalgia to prompt people to reflect and reconsider present-day issues and realities facing communities on a micro and macro scale, locally and globally. While a people-centred living history approach can be inclusive and help museums to engage with diverse issues and audiences (as discussed in Bain's work, 'Peopling the past'), nostalgia can also become an empowering and positive catalyst for change.[55]

Dressmaking has emerged as a key theme during object-based group reminiscence sessions for elderly South Asian women held at BCLM between 2019 and 2022. Many of the participants were skilled sewers and recalled making their own garments upon arrival to the United Kingdom during the 1960s. BCLM is continuing to explore this thread of research and interpretation. In 2022–2023, it created two new historic characters named Praveen Singh and Surinder Kaur, a brother and sister who migrated to the Black Country. Praveen arrived first and set up a textiles market stall. Surinder followed her brother to the region a few years later and also worked on the stall. These historic characters are based on oral history, secondary research and community consultation. Praveen Singh and Surinder Kaur provide opportunities to challenge nostalgia and views on migration, as well as a mirror to the modern day as visitors are prompted to question how they view multicultural societies.

The Hodson Shop and Minett's provide accessible places to start conversations about women's history and challenge sexist and class-based stereotypes about women, consumption, retail and community. Scripted interactions between historic characters, taking on the roles of retailer and customer, can communicate to visitors that gossip was a mechanism for sharing valuable information and for creating a network of supportive women that would look after and care for one another. BCLM can also highlight the Hodsons and Minetts as successful women running retail businesses. A historic character based on Brenda has been developed, highlighting women's involvement in business and changing fashions during the 1950s.

Clothing retail offers a familiar and appealing entry point to more challenging histories. By communicating these ideas through its events programme, living history interpretation and scripted interactions between historic characters, BCLM can challenge preconceived notions of women in business, the role of shopkeepers, and the community-focused social roles of these shops. *Forging Ahead* provides an opportunity for BCLM to take inclusive storytelling further, by exploring non-White working-class women's experiences of clothing retail, or as was often the case, of making their own clothing. The obtaining, caring for and wearing of clothing are near universal, embodied and everyday acts that connect past with present. As the recreation of Minett's is completed and as the new town emerges, the gathering of experiences of women who have migrated to the Black Country, and their relationship with clothes and fashion, will be prioritized. Minett's and Praveen Singh's market stall open opportunities to explore the wardrobes of migrant women, and the sartorial similarities and differences they encountered upon moving to the Black Country.

Conclusion

This chapter has demonstrated that the Hodson Shop and Minett's were Black Country businesses, embedded in their local communities. They had similar operating models, with services such as credit systems, personalized shopping experiences and relying on word of mouth rather than advertising. The key to their success and longevity was their relationship with their local communities. Both shops were run by Black Country people, for Black Country people. Both businesses understood the needs and problems faced by their customers and highly valued the customer–retailer relationship. They understood that, by offering high-quality service and products, they would have customers that would come to them time and time again and tell their friends. Furthermore, many of the relationships were supportive friendships, as retailers and customers shared stories and memories. These bonds, often formed through conversation or gossip, were fundamental to the successes of both the Hodson Shop and Minett's, which were appreciated for operating with what customers considered to be Black Country values: high quality products and exemplary service.

The two businesses offer BCLM the opportunity to represent hardworking and community-spirited Black Country businesspeople and create immersive experiences. *Forging Ahead* presents an unprecedented opportunity to explore challenging aspects of Black Country histories through the frame of retailing, clothing and community. Through historic characters recreating the shopping experience of Minett's and the Hodson Shop, visitors can be fully immersed, and learn about the value of local, community-focused retail. There is also an opportunity to provide a thought-provoking comparison between this type of retail and modern retailing and consumption habits. BCLM and other living history museums have a responsibility to use these experiences to discuss challenging histories and current social and political issues. The Hodson Shop and Minett's are perfect venues to explore and challenge themes of women's history, community and sexist and class-based stereotypes. Living history museums can tell powerful stories through immersive programming and thoughtfully scripted interactions, giving visitors the opportunity to reconsider preconceived notions they may hold. By doing this, museums like BCLM will engage audiences, provoke thought and debate, and endeavour to be a positive catalyst for change.

Notes

[1] E. Burritt, *Walks in the Black Country and its Green Border-Land* (London: Sampson Low, Son and Marston, 1868), 1.

[2] M. Blockley and BCLM, *BCLM: Forging Ahead Interpretation Plan* (2018).

[3] F. Tilden, *Interpreting our Heritage* (Chapel Hill: The University of North Carolina Press, 1977), 9.

[4] 'Museums are failing to address working class experiences', Museums Association, https://www.museumsassociation.org/museums-journal/opinion/2022/07/museums-are-failing-to-address-working-class-experiences/ (accessed 17/03/2023).

[5] BCLM Audience Finder Survey Report (2021–2022), internal document BCLM.

[6] A. Bain, 'Peopling the past: living history and inclusive museum practice', *Theory & Practice: The Emerging Museum Professional Journal*, 2 (2019), https://articles.themuseumscholar.org/tp_vol2bain (accessed 17/03/2023).

[7] J. Anderson, 'Living history: simulating everyday life in living museums', *American Quarterly*, 32:3 (1982), 291.

[8] D.B. Allison, *Living History: Effective Costumed Interpretation and Enactment at Museums and Historic Sites* (London: Rowman & Littlefield, 2016), 1.

[9] A. Naumova, 'Touching the past: investigating lived experiences of heritage in living history museums', *The International Journal of the Inclusive Museum*, 7:3–4 (2015), 1–8.

[10] Allison, *Living History*, 8.

[11] Anderson, 'Living history', 290–306.

[12] See S. Briercliffe, *Forging Ahead: Austerity to Prosperity in the Black Country 1945–1968* (Warwickshire: West Midlands History Limited, 2021); S. Hirsch, *In the Shadow of Enoch Powell: Race, Locality and Resistance* (Manchester University Press, 2018).

[13] For a comprehensive history of the Hodson Shop and collection, see S.B. Shreeve, 'The Hodson Shop', *Costume*, 48:1 (2014), 82–97.

[14] J. Gilbert, 'Better dressed than Birmingham? Wholesale clothing catalogues and the communication of mass fashion, 1920s–1960s', *Midland History*, 45:2 (2020), 258–274.

[15] J. Gilbert, 'Everyday and unworn dress as museum pieces: a study of the Hodson Shop collection, Walsall Museum, 1983–2016', PhD thesis, University of Wolverhampton, 2016.

[16] Shreeve, 'The Hodson Shop'.

[17] Nick, oral history interview by Nadia Awal, 17/07/2018, BCLM.

18   Nick, interview.

19   J.B. Jefferys, *Retail Trading in Britain, 1850–1950* (Cambridge University Press, 2011), 92.

20   Jefferys, *Retail Trading in Britain.*

21   R. Worth, *Fashion for the People: A History of Clothing at Marks and Spencer* (Oxford: Berg, 2007); Jefferys, *Retail Trading in Britain.*

22   S. Barbara, oral history interview by N. Awal, 16/07/2018, BCLM.

23   Nick, interview (emphasis added).

24   J. Hammond, 'A summary of the oral evidence on the Hodson Shop', Museum information document (Walsall Museum, 1998), np.

25   J. Hammond, 'Memories of the Hodson Shop', Museum information document (Walsall Museum, 1998), np.

26   C.P. Hosgood, 'The "pigmies of commerce" and the working-class community: small shopkeepers in England, 1870–1914', *Journal of Social History*, 22:3 (1989): 439–460.

27   Nick, interview.

28   A. Taylor, 'Funny money, hidden charges and repossession: working class experiences of consumption and credit in the inter-war years', in L. Ugolini and J. Benson (eds), *Cultures of Selling: Perspectives on Consumption and Society since 1700* (Abingdon: Routledge, 2006), 174.

29   J. Hammond, 'The history of the Hodson Shop collection' (Museum information document, Walsall Museum, 1998). *The Express & Star* was (and remains) a popular newspaper, serving the West Midlands and Staffordshire regions.

30   Despite not paying for advertising, Minett's did use branded paper bags. Examples from the 1950s and 1960s are held in the BCLM museum and archive collection, object number 2006/004/136.

31   Nick, interview.

32   Jefferys, *Retail Trading in Britain*, 334.

33   The Pilgrim Trust, *Men Without Work: A Report Made to the Pilgrim Trust* (Cambridge University Press, 1938), 125, quoted in Taylor, 'Funny money, hidden charges and repossession', 168.

34   J. de Vries, *The Industrious Revolution: Consumer Behaviour and the Household Economy, 1650 to the Present* (Cambridge University Press, 2008), 175.

35   Pauline, oral history interview with Nadia Awal, 06/11/2018, BCLM.

36   Hammond, 'Memories of the Hodson Shop'.

37   Customer account sheet, c.1939–1941, HSA4.35, Personal Handwritten Notes to and from the Hodson Sisters, The Hodson Shop Archive, Walsall Leather Museum.

38   Edith Hodson to Mr J. Griffiths, undated c 1922, HSA4.30, Personal Handwritten Notes to and from the Hodson Sisters, The Hodson Shop Archive, Walsall Leather Museum.

39   Edith Hodson to Mrs F. Ely, 10/07/1935, HSA4.31, Personal Handwritten Notes to and from the Hodson Sisters, The Hodson Shop Archive, Walsall Leather Museum.

40   P. Horn, *Behind the Counter: Shop Lives from Market Stall to Supermarket* (Stroud: Sutton Publishing, 2006), 52.

41   P. Collinson, 'Klarna: shopper's best friend or a fast track to debt?', *The Guardian*, 03/10/2020, https://www.theguardian.com/money/2020/oct/03/klarna-debt-buy-now-pay-later-fees-interest (accessed 28/04/2023).

42   Nick, interview.

43   Hammond, 'Summary of the oral evidence'.

44   Hammond, 'Memories of the Hodson Shop'.

45   M. Tebbutt, *Women's Talk: A Social History of Gossip in Working-Class Neighbourhoods, 1880–1960* (Aldershot: Scolar Press, 1995), 1.

46   Tebbutt, *Women's Talk*, 7.

47   Tebbutt, *Women's Talk*, 11.

48   Tebbutt, *Women's Talk*, 64.

49 See also S. Cotts and A. Danzi, 'Women's gossip and social change: childbirth and fertility control among Italian and Jewish women in the United States, 1920–1940', *Gender and Society*, 9:4 (1995), 469–490.

50 Nick, interview.

51 S. Barbara, interview.

52 Southalls Sanitary Towels, HSD15-16, Hodson Shop Collection – Household Cleansers, Polishes etc., Walsall Leather Museum.

53 The Vagina Museum, https://www.vaginamuseum.co.uk/ (accessed 18/04/2023); 'Menstruation and modern materials', Science Museum, 07/05/2020, https://www.sciencemuseum.org.uk/objects-and-stories/everyday-wonders/menstruation-and-modern-materials (accessed 28/04/2023).

54 Blockley and BCLM, *Forging Ahead Interpretation Plan*.

55 Bain, 'Peopling the past'.

8

Charity, Community and Trade: The British Charity Shop, 1940s–1970s

George Campbell Gosling

Introduction

The charity shop became a familiar fixture on the British high street over the second half of the 20th century. The number of charity shops increased notably in the 1980s and 1990s, but the distinctive model of largely volunteer-run shops selling primarily donated second-hand goods as a fundraising initiative, usually with multiple stores under the banner of a single charity, was not new. This chapter puts a spotlight on the decades between the Second World War, when this model of charity retailing was standard practice for the British Red Cross and others in communities across the country, and the late 1960s and 1970s, when the highly publicized success of Oxfam's flagship store served as the inspiration for an intense period of mass expansion of shops raising funds for local and national charities of all kinds.

The charity shops of this time have received only very limited scholarly attention.[1] Jessica Field and Tehila Sasson have both considered the charity shop and the charitable consumer as part of the wider adaptation of humanitarian activity to the postwar period and the end of empire. For Sasson, charity shoppers 'saw themselves as sharing the responsibility to a global rather than merely their immediate national community'.[2] For Field, the charity shop, specifically Oxfam's Broad Street shop, offered a novel form of engagement with the charity through consumption. Moreover, she suggests 'the symbolic value of these retail relations and the practice of charity consumption have constituted a level of social participation and belonging to the organization that has substituted membership for the majority of the general public'.[3] What this chapter seeks to do is shift the focus from the elusive charitable consumer and onto those Britons who continued to be members of various charities, and as part of their active membership set up and ran those shops where consumers could hunt for a bargain while embracing, to a greater or lesser degree, this new form of philanthropic engagement.

This chapter traces the emergence of the now familiar *charity shop* out of the myriad forms of bricks-and-mortar charity retail operating in Britain and more widely. From the 1940s, we see fundraising charity *gift shops* incorporating the functions and traditions of the British *jumble sale* and the North American *thrift store*. Their success by the end of the 1960s made them desirable sales outlets in the eyes of British charities' newly appointed trading officers, where their European counterparts in the *alternative trade* (later *fair trade*) movement would seek to establish their own shops dedicated to the cause of selling goods produced ethically in the Global South in the spirit of *trade not aid*. As Matthew Anderson has noted, however, charity shops played only a marginal and contested role in the early movement, leaving their fair trade potential largely untapped until much later.[4]

The central argument of this chapter is that we can only understand this by viewing the charity shops of this period on their own terms, instead of in relation to the charity shops of more recent decades. Earlier charity shops were different in two important respects. First, they were almost always the independent fundraising initiative of a local branch of the charity and therefore part of the associational culture of the local community, rather than any professionalized fundraising venture. This was likely a factor in the more positive, even collaborative, relationships with local traders, which offer a striking contrast from the tensions and even hostility that had set in by the end of the century. Second, despite the Broad Street example of a heavily commercialized approach to sales, most charity shops in this period focused far more on selling cheap, although they were still often very successful financially. This presented a challenge to the parent charities' trading officers, who saw the potential of expanding the merchandising mix of these shops as an accompaniment to selling through mail order catalogues. In the 1970s, this agenda lay behind the first serious efforts by charities to coordinate and professionalize the shops trading under their name, which ultimately fell short when local branches proved to be fiercely independent and resistant to central direction.

The research underpinning this chapter draws upon a variety of different archival collections. Extant charity records can be useful, so long as the ways they reflect the charity's power dynamics, organizational culture and administrative structures are understood.[5] Founders, leaders and central committees tend to be well represented, which can encourage a view of charity history *from above*. A history *from below* would prioritize the voices and experiences of ordinary members, supporters, recipients, volunteers and paid staff, usually poorly represented in archival collections. Some collections include regular reports and other materials relating to branches, but the business records of charity shops are rarely part of surviving collections for the branch or the parent charity. Local members' protectiveness over their shops and the funds they raised mean those aspects of their reports were often limited, while the trading officers working from central or regional offices are unusually visible for paid staff in charity archives. As a result, such collections are more useful for understanding the central direction of retailing and trading operations than what was happening in the shops themselves. Charity archives must therefore be complemented by other sources when researching the retailing operations of local branches and volunteers. One option is newspapers. Reporting in local newspapers, which included stories on the opening of new shops and seasonal milestones as well as shops closing down, put on display decision making around when to trade or not and what was considered a success. In many cases local papers continued to report on various aspects of charity shops' ongoing operations, putting a spotlight sometimes on local developments but more often the typical challenges faced by charity retailers. This reporting can provide further glimpses of what might be missing from the fragile and fragmentary archives of the charity sector.[6]

Even combined, however, these sources offer an historical record that is far from comprehensive. What we have, instead, is an extensive series of indicative examples showing that by the 1970s the charity retail sector was both expanding and contested. What was contested was the degree to which the charity shop should be professionalized, how it should balance new and purpose-made items with donated goods, and the extent to which each shop should be independently run by local volunteers or coordinated as part of a wider retailing operation. We need to understand how these tensions were resolved or managed if we want to understand the charity shop, which is such a distinctive feature of British retailing culture today.

The development of the charity shop

British charities traded throughout the *long 20th century*, with the selling of second-hand donated goods occupying a significant place. By the end of the 19th century, charity bazaars of the kind discussed by Papini in Chapter 2 were a well-established feature of British community life.[7] Charities selling from bricks-and-mortar shops, however, were more likely to focus on new purpose-made items, as in the case of the Salvation Army discussed in Chapters 5 and 6. Moving into the early 20th century, we also see shops opened by disability charities, including those of St Dunstan's described in the opening pages of this book.[8] This variety of charity-run shop tends to be missing when the Salvation Army 'salvage stores' are singled out as precursors of the modern charity shop.[9] These included the store at the Leeds Elevator profiled in *War Cry*, the Salvationist newspaper. As sites of *elevating* people to a better life by means of accommodation, work and faith, the Elevators were centres for the Salvation Army's social work across the country – with similar initiatives established in the United States and across the Empire. Unemployed men could be set to many different tasks, including going door to door in well-to-do neighbourhoods and offering to take away any unwanted household items. What the *War Cry* article described was the sale of those items and others collected as part of their 'salvage' operations.[10] At the same time, the Anglican Church was taking the lead in the smaller-scale social scheme of running *rummage* or *jumble sales* as 'local charitable endeavours selling second-hand goods to the poor'.[11]

This model of reselling unwanted goods at cheap prices to make them affordable for those struggling to make ends meet, while also serving fundraising or work creation objectives, is similar to parallel developments elsewhere around the world. Over the early part of the 20th century, the Salvation Army and another Protestant charity, the Boston-based Goodwill Industries, established chains of thrift stores primarily selling second-hand clothes across the United States, where they were sometimes also referred to as 'family service stores' or 'social service stores'.[12] In New Zealand, churches and charities followed the lead of the Auckland City Mission, which decided in 1927 to begin charging a nominal fee for what had previously been a free distribution of second-hand clothing. This was intended to 'remove the stigma of charity' from the items acquired, but it also provided a valuable source of income for the mission.[13]

In Britain, enterprises with a more explicit fundraising purpose in the early 20th century included those at the other end of the social spectrum, such as the high-end *gift shops* established by society women during the First World War. By the summer of 1918, the *Sunday Mirror's* gossip columnist was reporting that in London:

> Bond-street is lined with charity shops piled with gold, silver and jewelled treasures, of which Miss Elizabeth Asquith's is perhaps the greatest lure. I met Lady Curzon going in there on Friday afternoon nearly hidden behind a huge disc she was carrying. It turned out to be—no, not a new hat, but Lord Curzon's biggest silver salver, as a gift to the fund.[14]

This particular type of charity shop does not appear to have continued after the war. It would be another two decades before Lady Dawson would return from the United States with the idea of imitating the Bargain Box second-hand fundraising shop she had visited on New York's Third Avenue. Early in 1939 the *Daily Mirror* reported that she, along with Lady Baldwin and Lady Runciman and a team of volunteer store assistants, was opening a 'charity shop' on Bucking Palace Road. Where the New York store had been raising funds for hospital social service, the London shop used a system of differently coloured stickers to allow supporters of five different charities to raise funds for each of them through the sale of their donations.[15]

Second-hand fundraising *gift shops* during the Second World War operated in a similar vein, though usually raising funds for a single charity. The British Red Cross led the field here, running bazaars and 'around 150 pop up shops'.[16] In addition to sales, lasting up to a few weeks, there were a great many Red Cross shops trading daily for months or years until the end of the war. In some cases, they then moved to opening 'only on selected days when there would likely be a good trade'.[17] In others, difficulties in continuing to trade from the same premises forced them to move or close.[18] In Oxford, the Red Cross took over the Indian Famine Relief Organisation shop in 1943, with the intention of running 'a permanent Gift Shop'.[19] It was only the premises being needed again for peacetime trading that meant they had relocated away from the city centre by the time Oxfam opened its own shop on the same street in 1947.[20]

Some of the Red Cross shops raised funds for specific projects, such as the Angus Prisoners of War shop in East Central Scotland, profits from which were donated to the Prisoner of War parcels fund.[21] The range of items on sale – including jewellery, books and bric-a-brac – shows clearly that the jumble sale tradition was by now being brought into the charity-run shop.[22] Donations to the shop in nearby Forfar, which raised money to support occupational therapy work with disabled prisoners of war, were given a boost when on opening they received the gift of 'a beautiful canteen from Her Majesty the Queen'.[23] Royal patronage indicated that this was, in certain respects, a recognizably traditional form of philanthropic fundraising. It could also be a lucrative one. Individual shops in cities including Cambridge and Edinburgh recorded raising, in four years of trading, amounts in the range of £25–30,000 (the equivalent of around £1.5million in today's money).[24] The Oxford shop in particular was a major retailing operation, involving a team of 51 sellers, seven of whom were on the rota for each shift.[25] In only 18 months of trading for the Red Cross, it raised £16,880 (the equivalent of nearly £1million).[26]

During this time Oxfam ran a 'gift shop' as part of its Greek Famine Week in October 1943. Four years later, the ground floor of its Broad Street office was given over to selling donated second-hand goods – 'including fancy goods, evening bags, handbags, plates, cutlery, books, etc.' – to raise funds for the 'transport of clothing to Europe'.[27] It was only in the 1960s, after the shop was given a second floor in 1958,[28] that it was able to become as financially successful as the Red Cross had been during the war, when its shop was less than 150 yards away. By 1971, the Oxfam shop's highly publicized success had earned the manager, Joe Mitty, a host of plaudits including a two-page feature in *The Telegraph* dubbing him 'the salesman on the side of the angels'.[29] The publicity surrounding Oxfam, and especially its flagship store, fed a growing interest in charity retail operations more generally. From the late 1960s, local newspapers were reporting on a noticeable boom in the number of charity shops being opened across the country. The fact that journalists did not need to explain them is an indication that this model of charity retail was familiar by this time, while their growing number was still considered newsworthy.

The associational culture of second-hand selling

The mass expansion of charity shops in the late 1960s and early 1970s was not driven from the centre. For many charities, including those whose shops were appearing on more and more high streets across the country, this was a time when fundraising was undoubtedly important in their transformation 'from small-scale voluntary organizations to massive non-profit enterprises'.[30] However, the shops were almost always the independent initiative of local branches, which typically kept the funds raised, rather than as part of any top-down plan to grow the number of a charity's fundraising retail outlets. While the local members setting up and running shops had to work with, answer to, or resist the interference of, the central committees and paid trading directors of their transformed parent charity, they were distinct from them. It was local members who decided where and when to open a shop; whether to trade for days, weeks or months; seasonally or year-round; what to sell; and whether to pitch this more in the tradition of a jumble sale or a high-end charity auction.

Charity shops in this period therefore need to be understood as one aspect of the associational life of local communities in postwar Britain, the vibrancy of which has only recently been appreciated by historians. Narratives of decline, which saw secularization and the rise of the welfare state undermining associational and philanthropic cultures, have been challenged by those emphasizing continuity and adaptability in the face of change.[31] The importance of local associational culture to this adaptability in the 1960s has been identified in fields of voluntarism ranging from local civic associations and women's organizations to global humanitarianism.[32] Reflecting this, it was not only members of the charity's local branch but also members of the wider local community who took on the running of charity shops. Christian Aid recommended enlisting shop volunteers 'from the surrounding churches, Towns Women's Guild, Women's Institute, etc.'.[33] Oxfam similarly recruited from 'donors, with the aid of local churchmen or just as the result of canvassing', leading to volunteers who were 'usually middle-aged women with grown-up families'.[34] 'Spread the load as fairly as you can' among these volunteers, Christian Aid recommended, as 'mothers and housewives have many commitments'.[35] Such volunteering offered the opportunity to combine acting upon the Christian duty to help tackle global suffering with 'the social elements of fundraising' in what Anna Bocking-Welch calls the 'humdrum internationalism of parish life'.[36]

These shop volunteers had to navigate an identity and a place in the charity which was uncertain. Were they sales specialists working (even if unpaid) for a fundraising retailer, or, where they were members, was this simply one aspect of their involvement with the charity? The issue was raised at a 1968 meeting of Save the Children's trading committee. A former chair:

> criticised some of the sales staff, vis a viz their lack of knowledge of the work undertaken by the Fund. The Manager explained the difficulty in recruiting staff at a few days [sic] notice but it was agreed that consideration should be given to the possibility of engaging a Manageress during the summer months to enable her to spend some time at Headquarters learning something about the Fund's work.[37]

Oxfam's Bordon shop closed for a day in 1970 so staff could attend the charity's regional conference in Southampton, suggesting their being active local branch members was both expected and supported.[38] A few weeks later, volunteers became more closely involved in Oxfam's core work, when its shops across the country became collection depots for blankets to be sent to East Pakistan for the hurricane relief efforts.[39] It was these shop volunteers, with their dual identity as (unpaid) sales staff and members of the charity and community, who were responsible for establishing the retailing culture of most charity shops.

Most well-known here was the distinctly entrepreneurial approach of Joe Mitty, paid store manager at the Oxfam Broad Street shop:

> I look at my job in this light. I see myself as the steward entrusted with getting a responsible amount of money from gifts people give to benefit others. The Oxfam shops are a clearing house for compassion, an end I promote. … Do people get bargains in Oxfam shops? If you pay £5 for something you could get for £4 in another shop it is still a bargain because your money will go to the needy.[40]

Taking a longer view, we might see Mitty's approach as a continuation of the Victorian charity bazaar or the high-end fundraising *gift auctions* of the earlier 20th century. Such approaches to second-hand selling are different from that of the jumble sale, which prioritized the social value of affordable provisioning, even while raising funds. It is largely for this hard-nosed fundraising focus that the Oxfam shop has been viewed as the 'prototype for future shops'.[41] Where this view runs into difficulty is that, inasmuch as the Broad Street shop was doing something new, it was an outlier. This particular charity shop was an example of 'professional(ising) fundraising practices', as Field has noted.[42] Yet its relationship with other charity shops, even other Oxfam shops, was more one of inspiration than imitation.

A rather different impression of charity retailing had been given the year before when the *Yorkshire Evening Post* reported that the Oxfam shop on Church St in York was running low of stock and put out the appeal: 'We really do need some [bric-a-brac] quite urgently – anything will do, whatever condition it's in.'[43] There was a clear cultural difference between the aims of Mitty or the trading directors of leading charities and the attitudes of the local branch members running the vast majority of charity shops. 'Branches feel that if they have too professional an appearance it could inhibit their "second-hand" clientele', reported Save the Children's trading director in the mid-1970s, explaining their reluctance to sell the trading company's line of commissioned goods.[44] Christian Aid was also alert to the difficulties of mixing donated and new goods, advising supporters running shops that although they could order new goods from the charity's central London shop: 'Be very careful if you do. Never mix them on the same counter as second-hand stuff. Try to keep them in a separate section of the shop and the window. Make it clear they are NEW.'[45] This chimes with the emphasis placed in local press articles, which time and again highlighted the range of items and the bargains on offer. Impressive fundraising totals were often mentioned but, beyond naming the charity, the cause for which funds were being raised was often left implicit.

Parent charities were experimenting at this time with how much central direction could be asserted. If Oxfam's 29 regional organizers decided 'a shop would be a going concern in a town' (defined as having an estimated 5:1 ratio of income to expenses), they would then be responsible for securing premises, recruiting staff including a 'manageress' and a small 'pricing group', while more valuable items would be referred for pricing to a regional organizer or Mitty at the Broad Street shop.[46] Save the Children's trading committee misjudged the appetite for still greater involvement when they created the new post of Shops Area Supervisor in 1978. After a year of minimal progress they made him redundant and abandoned this effort to professionalize their shops.[47] These difficulties, like the previously mentioned unhappiness with introducing trading companies' lines into shops' merchandising mix, are in keeping with the complaints about central guidance over professional behaviour found by contemporary researchers in the 21st century.[48]

A notable difference, however, was the lack of tension in this period between charity shops and local traders. Moreover, commercial retailers were often among those in the community providing assistance with key challenges, including finding and securing suitable premises. The longevity of Oxfam's Broad Street shop is in no small part due to the fact that it could give over the ground floor, and later a second floor, of its offices to the experiment. In many cases, the goodwill of property owners in the local community was required to open a shop. When Save the Children opened its first two gift shops in the 1960s, the premises were made available by an 'anonymous benefactor'.[49] Oxfam developed the practice of moving in with as little as 48 hours' notice when empty premises were made available by multiple (or chain) retailers including Boots, WH Smith, Watney Mann and Sainsbury's.[50] In Mansfield, Oxfam was able to establish a shop 'through the generosity of the Co-operative Society', whose empty butcher's shop was taken over by the charity at 'acorn rent'. In addition to the premises, the Co-operative Society's maintenance department loaned buckets and brushes which were used by a local painter, while coat rails were supplied by Marks & Spencer.[51] 'Big multiples can sometimes be very helpful', Christian Aid told its supporters, 'even lending a member of their display staff' in some cases, while local stores might provide stock from discontinued lines.[52] The *Daily Telegraph*'s profile of Joe Mitty in 1971 noted that half of Oxfam's shops paid no rent: 'These are usually donated by business houses, property companies, banks, local authorities, often premises they themselves will require back later for some scheme or other.'[53] As the Red Cross repeatedly found at the end of the Second World War, this meant the continued trading of even the most successful charity shops was at the mercy of the whim of local businessmen as property owners. Yet these relationships with local traders and branches of larger retailers was generally positive. This is strikingly at odds with the situation 30 or so years later, when the small business lobby was clear that charity shops were the competition – and competing with an unfair advantage.[54] It is in this changed landscape that the rather different cross-sectoral partnerships of the 21st century, discussed by Fitton in Chapter 13, take place.

It would not quite be accurate to say there was no earlier criticism of charities competing with commercial retailers, though this was very heavily focused on the long-standing but increasing charity trade in Christmas cards. The Grenfell Association started selling cards in 1926 to raise funds 'for medical and educational aid to fishermen and Eskimos in North America'.[55] It was still selling its cards 40 years later, when the *Birmingham Post* was asking: 'do commercial firms resent the charity invasion' of '130 national charities, from animal welfare societies to cancer research' who had entered 'what has become a highly competitive business'? Instead of direct criticism, the article quoted an anonymous 'Birmingham company spokesman' as saying 'many retailers were stifling their objections because they felt an attack against charities would be misinterpreted by the public'.[56] By 1970, charities were being said to account for 15 per cent of all Christmas cards on sale.[57] As well as those charities new to seasonal trading, this included the Grenfell Association, which was by now also selling 'tea towels decorated with polar bears and stationery showing typical snow scenes'.[58] As the focal point of the criticism from commercial competitors, the scale of seasonal retailing made it a rather different issue from the regular trading of year-round charity shops.

Trading charities

In the mid-1960s, a small number of already-professionalizing charities began appointing trading officers or directors, typically with three roles. First, to organize the supply of a chosen line of items for sale, the choice of which was sometimes related to the objects of the charity. For example, helping to find a market for craft items made in countries where international aid charities were operating. Second, to sell these items via a mail order service. And third, to centrally direct (and, if necessary, establish) a chain of fundraising stores, which would usually combine the sale of these items with the sale of donated second-hand goods. In some cases, there was a mix of stores run by the trading director and those run by local branches, which might sometimes have carried items supplied centrally. In others, all stores were run by local volunteers with the trading director attempting to provide some degree of coordination and oversight. These developments built on longer traditions of charities selling items made in their workshops and seasonal trading focused on Christmas cards and other festive items, tapping into the interest in the emerging *alternative trade* movement.

Anderson has argued that we cannot understand the origins of the British fair trade movement without seeing 'the consumer within the context of social networks' and recognizing the importance of voluntary organizations and other alternative traders in the Global North in 'launching international trading ventures, providing assistance to producers, setting up church stalls, campaigning on the streets and lobbying government'.[59] To this list we could add *finding a market for the goods produced*. It was largely for this purpose that Oxfam Trading was established in 1964, initially called Oxfam Activities Ltd. The fact this was established as a separate trading company, however, had more to do with avoiding income tax on trading activities than it did reimagining the British consumer's relationship with producers in the Global South.[60] Christian Aid followed suit shortly after, as did Save the Children, whose *Christmas Card Committee* was rebranded as its central *trading committee*, with its *Christmas Card Controller* replaced by a *trading director*.

By the end of the decade, Barnardo's was one of the many charities to have joined them, demonstrating that charity mail order operations were therefore not exclusively for radical trading initiatives. The Barnardo's catalogue featured a wide variety of novelty and domestic items, including a Moka espresso coffee maker, Moulinex liquidizer, kitchen knife sets and Christmas tree lights. In the toy section were Cluedo and Monopoly, paint sets, a doctor's bag and tennis set. There was DIY equipment and gas lighters 'for men'. Alongside a range of small handbags were 55 watches, including one 'fashion watch, on dashing, red mock patient band', which the catalogue promised 'would go down well with girl friends and student nieces'. While the World Wildlife Fund sold children's stationery and mugs with different nature designs and the Association for Spina Bifida focused on soft toys and fancy-dress outfits, Christian Aid commissioned the same designer for its Christmas cards as for its cheese boards and bread boards.[61] As late as 1974, Christian Aid was pleased to be expanding its number of 'goods from developing countries' to occupy as much as three pages of its mail order catalogue.[62]

None of this was new in the 20th century. As early as the 1880s, the Salvation Army was running a 'Salvation Emporium' at its Trade Headquarters in the run up to Christmas. This was an opportunity for Salvationists to buy seasonal 'text cards', but otherwise the range of items on sale reflected the department store they were effectively operating year-round, kitting people out to live a good Salvationist life with uniforms and boots, instruments and sheet music for playing in the Salvation Army band, as well as bibles and the books written by the Army's General, William Booth.[63] Customers could also purchase a toast rack or slippers, knowing they were made by Salvationists and the profits were going to support the work of the Salvation Army.[64] In the early 20th century, the same could be said for disability charities, such as St Dunstan's, which promoted as seasonal gifts the same items it sold year-round. The late 1960s therefore saw a revival of late-Victorian and Edward philanthropic entrepreneurialism, with a new readiness to have goods manufactured or supplied specifically for the Christmas market.

Oxfam's trading company combined the seasonal sale of Christmas cards, children's toys and tea towels with selling 'crafts and clothes which are made by producers overseas' to a British market both in its shops and via mail order catalogues 'to help support their efforts to build a better future for themselves and their children ... through trade rather than through aid'.[65] This was a more sustained initiative than the previous selling of 'beads, bowls, and ornaments from Bechuanaland' (soon to become independent Botswana) or the range of pincushions and embroidered boxes made by Chinese refugees in Hong Kong and supplied to both Oxfam and the Huddersfield Famine Relief Committee by the Lutheran World Service. As celebrated as these early sales have been, Anderson has cautioned against overstating their alternative trading credentials, leading to 'an idealised interpretation of the 1960s as the heyday of Fair Trade'.[66] Oxfam's *Bridge* programme went further by not only 'paying a fair price for the goods' of producers in Asia, Africa and Latin America, but also 'providing marketing and technical expertise and support' and then using profits to fund 'development grants and social dividends'.[67] Between 1970 and 1975, these *Helping by Selling* items grew from 9 to

46 per cent of Oxfam Trading's sales, making them central to the overall growth in annual sales from a little under £300,000 to almost £750,000 (the equivalent of roughly £5 million to nearly £8 million given the high inflation in the 1970s).[68] Others adopting a *trade not aid* approach to international development included Tear Fund, whose first Tearcraft catalogue in 1975 promised production and consumption that was both ethical and evangelical. This set the stage for its less overtly or exclusively evangelical offshoot, Traidcraft, at the end of the decade.[69]

Attempts to combine the selling of new and donated goods in the same shops were not always harmonious, as in the case of Save the Children. When its trading company was established in 1966, it was imagined to be a welcome partner to its shops. The trading company would supply wallets and slippers from Hong Kong and Morocco, as well as a regular supply of 'children's clothes, rag dolls, water bottle covers, kettle holders, oven gloves and similar items' produced internationally, while the branches would be credited with the profits from their sale.[70] A decade later, however, it was noted by the charity's central trading committee that '[m]ost shops devote their efforts to selling donated items which give 100% profit rather than Trading Company goods on which only 30% of the selling price accrues to the Branch'.[71] This balancing became more difficult for the central London shop when, in 1972, a 50 per cent reduction in rates for shop premises was made available only to the charity and not its trading company, limiting what they could sell and placing greater importance on their ability to generate income from 'high-class donated gifts'.[72]

By this time, Christian Aid had closed the upmarket 'outlet for products of developing countries' its paid manager and assistants had run for six years, between 1964 and 1970.[73] The costs of running a shop on Sloane Street in the fashionable West London area of Belgravia, in premises today occupied by Chanel, meant the shop ended up essentially subsidized by the sale of Christmas cards and the mail order operation. Women's magazines and its own leaflets advertised a range of Kenyan crafts including soft toy animals and copper pendants adorned with 'local seeds' alongside ponchos and dresses from the Home Industries Centre in Mombasa, which used traditional prints and patterns but in distinctly Western styles, with prices reaching the equivalent of over £30 in the 2020s.[74] Yet by the end of 1976, with inflation soaring, Christian Aid's Postal Sales department had closed as well.[75]

These difficulties and failures represent the limits of 'a new consumer behavior' created by developments in 'the connection between humanitarianism and capitalism' in the 1970s. Certainly, Sasson is right to identify 'something novel happening in this decade, when mass consumer culture, globalization and a de-regulated economy influenced humanitarian action'.[76] While there was both a boom in philanthropic entrepreneurialism and notable energy to the emerging alternative trading movement, the extent to which the social and political agendas of these retailing operations were shared by the consumer remains unclear. Moreover, as we have seen, these developments were largely separate from the mass expansion of charity shops at the same time.

Conclusion

Charity shops experienced their first phases of mass expansion in Britain during the Second World War and then in the late 1960s and 1970s. During this time, they remained for the most part, whether seasonal or year-round shops, firmly rooted in and fuelled by local communities' associational cultures of second-hand selling. There were numerous innovations in charity retail, variously commercial and radical, yet charity shops were spaces where innovative approaches to fundraising were moderated by the shops' social function. Even Joe Mitty eventually overcame his concerns about giving the impression of a jumble sale and accepted selling second-hand clothes, bringing the Broad Street shop more in line with the other Oxfam shops around the country.[77] Meanwhile, dedicated *alternative trade* shops were short-lived and local volunteers were reluctant to give over too much space to such goods in their shops. Perhaps even today, it would be easy to overestimate the radicalism of the charity shop.

At the same time, the very existence of so many charity shops and the establishment of those trading companies were in themselves notable innovations. On high streets across the country, the multiple traditions of charity retailing were brought together in a newly unified model. Running or donating to a shop (more than buying from one) became ways of building and providing support for the charity and its cause at the community level. Despite efforts to coordinate and professionalize them, at this time they remained stubbornly local – independent of the charity whose name was displayed over the shop window and door. In these wartime and postwar phases of expansion, the charity shop was for the most part a distinctly grassroots initiative. The reason more businesslike or radical models were absorbed into this one was precisely because the early British charity shop was not a top-down third sector fundraising innovation but a widely popular type of community project.

Acknowledgements

The research presented here would not have been possible if not for the archivists maintaining charity archives and providing such valuable assistance to historians. Particular thanks go to those at the British Red Cross, the University of Birmingham's Cadbury Research Library, the University of Oxford's Bodleian Library and SOAS. I am also grateful for the support and advice offered by participants at the various Centre for the History of

Retailing and Distribution workshops at the University of Wolverhampton where versions were presented as the research developed.

Notes

[1] J. Field, 'Consumption in lieu of membership: reconfiguring popular charitable action in post-World War II Britain', *Voluntas: International Journal of Voluntary and No-Profit Organizations*, 27:2 (2015), 979–997. See also S. Horne and A. Maddrell, *Charity Shops: Retailing, Consumption and Society* (London, Routledge: 2002), 4; T. Sasson, 'In the name of humanity: Britain and the rise of global humanitarianism', DPhil thesis, University of California, Berkeley, 2015, 100.

[2] Sasson, 'In the name', 96.

[3] Field, 'Consumption in lieu', 995.

[4] M. Anderson, 'The British fair trade movement, 1960–2000: a new form of global citizenship?', PhD thesis, University of Birmingham, 2008, 48. See also M. Anderson, *A History of Fair Trade in Contemporary Britain: From Civil Society Campaigns to Corporate Compliance* (Basingstoke: Palgrave Macmillan, 2015).

[5] On the value and use of charity archives, see G. Brewis, 'Using archives and objects in voluntary sector research', in J. Dean and E. Hogg (eds), *Researching Voluntary Action: Innovations and Challenges* (Bristol University Press, 2022). On charity power dynamics, see A. Kidd, 'Philanthropy and the social history paradigm', *Social History*, 21:2 (1996), 180–192.

[6] M. McMurray, *Charity Archives in the 21st Century* (Cardiff: Royal Voluntary Service, 2014).

[7] F.K. Prochaska, 'Charity bazaars in nineteenth-century England', *Journal of British Studies*, 16:2 (1977), 62–84; P. Gurney, ' "The sublime of the bazaar": a moment in the making of a consumer culture in mid-nineteenth century England', *Journal of Social History*, 40:2 (2006), 385–405; I. Mitchell, 'Innovation in non-food retailing in the early nineteenth century: the curious case of the bazaar', *Business History*, 52:6 (2010), 875–891.

[8] On the workshops of disability charities, see A. Borsay, *Disability and Social Policy in Britain since 1750* (Basingstoke: Palgrave, 2005), 123–128.

[9] Horne and Maddrell, *Charity Shops*, 1–3; 'Elevator salvage store: waste turned to good account', *The War Cry*, 08/02/1908, 3.

[10] 'The Salvage Wharf', *The Deliverer and Record of Salvation Army Women's Social Work*, Vol. III: 7, January 1892, 126; Salvation Army International Heritage Centre, IFD/2/2/2: W. Bramwell Booth, *Light in Darkest England in 1895*, 33.

[11] V. Richmond, 'Rubbish or riches? Buying from church jumble sales in late-Victorian England', *Journal of Historical Research in Marketing*, 2:3 (2010), 327. See also V. Richmond, 'The English church jumble sale: parochial charity in the modern age', in I. Van Damme and J. Stobart (eds), *Modernity and the Second-Hand Trade: European Consumption Cultures and Practices 1700–1900* (Basingstoke: Palgrave Macmillan, 2010).

[12] J. Le Zotte, ' "Not charity, but a chance": philanthropic capitalism and the rise of American thrift stores, 1894–1930', *The New England Quarterly*, 86:2 (2013), 169–195. See also J. Le Zotte, *From Goodwill to Grunge: A History of Secondhand Styles and Alternative Economies* (Chapel Hill: University of North Carolina Press, 2017).

[13] H. Dollery, 'Social service, social justice or a matter of faith? The Palmerston North Methodist Social Service Centre 1963–2000', MA thesis, Massey University, 2005, 42; B. Labrum, 'Hand-me-downs and respectability: clothing the needy', in B. Labrum, F. McKergow and S. Gibson (eds), *Looking Flash: Clothing in Aotearoa New Zealand* (Auckland University Press, 2007), 127–128.

[14] KIKI, 'Gossip mainly for and about women: a week of engagements', *Sunday Mirror*, 02/06/1918, 10.

[15] 'Ivor Lambe's tales', *Daily Mirror*, 08/02/1939, 11; 'Social news', *New York Times*, 19/12/1932, 12.

[16] Sasson, 'In the name', 99–100.

[17] British Red Cross Archive, RCB/2/38/17/150/1, Angus Branch meeting minutes, Shop Committee, 22/06/1945.

[18] British Red Cross Archive, RCB/2/39/1/7, Minutes of the Cambridgeshire & Isle of Ely Grand Council and Executive Committee, 1937–1944, War Executive Committee, 14/07/1944.

[19] British Red Cross Archive, RCB/2/12/1/2, Oxford Red Cross & St. John Gift Shop, Minute Book, 1943–1945, 07/12/1943 and 13/12/1943.

[20] British Red Cross Archive, RCB/2/12/1/2, Oxford Red Cross & St. John Gift Shop, Minute Book, 1945.

[21] British Red Cross Archive, RCB/2/38/17/150/1, Angus Branch meeting minutes, War Fund Finance Committee, 03/12/1943.

[22] Scottish Red Cross News, 07/03/1944, 3.

[23] Scottish Red Cross News, 12/05/1944, 2.

[24] British Red Cross Archive, RCB/2/39/1/7, Minutes of the Cambridgeshire & Isle of Ely Grand Council and Executive Committee, 1937–1944, War Executive Committee, 17/11/1944; Scottish Red Cross News, November 1944, 3; May 1945, 6.

[25] British Red Cross Archive, RCB/2/12/1/2, Oxford Red Cross & St. John Gift Shop, Minute Book, 1943–1945, 04/02/1944 and 27/04/1944.

[26] British Red Cross Society, Oxfordshire Branch, Annual Report and Statement of Accounts 1945, 17.

[27] Bodleian Library, MS. Oxfam DON/1/2, folder 1, 1949 local press cutting. For a fuller discussion of Oxfam's Broad Street shop see Field, 'Consumption in lieu'.

[28] M. Black, *A Cause for Our Times: Oxfam the First 50 Years* (Oxfam and Oxford University Press, 1992), 98–99.

[29] Bodleian Library, MS. Oxfam DON/1/3, folder 4. Oxford Committee for Famine Relief, *Gift Shops News*, nd; B. Rogers, 'Salesman on the side of the angels', *The Daily Telegraph Magazine*, 354, 06/08/1971, 7–8.

[30] M. Hilton, J. McKay, N. Crowson and J.-F. Mouhot, *The Politics of Expertise: How NGOs Shaped Modern Britain* (Oxford University Press, 2013), 54.

[31] For the declinist view, see F. Prochaska, *Christianity and Social Service in Modern Britain: The Disinherited Spirit* (Oxford University Press, 2006). For the counter, see Hilton et al, *The Politics of Expertise*.

[32] L. Hewitt and J. Pendlebury, 'Local associations and participation in place: change and continuity in the relationship between state and civil society in twentieth-century Britain', *Planning Perspectives*, 29:1 (2014), 25–44; C. Beaumont, 'Housewives, workers and citizens: voluntary women's organisations and the campaign for women's rights in England and Wales during the post-war period', in N. Crowson, M. Hilton and J. McKay (eds), *NGOs in Contemporary Britain: Non-State Actors in Society and Politics since 1945* (Basingstoke: Palgrave Macmillan, 2009); G. Brewis, 'From service to action? Students, volunteering and community action in mid-twentieth century Britain', *British Journal of Educational Studies*, 58:4 (2010), 439–449; A. Bocking-Welch, 'Youth against hunger: service, activism and the mobilisation of young humanitarianisms in 1960s Britain', *European Review of History*, 23:1–2 (2016), 154–170.

[33] SOAS, CA/CA1/07/194/011, Running a Christian Aid Gift Shop, c1969.

[34] Rogers, 'Salesman on the side', 8.

[35] SOAS, CA/CA1/07/194/014, Running a Shop for Christian Aid, October 1976.

[36] A. Bocking-Welch, *British Civic Society at the End of Empire: Decolonisation, Globalization and International Responsibility* (Manchester University Press, 2018), 178, 175.

[37] Cadbury Research Library, Save the Children Archive, A376 Trading Committee (ex-Christmas Card Committee), Save the Children (Sales) Limited, Trading Committee, 25/1/1968.

[38] Bodleian Library, MS. Oxfam COM/2/4/13 (folder 3) – extract from *Alton Herald*, 02/10/1970.

[39] Bodleian Library, MS. Oxfam COM/2/4/13 (folder 3), newspaper cuttings, c1970.

[40] Rogers, 'Salesman on the side', 7.

[41] Sasson, 'In the name', 100.

[42] Field, 'Consumption in lieu', 981.

[43] 'Call for bric-a-brac': Bodleian Library, MS. Oxfam COM/2/4/13 (folder 3) – extract from *Yorkshire Evening Press*, 13/10/1970.

[44] Cadbury Research Library, Save the Children Archive, A376 Trading Committee (ex-Christmas Card Committee), Save the Children (Sales) Limited, Trading Committee, 15/01/1976.

[45] SOAS, CA/CA1/07/194/011, Running a Christian Aid Gift Shop, c1969.

[46] Rogers, 'Salesman on the side', 8.

[47] Cadbury Research Library, Save the Children Archive, A376 Trading Committee (ex-Christmas Card Committee), Save the Children (Sales) Limited, Trading Committee, 28/07/1977, 20/07/1978 and 24/10/1979.

[48] Horne and Maddrell, *Charity Shops*, 88.

[49] Cadbury Research Library, Save the Children Archive, A376 Trading Committee (ex-Christmas Card Committee), Christmas Card Committee, 27/11/1964.

[50] 'East Lancs men in Oxfam sales drive': Bodleian Library, MS. Oxfam COM/2/4/13 (folder 3) – extract from *Lancashire Evening Telegraph*, 22/10/1970.

[51] Bodleian Library, MS. Oxfam COM/2/4/13 (folder 3) – extract from *Mansfield & North Nottinghamshire Chronicle*, 01/10/1970, 'Just Chatting' column.

[52] SOAS, CA/CA1/07/194/014, Running a Shop for Christian Aid, October 1976.

[53] Rogers, 'Salesman on the side', 8.

[54] Horne and Maddrell, *Charity Shops*, 84–87.

[55] 'Suzanne Jeffries goes shopping: now the robin is fighting a rearguard action': Bodleian Library, MS. Oxfam COM/2/4/13 (folder 3) – extract from *Yorkshire Post*, 24/11/1970.

[56] C. Curtis, 'Effects of the causes on cards', *The Birmingham Post* (*Birmingham Daily Post*), 19/11/1966, 6.

[57] 'Suzanne Jeffries goes shopping'.

[58] 'Presents and cards which can help a charity': Bodleian Library, MS. Oxfam COM/2/4/13 (folder 3) – extract from *Northern Echo*, 19/11/1970.

[59] Anderson, 'British fair trade', 2.

[60] Anderson, *History of Fair Trade*, 26.

[61] S. Lewis, 'Charity for stay-at-homes': Bodleian Library, MS. Oxfam COM/2/4/13 (folder 3) – extract from *Guardian*, 22/10/1970.

[62] SOAS, CA2/D/15 – Christian Aid, Staff Correspondence: Postal Sales 1973/4, Memorandum from Alex Barrie, 18/02/1974.

[63] 'Prepare for the winter siege', *War Cry*, 18/11/1893, 14.

[64] S. Roddy, J.-M. Strange and B. Taithe, *The Charity Market and Humanitarianism in Britain, 1870–1912* (London: Bloomsbury, 2018), 40.

[65] Bodleian Library, MS. Oxfam COM/3/1/11, folder 4. 'Bicester-based charity celebrates Anniversary. Oxfam celebrates 25 years of fair trade', 14/03/1990, 1.

[66] Anderson, 'British fair trade', 47.

[67] 'Bicester-based charity', 2.

[68] Black, *A Cause*, 165. For an in-depth analysis of the development of Oxfam's international trading programmes, see Anderson, 'British fair trade', 49–55.

69 Anderson, *History of Fair Trade*, 56.
70 Cadbury Research Library, Save the Children Archive, A376 Trading Committee (ex-Christmas Card Committee), Save the Children (Sales) Limited, Trading Committee, 04/01/1967.
71 Cadbury Research Library, Save the Children Archive, A376 Trading Committee (ex-Christmas Card Committee), Save the Children (Sales) Limited, Trading Committee, 15/01/1976.
72 Cadbury Research Library, Save the Children Archive, A376 Trading Committee (ex-Christmas Card Committee), Save the Children (Sales) Limited, Trading Committee, 06/10/1971; 25/07/1972.
73 SOAS, CA/CA2/03/016 – Christian Aid, Shop: General, Confidential Memorandum: The Christian Aid Shop, from AR Barrie to Mr Hugh Samson and Mr BJ Dudbridge, 08/01/1970, 2.
74 SOAS, CA/CA2/03/016 – Christian Aid, Shop: General, Confidential Memorandum: The Christian Aid Shop, from AR Barrie to Mr Hugh Samson and Mr BJ Dudbridge, 08/01/1970, 1; SOAS, CA2/D/15 – Christian Aid, Staff Correspondence: Postal Sales 1973–4.
75 SOAS, CA2/D/23/4 – Christian Aid, Postal Sales: Refugees 1975, Letter from Kenneth Slack, Director, to Jenny Gordon, 19/12/1975.
76 Sasson, 'In the name', 96.
77 Black, *A Cause*, 99.

9

Empire of Charity: The British 'Helping Hand' in South African Charity Shops, 1971–1972

Jessica Field

Introduction

In 1943 Cecil Jackson-Cole, a philanthropic estate agent and second-hand furniture salesman from London, opened a temporary charity shop on Broad Street in the centre of Oxford to raise money for Greek famine relief, a Second World War appeal run by the Oxford Committee for Famine Relief.[1] It was a fundraising method that proved successful and over subsequent decades, Oxfam (as the Committee became later known) opened several hundred permanent shops throughout the country. While the Broad Street Oxfam shop was not the first example of charity retail in Britain or overseas, it became one of the more iconic. The success of the Oxfam branding was such that, at least until the turn of the 21st century, 'Oxfam shop' was frequently used as a generic name for any charity shop.[2] Similarly, Oxfam as a whole became synonymous with its shops for many people in Britain and elsewhere in the Global North.[3]

Building on Oxfam's early shop successes, Jackson-Cole and his charity colleagues opened a number of other UK shop franchises for other causes as part of the wider expansion of charity shops discussed in Chapter 8. By the late 1960s, they had set their sights on expanding charity shop fundraising overseas. Jackson-Cole saw an opportunity to raise money from the growing middle classes in both developed and developing countries, and he also saw fundraising as a spur for national governments to focus on welfare issues. Writing in 1976, Jackson-Cole stated:

> Many do not realise that the Welfare State in the U.K. arose out of the efforts of the Charities here in first calling attention to the distressing

needs of great sections of the population. … [T]he same sort of work is necessary by Charities in the poorer countries in order to wake up the conscience of middle and better-off people in those places so that eventually their governments will do more in the same way as the British Government, and other Governments, have come to do for their own people.[4]

In India, Jackson-Cole and his long-time business and charity colleague John Pearson organized the hiring and training of salaried fundraisers to run sponsored events for initiatives supporting the aged.[5] In South Africa in the early 1970s, Jackson-Cole and another charity colleague, Charles Norman, oversaw the opening of four charity shops in Cape Town, which expanded to at least 16 across the country by the end of the decade. The first handful of gift shops in the apartheid state were associated with a national elderly welfare association and initially attracted a stream of donations and press attention. However, within a year the shops were struggling to continue because of clashes between management in London and Cape Town, difficulty attracting volunteers to run the shops, and limited donations from the public. This chapter examines what fed into such operational difficulties between Britain and South African shop management and, spring-boarding from Jackson-Cole's own assertions about the links between fundraising and governance, uses the case study to highlight how British charity retail – like its relief programming counterparts – maintained distinctive neo-colonial characteristics long into the 20th century. It is less a story of retail community actions in Britain, and more an exploration of how a group of British charity retailers saw and acted on their sense of global responsibility.

Scholarly research linking local and global social causes with retail and shopping has grown in recent decades – with works highlighting social justice boycotts of consumer products in the 18th and 19th centuries, the development of second-hand clothes markets over the 19th century, and the emergence of fair trade stores and modern charity shops in the 20th century.[6] I have written elsewhere about how Oxfam shops, and charity shops in general, cemented consumption as a form of popular engagement with international humanitarianism and membership to aid agencies in Britain.[7] For Oxfam, its shops not only raised money and fostered support from the general public, the stores which sold handicrafts also provided a sales (and marketing) outlet for goods, which in turn contributed to the charity's employment-focused development activities in the Global South.[8] These shops have long been deeply entwined with social transformation work overseas.

Many studies (particularly in geography) have examined the moral linkages of charity and socially conscious retail practices, analysing the asymmetrical relationships between producer, consumer, beneficiary and the mediating organizations in between.[9] Historians of humanitarianism have analysed the expansion of imperialism through practices of caring for distant strangers, and have highlighted how (neo-)colonial sentiments and action have been implicated in humanitarianism.[10] Emily Baughan argued that relief activities run by British aid agencies in Kenya in the 1950s and 1960s enabled and colluded in the violence of the British colonial state and 'continue[d] to ensure that the ideals of British colonialism remained embedded in postcolonial states'.[11] In their research on famine relief, Tehlia Sasson and James Vernon highlighted that during decolonization, aid workers invariably reproduced colonization, as they used colonial knowledge, expertise and connections in order to plan their relief schemes – not least because many were former British officers.[12]

This chapter seeks to link those threads – British charity retail and humanitarian neo-colonialism – through a case study of Jackson-Cole's South African network of charity shops in the early 1970s. It argues that the organization and management of international fundraising by a group of British aid figures and their charity organizations exemplifies another, lesser explored, way that British humanitarian organizations propagated the ideals and technologies of British colonialism. It also argues that there was a clear racialized character to those giving and receiving ideals and technologies. While those gift shops in South Africa represent only a relatively small part of charity retail history, their British origins and contested transnational management offer opportunities to explore the linkages between fundraising (communities) in Britain and neo-colonialism.

This chapter uses diaries, notes and organizational documents from Jackson-Cole's personal papers, which required family permission to access.[13] Jackson-Cole chose what documents he saved and his archive was then further shaped by his wife, Theo Jackson-Cole, who collated and donated the collection to West Sussex Records Office many years after her husband's passing. As such, there will inevitably be bias in the selected preservation of certain papers at the expense of other material not deemed worthy, interesting or safe enough to catalogue.[14] The South Africa gift shops collection is a relatively small part of the collection and is not comprehensive. Yet, where there are limitations in the source material as a result of source selectivity or bias, there are also strengths as they reveal correspondents' personal perspectives, motivations and values – key themes of this analysis.

The chapter begins by exploring the organizational and personal factors that led Jackson-Cole and colleagues to expand the charity shop model in Britain and then to open shops in South Africa. This is followed by an examination of some of the Cape Town gift shops' early challenges with management and charity law and culture in South Africa. The third part of this chapter contextualizes these challenges in relation to the neo-colonial and missionary motivations and attitudes of Jackson-Cole and his colleagues, as the shops became a contested site of control within the first year of their opening. These neo-colonial dynamics are set against the backdrop of South Africa's apartheid system, which institutionalized racial discrimination and governed social structures and everyday life within the country across the period.

Charity shops in service of 'the Cause'

The mandate of Oxfam's first shop was to sell donated goods, such as clothing, jewellery or homeware, in order to raise money for victims of the Greek famine during the Second World War. At the peak of the appeal, the gift shop made £2,800 in one week. Jackson-Cole wrote that if customers laid down their own umbrellas and parcels 'other members of the public were taking them away paid for – so keen was the rush to buy!'[15] When the war ended several members of the Committee felt that both Oxfam and the shop were no longer needed, but Jackson-Cole, along with a few other co-founders of the Committee, sought to continue operations in order to raise funds to tackle ongoing humanitarian suffering.[16] As a result, in 1947, a permanent shop-cum-headquarters was opened at 17 Broad Street in Oxford. Oxfam opened four more permanent stores over the course of the 1950s and early 1960s. Each of these was modelled on the original Broad Street premises because, according to the shop's first salaried manager, Joe Mitty, 'we thought we had got the right formula'.[17]

Jackson-Cole also established two gift shop franchises independent of any single charity – Helping Hand and Acorn – which raised money throughout the 1960s and 1970s for a number of causes including Help the Aged, ActionAid, Age Concern, Churches' Council for Health and Healing, the National Council of Social Service and Shelter (the first two of which were also co-founded by Jackson-Cole). Helping Hand had one permanent outlet in central London on Upper Street and operated as a network of temporary stores throughout the 1960s and 1970s. This network of shops displayed a poster in their windows informing customers of their support for several causes.[18]

Central to Jackson-Cole's efforts to expand these shops and other fundraising initiatives was the Voluntary and Christian Service group (VCS). Originally called Voluntary and Christian Causes, Jackson-Cole founded VCS with a handful of other business and charity colleagues in 1953.[19] As a fundraising and grant-giving body the VCS kickstarted or supported many of Oxfam's appeals, as well as the charity work of Toc H (an international Christian movement), Help the Aged and Age Concern. It also assisted in the development of a housing association, contributed to the foundation of ActionAid, and supported smaller projects throughout the world.[20] VCS was funded through the profits of Jackson-Cole's estate agency business, Andrews and Partners, sharing an office with them in London.[21] Its trustees – which included Charles Norman (a key figure in the South African shops whom we shall meet later) – played central roles in the governance of many of the charities it supported.

The VCS was a sprawling network of business and charity organizations, underpinned by a sense of mission encapsulated in six principles. First, to relieve suffering in line with the Christian injunctions to feed the hungry, clothe the naked, shelter the homeless and heal the sick; second, to kickstart new ventures for other charities if they did not have the upfront funds or momentum; third, to champion the use of entrepreneurial skills and business experience; fourth, to involve business-like people whatever their religious persuasion and give them a vocation; fifth, to focus on unpopular causes; and, finally, to 'experiment, to test, to keep innovating, to maintain momentum, and continually to challenge the accepted limits of ordinary achievement'.[22] Jackson-Cole was deeply spiritual and committed to the Christian faith himself, and he sought a sense of Christian-like mission in those he worked alongside in VCS and across all his charities (whether they had a personal faith or not).[23]

This interweaving of a Christian ethic and modern entrepreneurial business practices was certainly not unusual in Britain across the 1950s and 1960s. Many leading business figures held a strong, private faith and pursued their faith-inspired injunctions through organized charity work.[24] Christian charities – such as Christian Aid (1957), the Catholic Fund for Overseas Development (1961) and Tear Fund (1960) – were founded and expanded in those decades, as their founders sought to run professional, secular organizations that could 're-establish the relevance of Christian values within modern society'.[25]

Jackson-Cole and other trustees saw the VCS's key responsibility as a Christian-inspired influence for wider social change. A note written in 1977 reflecting on Jackson-Cole's life's work explained that government welfare had arisen 'first through individual efforts in voluntary charity'.[26] In his retirement speech from the role of Honorary Secretary of Oxfam in December 1966, he stated that: 'Fund-raising is very important because it is more than fund-raising (a) each donation is equal to vote [sic] in favour – (b) because it attracts publicity.'[27] Jackson-Cole saw consumer participation through charitable donation and purchase as a form of conscious engagement in and of itself, and a means to influence social change and improve the wellbeing of society. In his view, charity could not be divided into sub-causes. Rather, it was part of a 'the Cause' – organized efforts to remedy suffering, wherever or however it occurred in the world.

Ideas of social progress are embedded within (particularly Protestant) Christianity and are central to the work of many faith-inspired non-governmental organizations (NGOs).[28] Religiously inspired ideals underpinned British imperial humanitarianism throughout the 19th century and well into the 20th.[29] Christian-inspired progress infused Jackson-Cole's charitable work – he frequently declared throughout his personal papers that 'there is a responsible spirit behind the Universe who is seeking to remedy the suffering'. In 1967 he reflected: 'we have seen God's acts in Oxfam and should try with the help of others to trace how He [God] has been working from 1870 onwards (the Irish famine) to bring about the present international position'.[30] While Oxfam and the like had been undertaking relief and development work for many years in the Global South, the funds that paid for these efforts were largely raised in and by publics in the Global North. Jackson-Cole saw this as a missed opportunity to further 'the Cause' and, by 1971, the VCS had turned to fundraising directly in South Africa and elsewhere overseas.

From Britain to South Africa

South Africa – previously a Dutch and then British colony – became a republic in 1961. The governing White Afrikaner minority were fervently nationalist and violently segregationist.[31] From 1948 to the early 1990s, the National Party implemented a national system of apartheid that institutionalized racial discrimination and the marginalization of non-White (particularly Black) communities. After an escalation of apartheid violence across the 1960s, the segregationist system began to weaken in the 1970s – though the wealth and privilege of White South Africans, and the poverty and inequality faced by Black South Africans and other non-White populations, was already well-entrenched.[32]

Against this backdrop, in 1971, the VCS initiated and financed the establishment of South Africa's first four gift shops, in the Claremont, Sea Point, Observatory and Wynberg areas of Cape Town.[33] The shops were to raise funds primarily in the name of the South African National Council for the Welfare of the Aged (SANCWA), who were then to distribute it to local charities.[34] The shop set-up was modelled on British charity shops: the public were encouraged to donate second-hand clothes, books, shoes, homeware and jewellery, all to be sold in the stores, which were run by dedicated volunteers and a salaried manager. Marketing techniques for soliciting donations included shop appeals and the production of brochures, and these administration costs were taken out of shop funds. Charles Norman – a Help the Aged and VCS trustee (and a White South African based in Britain) – visited South Africa to lead the set-up, in collaboration with Cape Town-based Dr William Slater (Chairman of SANCWA), Mrs Droskie (Director) and Mr Yeld (Vice Chairman).[35]

William Slater described the South African gift shops as among the first charity shops in the country in correspondence with Jackson

Cole.[36] Second-hand retail was not new in South Africa, as shops and rummage stalls had long-served poorer communities. An early evaluation of the SANCWA gift shops noted that Jewish-run rummage sales and a second-hand outlet selling cheap clothing to non-Whites on a delayed-payment basis as the SANCWA charity shop's main competition in the Sea Point area of Cape Town.[37] However, implicit in Slater's suggestion of novelty is in the professionalized nature of the venture, with salaried managers trained in fundraising appeals and with a business strategy for shop management.

Mrs Droskie, Director for SANCWA, recruited some of the first (primarily female and White) volunteers to run the Cape Town shops, and their management was supported by the part-time efforts of Major Aubrey Smith. By October 1971, Smith had been hired on a full-time basis by Slater and Droskie, partly to account for the gap left by the departure of Charles Norman and partly 'to safeguard the future of the shops' as the administrative workload increased.[38] The Wynberg shop opened to some fanfare in early September 1971, with an inauguration by the Mayor, Richard Friedlander, and local newspaper coverage in *The Cape Times*.

The gift shops were not seeing the success that SANCWA hoped, however, and just as the Wynberg and Observatory shops were opened, Slater and Droskie corresponded with Jackson-Cole over several pressing issues. First, Sea Point was struggling to meet costs and donations were not coming in the quantity anticipated. Second, SANCWA pointed out that under South African law, charitable appeals could only be made by a registered welfare organization, that the funds had to be distributed to causes linked to the focus of the registered organization, and that strict reporting processes had to be followed. Despite this, Jackson-Cole was pushing for the raised money to be dispersed to prisoner and family welfare causes, as well as those focused on the elderly (in line with the VCS's imperative to support unpopular causes and mirroring the multiple causes approach of Helping Hand gift shops in Britain). SANCWA had lent its welfare registration number to the four gift shops and explained that 'no funds may be allocated to such other body',[39] otherwise it placed the organization at potential legal risk.

According to an evaluation by Yeld, the generalized approach to charity also dissuaded people from volunteering their time, as 'there are relatively few of what one may call "freelance" workers who are prepared to respond to appeals in aid of causes to which they are not already attached'.[40] There was an emerging tension between the organization of the four gift shops as modelled on British practice, and the culture and laws around volunteering and fundraising in South Africa.

Linking all of these concerns was the problem that 'uncertainty and vagueness remains as apparently there is no one in this country empowered to make decisions on your [Cecil Jackson-Cole's] behalf'.[41] Echoing the paternalistic relationships of imperial Britain, overarching control of the initiative was retained by the VCS in London, and actioned through various visits by Charles Norman, Chairman of the VCS, Jackson-Cole and Alec Churcher, a member of the VCS General Purposes Committee.

Jackson-Cole and his colleagues in the VCS viewed this need for control in expertise terms. On 10 September 1971, less than a week before William Slater sent his first letter outlining the Cape Town shop difficulties, Jackson-Cole had prepared notes for a speech where he explained the key components of success for a (Christian-inspired) charity.[42] Similar to the VCS's six principles, these included: a 'God-given urge' to help far away suffering populations, the 'undivided responsibility' of an experienced director, and business efficiency. 'In my experience', Jackson-Cole continued, 'it is impossible to attain this degree of efficiency on the fund-raising side of a National Charity if this particular responsibility is shared with a Committee'.[43] According to Jackson-Cole, 'the urge' suffered most within committee-led organizations; responsibility in these scenarios was diffuse and not taken by any single individual, and therefore failures could not result in termination of that individual. There was also an element of moral authority in this positioning, as Jackson-Cole declared an 'increased need for moral leadership', in both rich and poorer countries, 'which VCS/Help the Aged may come to give, on the problems of old age'.

Writing in 1975 about the need to develop fundraising skills in India, Jackson-Cole summarized this position: '*we have to teach* the individual who has exceptional insights what he has to do about it. ... [B]ut, of course, only to the right individuals' [emphasis in original].[44] For the Cape Town shops, Charles Norman was the trainer and, after his departure, when shops began struggling the VCS sought to provide 'training letters to each [Cape Town gift shop] manageress listing ways to improve matters'. The shops were required to regularly report their charity activities and takings to Mr Worby, one of the managers of the Helping Hand gift shops in the United Kingdom.[45] The training letters were opposed by SANCWA and never materialized, and the organization continued to press for the Board of Directors to be situated in Cape Town rather than routing information and decisions through London. Slater expressed deep gratitude to the VCS for initiating and financing the establishment of the first shops, but he and Droskie repeatedly explained that the shops would not be successful without SANCWA having autonomy in operations.[46]

According to Alec Churcher, however, the reason for this push back from SANCWA was that:

[T]here is a real resentment, founded on strong national pride and a distrust of anything international, against any implication that South

Africa is not capable of running its own affairs and solving its own problems without outside help. They are critical of Britain and do not think they have anything to learn from her.[47]

Churcher also surmised that Oxfam's difficulties were due to similar reasons, though no further explanation was given about the nature of these difficulties.[48]

Empire of charity

In many ways, efforts to centralize control (around Jackson-Cole in particular) were no different in South Africa to what was happening within the VCS's network of charities in Britain. In April 1975, Jackson-Cole wrote in his personal papers that he received a 'slap in the face'.[49] The Finance Committee of Help the Aged (UK) attempted to limit the organization's expansion overseas – undermining Jackson-Cole's plans. He expressed concern that a committee could attempt to override his decisions.[50] Nonetheless, the existence of the Committee was a check and balance on a singular authority. In contrast, the tensions that played out between London-based VCS members and the Cape Town-based SANCWA highlighted the persistence of a particular colonial paternalism in Jackson-Cole and colleagues' approach and attitudes towards contemporaries in the Global South. While the VCS's associates in SANCWA must have been viewed as having the requisite urge to tackle challenges facing the aged in South Africa – and the country was recognized as having a wealthy middle class with the capacity to give – control over the fundraising initiatives steadfastly remained outside of the country.

Skinner and Lester, in their article on humanitarianism and empire, note that a constant aspect of humanitarianism from empire to the end of the 20th century, 'is the power imbalances between those who "issue" humanitarian empathy and material aid and those who are in receipt of it'.[51] While the development of these gift shops in Cape Town was explicitly to empower those from South Africa to support their own poor (in other words, to issue their own material aid), the power imbalances between the VCS and SANCWA were such that SANCWA did not have the autonomy to work in its own way under its name, or even within the confines of South African law. It was, in many ways, the reproduction of a colonial relationship; one where the VCS infantilized its South African partners and remained inflexible in the administration of a British fundraising model in the South African context. Writing later about a different set of VCS-supported charity shops in Johannesburg, Charles Norman (a White South African himself, though based out of Britain) stated that: 'like many South Africans they [colleagues of their other partner charity] think that Britain is a soft number and they will just take all that can be given without making a contribution themselves' (the contribution in this case referred to repaying shop promotion costs that had been initially fronted by the VCS).[52]

Moreover, the recipients of the VCS's humanitarian attentions were not homogeneous and received differing forms of targeting, support and training depending on the VCS's views of their needs and abilities. The SANCWA members in communication with the VCS about the shops and fundraising were White South African, as were the managers of the VCS's South African gift shop partner from 1973, Toc H.[53] The prosperous suburban locations of the four first shops – Claremont, Sea Point, Observatory and Wynberg – had been designated as 'White' areas under South Africa's Group Areas Act.[54] Non-White people were not permitted to live in these areas, though they could commute to, and work in, them with relevant permissions. As such, the donors and customers of these shops were likely majority White, too.

At least one of the Johannesburg shops had a Black South African volunteer. Rose volunteered in the Rosebank shop in Johannesburg in 1973. Unlike her White colleagues, Rose's surname was not mentioned in the Gift Shop Committee Meeting Notes and she is also referred to in the notes as 'the African saleslady'. There is a second depersonalized reference to 'the African saleslady from Kensington' in relation to the Orange Grove shop. It is unclear whether Rose and this unnamed 'African saleslady from Kensington' are the same person.[55] These depersonalizing references to Black volunteers in contrast to White volunteers and managers in the notes highlights prevalent othering in these shop spaces.

In contrast, different engagements with non-White South Africans were planned. Two of the charitable causes considered as potential recipients of the Cape Town charity shops' profits were elderly welfare organizations that were doing 'immense work' with 'white and coloured aged folk' (Coloured [mixed-race] being one of the four racial classifications under the apartheid system: Black, White, Coloured and Indian). Separate to the shops, Alec Churcher – while in the country mediating between the VCS and SANCWA over the running of the gift shops – explored the possibility of 'the selling of Bibles to African mine workers'. Writing to the Phyllis Trust (also founded by Jackson-Cole) in February 1972, Alec Churcher noted:

> I was able to talk with a fairly wide variety of people about this whole question, seeking their views as to the possible dangers of putting Bibles into the hands of ill-educated and semi-literate Africans without at the same time giving any instruction as to its right use and/or guidance in the understanding of the Old Testament in particular. ... The majority of those I consulted ... were of the opinion that it would be best to sell New Testaments only.[56]

The explanation given for New Testament preference was lack of Bible literacy among African mine workers and wrong or over-literal interpretations of biblical passages. In the view of Alec Churcher and his correspondents, the New Testament provided more guidance and religious instruction than the Old.

South Africa during the 1970s experienced relatively strong economic growth due to the success of the country's extractive and manufacturing industries. This success was built upon the apartheid system, which exploited low paid, and heavily controlled, Black labour.[57] Therefore, the miners Churcher was referring to were likely Black South Africans. The Bibles were to be sold by travelling book sellers rather than in the gift shops, which were situated in relatively affluent and 'White'-classified suburbs of Cape Town. For Jackson-Cole and Alec Churcher, their charity work in South Africa from 1971 was civilizing in purpose. Black South Africans were targeted for evangelical education, Coloured and White South Africans were imagined as the beneficiaries of shop funds, and the White middle class were sought out for training in fundraising. To quote Jackson-Cole: 'once they [local fundraisers] are shown how to do it they respond by raising money themselves in a wonderful way for their poorest of the poor'.[58] It was a holistic and heavily racialized mission in the name of 'the Cause' that should, Jackson-Cole hoped, foment social change at all levels and spur the South African government to develop welfare safety nets 'the same way as the British Government, and other Governments, have come to do for their own people'.[59]

With these social transformation sentiments and a clear consciousness of inequality, it seems striking that Jackson-Cole and his VCS colleagues made no overt references to anti-apartheid resistance, at least in the documents available. During this period, international opposition to apartheid was growing and Britain was a key centre of global activity. The Anti-Apartheid Movement (AAM) – an international mass movement that emerged in 1959 – had made significant waves in the struggle against racial segregation in South Africa through boycott and disengagement activities, particularly across the early 1960s. However, lack of explicit reference in these records should not necessarily be taken as a lack of concern. In her article on AAM in the 1970s, Christabel Gurney notes that the AAM's radical boycott and withdrawal tactics were falling out of favour – particularly among churches, businesses and the Trade Union Movement.[60] These actors had misgivings about the social and economic impacts of wholesale disengagement, and instead encouraged actions like fair pay for African employees as a means to influence change from within.

It is by no means certain what Jackson-Cole's opinions on apartheid were. Jackson-Cole worked with church-linked networks within the country and championed South-African driven change – whether through the shops or through Christian education. This suggests, if he had any view about apartheid at all, he might have leant towards a change from within positioning. Moreover, it seems likely that Jackson-Cole did not take a stance *against* anti-apartheid resistance, as Judge J.H. Steyn, a social justice campaigner and public opponent of apartheid, was the chairman of one of the charity shops' proposed beneficiary charities and a figure floated as potential board member of the Cape Town charity shop network.[61] However, Jackson-Cole and the VCS operated a *charity*, rather than *social justice*, approach to alleviating suffering in the country, which would have failed to make headway against the deeply unjust and violent apartheid system.

Ultimately, regardless of Jackson-Cole's views, the VCS's efforts to tackle suffering through charity shop enterprise in Cape Town failed. On 15 December 1971, William Slater wrote to Jackson-Cole to announce that – because no compromise had been reached on the issues of management and London continued to be vague and chaotic in their dealings – SANCWA would withdraw the authority to use its Welfare Registration Number by 31 March 1972.[62] Internal memos in Jackson-Cole's personal papers suggested that he perceived SANCWA mismanagement of the shops to be the core of the problem, but the two organizations parted ways amicably in the end, letting 'bygones be bygones'.[63] It is not clear whether the shops continued independently under SANCWA, nor whether the Bible selling mission got off the ground.

After this, the VCS turned to the South African wing of the international Christian charity, Toc H, and supported the establishment of at least five gift shops under their name across 1973–1975 in Johannesburg. Managers of these also found it 'frustrating to work under such long range control'.[64] The VCS in their turn was frustrated by Toc H's apparently inefficient day-to-day running of the stores. Elsewhere in Jackson-Cole's papers, it is suggested that the VCS had a hand in opening at least 16 shops by the end of the 1970s.

Across South Africa today, the charity shop is a common site of fundraising and second-hand goods sale.[65] While further research in needed to explore how long the VCS-supported gift shops lasted, and the extent to which they shaped the broader domestic charity shop landscape in Cape Town and Johannesburg, the four gift shops in Cape Town certainly formed a key sense of Jackson-Cole and the VCS's humanitarian contribution back in Britain. It was a sense of contribution that affirmed British models of charity organization as the main (if not, *only*) route to national social progress, and the ideology involved overt forms of control through management, as well as indirect forms of domination through notions of expertise.

Conclusion

After the success of the first temporary Oxfam shop in 1943, Jackson-Cole sought to develop and expand charity shops to enable the general public in Britain to help the poor in distant places, and in doing so to encourage progressive global shifts in working towards supporting 'the Cause' and ending suffering. A community of Christian-spirited businesspeople (mainly men) converged around this idea, and around Jackson-Cole, through the formation of the VCS in Britain in 1953. The VCS defined itself as a Christian kick-starter organization, dedicated to supporting charities through funding initial appeals and offering fundraising expertise – first in the United Kingdom, and then overseas. It soon sought to replicate the success of the Oxfam and Helping Hand charity shop model in Britain in poorer countries where there was a burgeoning middle class that might be able to fundraise to help their own poor. In South Africa, between 1971 and 1972, the VCS partnered with the South African National Council for the Welfare of the Aged and opened four gift shops in Cape Town.

In literature exploring the expansion and impacts of British charity and humanitarian relief overseas, the British export of fundraising models to postcolonial contexts has received limited attention. This may be a result of its relatively small scale, diffuse nature and uneven impacts. Indeed, as this chapter has explored with regards to South Africa, these gift shops faltered not long after they got off the ground. It may also be because fundraising has always been a less visibly interventionist aspect of British humanitarianism than direct relief missions. What this small case study has shown, however, is that interventionism and ideas of social progress infused British charity shop operations overseas as much as their relief programme counterparts. Moreover, similar to many British NGO relief programmes in the Global South across the time period, the relationship between the VCS and SANCWA can be characterized as colonial and paternalistic; administrative control and notions of expertise flowed one way – from Jackson-Cole, Norman and Churcher towards their partners in Cape Town (and later, Johannesburg). While there is still much to understand about the longer-term impacts of the British charity shop model on the charity retail landscape in South Africa – including ways in which it manifested and reinforced apartheid segregations – what is clear from this study is that for a small community of British charity fundraisers in Britain, charity shops presented more than a financial means to a humanitarian end. Charity shops were a racialized governance tool that, in their own right, could be used to foment social change – whether in Britain, or globally.

Acknowledgements

Thank you to the tireless work of the editorial team of this volume and reviewers of my chapter, especially George Gosling, Alix Green and Grace Millar, whose thoughtful comments have significantly improved the piece. Many thanks to Bertrand Taithe and Rebecca Gill for inspiring me to pick up this particular thread of Jackson-Cole's work in the first place, and to

Virginie Le Masson for providing invaluable feedback and encouragement in the early stages. Any errors remain my own. Finally, a thank you and special mention goes to Theo Jackson-Cole, who sadly passed away in March 2021.

Notes

1. M. Black, *A Cause for Our Times: Oxfam the First 50 Years* (Oxford: Oxfam, 1992), 16.

2. L. Parson, 'The voluntary spaces of charity shops: workplaces or domestic spaces?', in C. Milligan and D. Conradson (eds), *Landscapes of Voluntarism: New Spaces of Health, Welfare and Governance* (Bristol: Policy Press, 2006), 234.

3. S. Ilcan and A. Lacey, 'Governing through empowerment: Oxfam's global reform and trade campaigns', *Globalizations*, 3:2 (2006), 217.

4. C. Jackson-Cole (hereafter in notes: CJC), 'Wither Help the Aged? And Action in Distress?', 20/09/1976, Box 3, Folder: CJC Writings (Charities) 1938–1979. CJC Personal Papers, West Sussex Record Office, Chichester ('CJC/WSRO').

5. J. Field, 'Charitable giving in modern India', in R. Ginty and J. Peterson (eds), *The Routledge Companion to Humanitarian Action* (Abingdon: Routledge, 2015), 457–467.

6. M. Hilton, *Consumerism in Twentieth-Century Britain: The Search for a Historical Movement* (Cambridge University Press, 2003), 15–16; J. Le Zotte, 'Not charity, but a chance': Philanthropic capitalism and the rise of American thrift stores', *The New England Quarterly*, 86:2 (2013), 169–195; M. Anderson, *A History of Fair Trade in Contemporary Britain: From Civil Society Campaigns to Corporate Compliance* (London: Palgrave Macmillan, 2015); M. Anderson, 'The British fair trade movement, 1960–2000: a new form of global citizenship?', PhD thesis, University of Birmingham, 2008; S. Horne, 'The charity shop: purpose and change', *International Journal of Non-Profit and Voluntary Sector Marketing*, 5:2 (2000), 113–124; S. Horne and A. Maddrell, *Charity Shops: Retailing, Consumption and Society* (London: Routledge, 2003).

7. J. Field, 'Consumption in lieu of membership: reconfiguring popular charitable action in post-world war II Britain', *Voluntas*, 27:2 (2016), 979–997.

8. Anderson, 'The British fair trade movement', 47; Ilcan and Lacey, 'Governing through empowerment', 217.

9. M. Goodman, 'Reading fair trade: political ecological imaginary and the moral economy of fair trade foods', *Political Geography*, 23 (2004), 891–915; C. Barnett, P. Cloke, N. Clarke and A. Malpass, 'Consuming ethics: articulating the subjects and spaces of ethical consumption', *Antipode*, 37:1 (2005), 23–45; A. Hutchens, 'Empowering women through fair trade? Lessons from Asia', *Third World Quarterly*, 31:3 (2010), 449–467; A. Brooks, *Clothing Poverty: The Hidden World of Fast Fashion and Second-Hand Clothes* (London: Zed Books, 2019); Anderson, 'The British fair trade movement'.

10. R. Skinner and A. Lester, 'Humanitarianism and empire: new research agendas', *The Journal of Imperial and Commonwealth History*, 40:5 (2012), 730–731.

11. E. Baughan, 'Rehabilitating an empire: humanitarian collusion with the colonial state during the Kenyan emergency, ca. 1954–1960', *Journal of British Studies*, 59 (2020), 78.

12. T. Sasson and J. Vernon, 'Practising the British way of famine: technologies of relief, 1770–1985', *European Review of History*, 22:6 (2015), 860–872.

13. CJC Personal Papers, ACC.6259, WSRO.

14. E.J. Webb, D.T. Campbell, R.D. Schwarz and L. Sechrest, 'The use of archival sources in social research', in M. Bulmer (ed), *Sociological Research Methods* (New Jersey: Transaction Publishers, 2003), 113–130.

15. CJC, 'Part memoirs of C. Jackson-Cole covering the earlier period of Oxfam' (circa 1979), 4, Private Collection of Mrs M. Theo Jackson Cole.

16. Black, *A Cause for Our Times*, 32.

17 Interview with Joe Mitty (transcript), June 2002, Oxfam Archives, Oxford.

18 CJC, Minutes of a meeting of the Gift Shop Committee, 139 Oxford Street, 27/11/1973. Box 15, Folder: Helping Hand, CJC/WSRO.

19 Voluntary and Christian Service, circa 1974, 'VCS. Report with a purpose: what now has to be achieved?'. Printed by J. E. C. Potter & Son Ltd, Stamford, Lincolnshire, England.

20 J. Field, 'Serving "the cause": Cecil Jackson-Cole and the professionalization of charity in post-war Britain', *Historical Research*, 93:260 (2020), 379–397; John Cole, interview with author, Stornoway, Scotland, 8 November 2011; United Nations Development Programme, 'Governing Council: Twenty-eighth Session' (Twenty-eighth session, June 1981), Reference: DP/561.

21 Cole, interview with author, 2011.

22 VCS [report], c1990. Personal archives of Roger Lees, UK.

23 Field, 'Serving "the cause"'.

24 M. Anderson, 'NGOs and fair trade: the social movement behind the label', in N. Crowson, M. Hilton and J. McKay (eds), *NGOs in Contemporary Britain: Non-state Actors in Society and Politics since 1945* (London: Palgrave Macmillan, 2009).

25 Anderson, 'The British fair trade movement', 74, 82.

26 Author unspecified, 'Some of the material for helping preparing the book "Ten Years Too Late"' (February, 1977), 11–12. Box 3, Folder: CJC Autobiographical Writings 1969–1978, CJC/WSRO.

27 CJC, 'By C. Jackson Cole on retirement from the office of Honorary Secretary of Oxfam' (15/12/1966), Box 3, Folder: CJC Writings (Charities) 1938–1979, CJC/WSRO.

28 E. Bornstein, *The Spirit of Development: Protestant NGOs, Morality, and Economics in Zimbabwe*, vol 2 (Stanford University Press, 2005), 3–4.

29 M. Barnett, *Empire of Humanity: A History of Humanitarianism* (Ithaca: Cornell University Press, 2011).

30 CJC, 'Books which need to be published, or, if already published, need to be further propagated for more intensive sale' (26/09/1967), Box 5, Folder: CJC Copy Letters 1967–1968, CJC/WSRO.

31 P.J. Henshaw, 'The transfer of Simonstown: Afrikaner nationalism, South African strategic dependence, and British global power', *The Journal of Imperial and Commonwealth History*, 20:3 (1992), 419–444.

32 C. Bundy, 'Poverty and inequality in South Africa: a history', in *Oxford Research Encyclopaedia of African History* (Oxford University Press, 2020).

33 W.B. Slater to CJC, 14/09/1971. Box 18, Folder: Gift shops SA (i), CJC/WSRO. Slater states that the shops are the first of their kind in the country.

34 Slater to CJC, 14/09/1971.

35 In a 1974/1975 VCS report, Yeld is also noted as being the General Manager of the Citizens Housing Association in South Africa and a key overseas associate of VCS.

36 Slater to CJC, 14/09/1971.

37 R.W.A. Yeld, 'Helping Hand gift shops: report and recommendations'. Contained in correspondence, R.W.A. Yeld to CJC, 22/11/1971, Box 18, Folder: Gift Shops SA (i), CJC/WSRO.

38 Mrs Z. Droskie to CJC, 21/10/1971, Box 18, Folder: Gift Shops SA (i), CJC/WSRO.

39 Yeld, 'Helping Hand gift shops', 4.

40 Yeld, 'Helping Hand gift shops', 2.

41 Slater to CJC, 14/09/1971.

42 CJC, 'Wither Help the Aged? And other charities dealing with the vital needs covered by some of the Christian injunctions', 10/09/1971, Box 3, Folder: CJC Writings (Charities) 1938–1979, CJC/WSRO.

[43] CJC 'Wither Help the Aged?'. Exempting the VCS, which was a successful committee precisely because its board was populated with 'conscientious' and successful businessmen.

[44] CJC to Frank Baker Esq, 15/05/1974, Box 3, Folder: CJC Writings (Charities) 1938–1979, CJC/WRSO.

[45] CJC/WRSO. VCS Committee note, 05/01/1972, Box 3, Folder: CJC Writings (Charities) 1938–1979.

[46] Slater to CJC, 14/09/1971. Also around this time, the UK charity Christian Aid approached the South African charity DEVCRAFT about selling their items in their mail order retail operation. However – expressing similar concerns around autonomy and a domestic focus – DEVCRAFT turned down the offer, explaining that they 'will concentrate in the immediate future on improving the effectiveness of our two retail outlets and developing a good wholesale marketing programme here in South Africa'. Memorandum from Alex Barrie, 18/02/1974, SOAS, CA2/D/15 – Christian Aid, Staff Correspondence: Postal Sales 1973/4. Special thanks to George Gosling for this source and insight.

[47] A. Churcher, 'Gift shops in Cape Town', 1, 18/12/1971, Box 18, Folder: Gift Shops, CJC/WRSO, SA (i).

[48] Churcher, 'Gift shops in Cape Town', 1.

[49] CJC, 'A reminiscence on one of my working weeks', 27/04/1975, Box 3, Folder: CJC Autobiographical Writings, 1969–1978, CJC/WRSO.

[50] CJC, 'A reminiscence on one of my working weeks'

[51] Skinner and Lester, 'Humanitarianism and empire', 740.

[52] Memo from Charles Norman to CJC, 09/01/1973, Box 15, Folder: Helping Hand, CJC/WRSO.

[53] CJC/WRSO. Gift Shop Meeting Committee Notes, 22/12/1973, Box 18, Folder: Gift Shops SA (ii).

[54] S. Oldfield, 'Urban networks, community organising and race: an analysis of racial integration in a desegregated South African neighbourhood', Geoforum, 35 (2004), 195.

[55] Gift Shop Meeting Committee Notes, 22/12/1973, Box 18, Folder: Gift Shops SA (ii), CJC/WRSO.

[56] Alec Churcher to The Trustees of the Phyllis Trust, 'Policy re bible selling in South Africa', February 1972, Box 18, Folder: Gift Shops in SA (i), CJC/WSRO.

[57] W. Beinart, Twentieth-Century South Africa (Oxford University Press, 2001), 171.

[58] CJC, 'Newsletter from the founder' (November 1977), Box 3, Folder: CJC Writings (Charities) 1938–1979, CJC/WRSO.

[59] CJC, 'Wither Help the Aged?'.

[60] C. Gurney, 'The 1970s: the anti-apartheid movement's difficult decade', Journal of Southern African Studies, 35:2 (2009), 473.

[61] Yeld, 'Helping Hand gift shops', 6.

[62] W.J.B. Slater to CJC, 15/12/1971, Box 18, Folder: Gift Shops SA (i), CJC/WRSO.

[63] VCS Committee note, 05/01/1972, Box 3, Folder: CJC Writings (Charities) 1938–1979, CJC/WRSO.

[64] Untitled document, an extract from a letter from John Goldfinch, of Toc H South Africa, to Charles Norman, circa September 1973, 4, Box 15, Folder: Helping Hand, CJC/WRSO.

[65] K.G. Watt, 'Valuing precarious commodities: an ethnography of trade in three charity shops in the Cape Metropolitan area', master's thesis, Stellenbosch University, 2014.

10

Race, Retailing and the Windrush Generation: Principle and Practice in the John Lewis Partnership's Recruitment of Commonwealth Arrivals, 1950–1962

Alix R. Green

Introduction

Retail is a distinctive and potentially productive space for historians seeking to understand the workings of racist and racialized thinking in policy and practice and the exclusionary centring of Whiteness in conceptions of national identity in Britain. It is a sector premised on display and the public transaction of business and one of hidden labour, for example in distribution, personnel, management or estates. Engaging with retail offers us a valuable opportunity to explore how businesses shaped and reshaped racialized notions of staff aptitudes, attitudes and appropriate conduct organizationally and within and in response to broader social change. The immediate postwar period compels our attention here: a period of expansion as retailers sought to meet rising demand fuelled by customers' new discretionary spending power and one in which companies were both selling to and recruiting from a pluralizing society as newly recognized citizens of the United Kingdom and Commonwealth arrived in Britain, as did migrants and refugees from continental Europe. We can gain critical purchase on big questions, such as how citizenship, identity and belonging were refracted through the lens of race, by exploring and connecting case studies of how retailers understood and responded to this moment of transition and transformation.

In late 1961, executives at the John Lewis Partnership (JLP) – a large UK department store and grocery business with a distinctive democratic employee-ownership model – assembled a policy document on the 'Employment of Coloured Workers'. It was intended to serve as a 'directive to employing officials throughout the Partnership' and as a statement 'where occasion demands, for publication to the Press, to customers, or in our own journalism'.[1] The policy was formulated in response to a newspaper article, published in February 1961, which revealed to the *Observer*'s readership the discrimination in employment faced by Commonwealth arrivals, naming the Partnership.[2] Critical press coverage was unwelcome to the business, but, as I will argue, central and branch managers believed larger and more fundamental issues to be at stake.

The policy document opened with a restatement of Rule 21(2) from the 1950 edition of JLP's written Constitution: to recruit those 'whose assistance is likeliest to be best for the Partnership's efficiency in the conduct of its business … without regard to age, sex, race, social position, family connection, religious or political views, with the sole exception of totalitarianism whether called Fascism or Communism or something else'.[3] Appropriating and adapting a provision conditioned by Cold War anxieties in a context of decolonization, the policy went on to suggest that any assessment of suitability must take account of customers' views. As no evidence of objection to African and West Indian workers was forthcoming, the Partnership was 'prepared to experiment in suitable circumstances with the employment of these particular coloured workers, either men or women, in selling departments where candidates of sufficient intelligence and education and suitable appearance offer themselves'.[4] Should such experimentation elicit unfavourable reactions from customers or 'from our normal sources of recruitment' (clarified elsewhere as 'the English white collar worker')[5] then prompt action should be taken to transfer those Partners to other work.

That the company prepared the document is itself significant and the multiple identified audiences point us to the anticipated sources of commentary on or objection to the employment of racialized people in the Partnership. The formulation is also notable for its silences, ambiguities and preconceptions. How would such principles of recruitment be interpreted on the ground at a time when the retail sector was expanding and diversifying within a broader context fraught with anxieties about the impact of migration on British society? We can detect the traces of pseudo-scientific taxonomies, giving hiring managers potential cover for decisions based on the assumed attributes of a people group rather than the credentials of an individual. But particularly striking is the way in which clarity of principle was immediately – and, apparently, easily and unproblematically – occluded. The provisions and caveats evidently made sense to the policy's contemporary architects but, looking back, we have to ask why they did so. This is the task of the chapter: to try to explain the contingencies with which equity of treatment was offered to prospective and serving Partners.

An apparently rapidly pluralizing society raised serious implications for JLP's sense of identity and community on three levels. First was the level of the Partnership itself; the selection of new members mattered more in a community of co-owners ostensibly held together by bonds of collective effort and reward than in a conventional retail business. A second level of community embraced customers and the wider public; fostering a sense of allegiance and belonging with customers through the provision of quality products and of expert, conscientious service was understood as key to commercial success. Communities formed around individual stores, many of which had strong roots in their localities that predated acquisition by JLP, but careful stewardship of the company's reputation for integrity allowed for some portability of customer loyalty. A sense of national community formed a third level. The founder, John Spedan Lewis, saw his design for JLP as evoking and strengthening the distinctive institutions of the British democratic system. The damage and dislocation of the Second World War and its aftermath and the shifting constellations of power emerging from the Cold War and decolonization seemed to lend this task a fresh urgency and significance.

To understand the policy and these broader questions of identity and community, I draw on records held in JLP's archives, to which I had unrestricted access: items published as part of the company's commitment to an internal 'free press' in the central *Gazette* and branch *Chronicles*; memoranda between senior managers; routine reports from individual stores. I have focused on files the business itself created and organized in terms of race and 'colour', still present in archival descriptions, and on specific references in the Partnership press. This source base is not as extensive as we might expect for a period characterized by intense debates about migration and the resultant social mixing. It also captures almost nothing of the everyday experiences of Partners of colour.[6] These absences are revealing, placing JLP within a context in which claims of British society's 'colour blindness' were in wide circulation. Records that show where and how colour was both seen and named are conspicuous and disruptive in this context. From them, we gain some insight into how the company interpreted and responded to those moments when the fault lines between principle and practice became unstable.

The chapter was written and revised in the early 2020s. It was assembled, and will be read, through the lens of a present characterized by enduring systemic racism and hostility to migrants and refugees. This history matters because the arguments that stand in the way of racial justice depend on its absence, whether by ignorance, marginalization or selective amnesia. Claims about British values such as equality before the law and tolerance – which are central to resisting demands for structural change – break down on historical inspection. The chapter aims to make two overarching contributions in this context. First, it seeks to show that histories of work and of business demand serious attention if we are interested in people's lives in the round; the experiences of Commonwealth arrivals in the pursuit of employment were conditioned by racial prejudice and it continues to affect the working lives of people of colour today – including in academe.[7] Second, the chapter proposes that case studies at this level of granularity are the necessary analytical complement to larger-scale enquiries about race, work and identity in postwar Britain. Historians of retail have much to offer on both counts.

Racializing citizenship and belonging

The John Lewis policy statement was formulated at a time when Commonwealth immigration was increasingly being framed as a problem. Political conversations on loosening Commonwealth ties and the prospects of population mobility if Britain joined the European Economic Community were conducted alongside an urgent social dialogue about integration and 'race relations' after the violence of 1958.[8] The battle lines of desegregation in Jim Crow America and violent policing of Black South African protesters made headline news and seemed to offer 'lessons' relevant to national debates about 'the stakes of urban racial violence and ... the politics of race, nation, citizenship, and Britishness'.[9] Increasingly racialized ideas of citizenship and belonging shaped these processes, which were given legislative expression in the 1961 Commonwealth Immigration Bill. Enacted in July 1962, the law required prospective migrants to apply for a Ministry of Labour voucher, with three categories dividing those holding a job offer (known as category A), 'skilled' (B) and 'unskilled' (C) workers. Employers do not appear as actors in the legislation itself, but with no limit set on the number of category A vouchers, they acquired a new role brokering entry to the country.[10] Indeed, the demand-led work-permit system made admission to the United Kingdom 'entirely employer based' until 2005.[11]

Legislative frameworks and formal government policies were only part of the picture. The British Nationality Act 1948 had codified a long-standing sense of imperial belonging and newly recognized citizens of the United Kingdom and Colonies travelled to the UK to realize a claim ostensibly built on a 'shared and universal category of subjecthood that made no distinction in regard to race'.[12] Yet, as Nadine El-Enany has pointed out, informal measures to 'curb the movement of racialised people' were pursued by the Colonial and Commonwealth Offices from the start, including withholding passports and warning prospective arrivals about the difficulties finding employment and housing in the United Kingdom.[13] Those who overcame these obstacles and made the journey then found the British promise of equality before the law to be hollow.

The experiences of Commonwealth arrivals were exposed in stark terms by Ruth Glass, a sociologist and director of research at the Centre for Urban Studies, in her analysis of West Indian migration, *London's Newcomers*, published in October 1960.[14] Prospective tenants faced 'the closed door', with overtly discriminatory advertisements or doorstep refusals; accommodation was largely to be found – as it had been for previous generations of migrants and outsiders, Glass observed – in high-density 'zones of transition'. In their search for employment, West Indians were subject to 'downgrading' of occupational status, particularly those who had previously undertaken skilled and non-manual jobs (see Chapter 11 in this volume for how the purchase of corner shops by 'Asian' communities reflected an urge towards both self-determination and self-protection in the face of such exclusions). In explaining the indignities and animosities faced by these newcomers, Glass characterized the majority attitude within British society as 'benevolent prejudice': 'a combination of passive prejudice and passive tolerance' that allowed individual members of the out-group to be accepted while powerful biases against the out-group as a whole were maintained. Discrimination was not always explicit – in the form of official colour bars – but it was widespread and 'tend[ed] to be rather erratic and shamefaced', with passive tolerance 'camouflaging' prejudiced behaviour practised casually and routinely in every aspect of public life.[15]

Glass and other early sociologists and anthropologists of race relations, as well as the theorists who shaped the field of cultural studies, laid the intellectual foundations for the historians and other scholars who started to weave new ideas and perspectives on race, identity and otherness into their accounts of modern Britain in the 1990s.[16] As Geoff Eley noted, this temporality is 'off'. He pointed to 'the continuing eruption of racialised conflicts into public life' during the 1980s as the jolt for historians to recognize race as a significant concern in understanding 'the shape of the social world and how it works': a decade or so later than for gender.[17] It is perhaps only in the last 20 years or so that sustained historical attention – in academic work and in programming aimed at public audiences – has been given to Black lived experiences in postwar Britain and to the racialization of citizenship.[18] The 2023 call by the editors of a thematic issue of *Twentieth Century British History* 'to notice the work that race and its absent presence does' and 'to consider what else thinking with and through race might show us' suggests a significant temporal drag persists.[19]

This history was placed momentarily in the foreground of public engagement with the past in 2018, 70 years after the arrival of the *Empire Windrush*. The anniversary was marked in parliament, in the media and by museums, archives, local councils and other organizations.[20] Community projects, many supported by Heritage Lottery Fund grants, captured and celebrated the contributions of Caribbean migrants to British culture and society – including in the world of work.[21] The contemporaneous scandal of government detentions and deportations of Windrush Generation members under hostile environment policies sharpened the critical edge of work done by academics and activists.[22] The use of 'Windrush Generation' in the title of this chapter consciously invokes the fraught duality of the term: belated recognition of the experiences and contributions of postwar Commonwealth arrivals amid state *de*recognition of theirs and their families' legal status – and with it, revocation of access to healthcare, education, employment, and all the protections and entitlements of citizenship.

Historians, but more often, sociologists and geographers, have studied the discrimination faced by Commonwealth arrivals finding work and the prejudice they encountered in performing their daily responsibilities.[23] Those interested in trade unions have explored Black self-organization and the shifting boundaries of solidarity.[24] Yet the retail sector is largely absent from these literatures, reflecting, in part, retailers' reluctance to employ Black staff on the shop floor.[25] Writing in 1979 about West Indian and Asian arrivals who had settled in Birmingham, J. Rex and S. Tomlinson observed that 'whereas the white woman typically becomes a secretary or shop worker, the immigrant woman works in a factory, or in a hospital, or rather less frequently in service industries'.[26] Retailing was not, however, just the shop floor. To understand how questions of colour played out in a large company we need to consider many contexts of practice: the warehouse, the canteen, the garage, the typing pool.

This organizational plurality – with its divisions between roles that are on, and those removed from, public display – makes retailing a compelling subject for historians interested in race, identity and belonging in modern Britain. This research requires the use of business archives, often dismissed by historians as 'too self-serving of the businesses they represent, difficult to access, or … too dry in terms of their holdings'.[27] The potential exposure of historical racial discrimination may be regarded as a risk for companies still in operation – and confronting prevalent and persistent issues such as hiring bias and pay gaps – although it would not necessarily preclude the granting of archival access. There is a long way to go, but some businesses are recognizing that open, critical engagement with histories of exploitation and discrimination can help build trust and confidence, externally and internally.[28]

Democracy and diversity in the Partnership community

Within these contexts, JLP is a productive case study – and not just as a large and complex multi-site retailer with rich archival holdings. It is also a company with a keen sense of its historical and philosophical distinctiveness, which engaged Spedan Lewis and his successors in exercises of comparison and contrast with other businesses and institutions. These points of contact make the Partnership of interest to a wide range of historians. For example, Spedan Lewis' commentaries on JLP as a producer co-operative served both to acknowledge a shared foundational critique of industrial capitalism and labour exploitation between the Partnership and the co-operative movement and to underscore the subsequent divergence of their pathways. He saw the benefits that the Co-op shop brought to customers (explored in Chapter 4 in this volume) as secured at the expense of staff. As he sharply put it: 'Private Enterprise says to the worker ... "I shall exploit you as far as I can but, if I do well enough for myself, you may find that you can get more out of me than you could out of the Cooperative Society of Consumers".'[29] By taking the co-operative spirit as animating not the community of *consumers* but that of *producers*, Spedan Lewis drew the company's attention to focus on the formal and informal systems and structures that shaped how its members connected and interacted.[30]

In this respect, the Partnership was a form of *political* community. Spedan Lewis saw his business as an expression of, and a bulwark for, the institutions of British democracy, most notably against the threat of Communism. Powers were balanced between three principal authorities: the Chairman; a Central Council, elected by secret ballot; and the Central Board (with five Directors chosen by each of the other authorities). He conceptualized the Partnership as a 'state within a state' – bound by UK law but otherwise free to act in pursuit of its own constitutionally defined aims – a striking formulation that connects the Partnership into a range of themes in postwar British history.[31] For our purposes, however, the particular relevance lies in the notion of 'membership ... [as] correspond[ing] quite genuinely to citizenship in our modern democracies'.[32] Read alongside his reflections on cooperation, we start to understand Spedan Lewis' Partnership as a distinctive kind of community. Recruitment to JLP was not merely transactional or contractual; gaining employment meant acquiring a new, meaningful and commanding status, bringing both obligations and entitlements. In this context, race and racial prejudice became for the company an issue of *belonging* rather than one of complaint and redress (the latter, an administrative approach, formed the basis of the 1965 Race Relations Act, extended in 1968 to include discrimination in employment).[33]

The integrity of the Partnership community was not premised on uniformity but, at least ostensibly, on 'variety of standpoint and background', which Spedan Lewis saw as beneficial for effective 'team-work' within the business.[34] For the Partnership, team-work was no less than the means by which the democratic community survived and thrived, an insight that helps explain 1950 Rule providing for ostensibly open and non-discriminatory recruitment. Marks & Spencer, another British retailer with clothing and food operations, formulated a similar though broader brush statement of principle in its 1954 Employment Policy:

> Tolerance is a marked feature of our organisation. In selecting staff for example, no prejudice is shown in regard to nationality, religion, or marital status, provided the applicant is a person of integrity with the right qualifications for the job. We have as a result been able to draw on a very wide field and to absorb unusual personalities whose talent, though not immediately obvious, we have recognised and developed.[35]

Fostering variety was not only consistent with, but nourished by, an assumption that particular groups favoured certain traits; in the Partnership, recruitment should be 'as wide as possible' to ensure a range of traits was represented across the company.[36] For example, Spedan Lewis saw the role of Registrar as particularly suitable for women. Registrars – one in each branch, overseen by a Chief Registrar – were the 'nervous system' by which the Partnership as a large company detected the small signals of '[i]nadvertence, ignorance, unawareness'. This responsibility called on the 'feminine abilities' of shrewd judgement and sensitivity that were the outcome of millions of years of 'females' being 'alert for danger and bent upon avoiding it'.[37]

The same line of reasoning saw the recruitment of 'a very wide range ... of sections of our national community with a sprinkling of Jews', of 'foreigners' with 'abilities ... much less uncommon outside our own country' and people 'from outside the trade' as parallel strategies of equivalent value.[38] Spedan Lewis did not elaborate on what these distinctive abilities might be, but it is worth noting the casual anti-Semitism that complicates any analysis of racialization.[39] In a long response to a 1944 letter to the *Gazette* reporting rumours circulating in two of the stores of 'Jew-owners in the background', he invoked the anti-Semitic notion of 'Jewish blood'.[40] After insisting on the lack of it in his family tree, he commented in an almost offhand manner:

> Jewish blood tends, as we all know, to have certain valuable abilities and certain unpleasant traits of character. I have always wanted to see the Partnership include in its team a moderate number of Jews but it remains to be seen whether that can be done successfully as a regular policy on a substantial scale.[41]

Spedan Lewis' commitment to the idea that traits and habits were cultivated and passed on within social groups was broadly in accord with the then emerging field of race relations, which rejected biological explanations and 'explored behavioral norms in order to chart cultural difference'.[42] In 1954, while still Chairman, Spedan Lewis reprinted in the *Gazette* under the heading 'No Colour Bar' a complaint from a customer refusing to shop with John Lewis should they employ people whom she called 'loathsome black creatures', along with his reply. Beginning with the observation that the sun had darkened human skin over generations among people living close to the Equator, he then commented: 'human beings do thus differ in colour and ... the characters of some coloured people are very high and the characters of some white people loathsome'. The presence of a 'handful [of Partners] whose skins are not white' may matter to her less – he suggested, in a characteristic non sequitur – 'than if the present development of the fixed-price system did not oblige us to charge our customers for many things more than we otherwise should'.[43]

The framing of the company as a community animated by difference is particularly interesting in the context of the Commonwealth. Indeed, the Commonwealth promise of open, co-operative relations of mutual benefit bears affinity with Spedan Lewis' notion of team-work. Marking Commonwealth Day in 1956, the John Lewis *Chronicle* encouraged its readers to befriend one or more of the 'large and valuable group of Commonwealth Partners among us ... by extending a friendly hand, you, in your small way, will be doing a lot to maintain and encourage the Commonwealth spirit which may be so sorely needed in the future'.[44] The parallel extends to the powerful paternalistic assumptions that conditioned both institutions. Spedan Lewis did not imagine equity between members of the Partnership to mean equality. The company was, as the *Gazette* masthead reminded Partners on a weekly basis, a constitutional monarchy. Hierarchy was the natural expression of a wide range of ability and necessary for the effective functioning of the business; it was, he thought, in the interests of the rank and file to ensure 'brain-workers' were paid 'handsomely' for their capabilities.[45] 'Commonwealth spirit' may have called on White British Partners to 'make the stay among us of our Dominion and Colonial colleagues a happy one', but they did so as hosts welcoming transient and grateful guests (the descriptors 'Dominion' and 'Colonial' are striking here, suggesting the enduring imprint of racialized imperial categorizations on organizational thinking).[46]

If variety was seen as conducive to the functioning of JLP as a democratic community in the abstract, the implications in practice for Partners embodying difference were less clear. The Constitution's rule on recruitment codified equity as a foundational principle, but, as we will see, it was also subject to informal interpretations that could undercut that commitment – inviting comparison with the contemporary immigration policy environment noted earlier. One of the principal criticisms of the 1962 Commonwealth Immigration Act, both at the time and subsequently, was the wide discretion allowed to immigration officers.[47] The parallel with JLP is not exact of course, but a highly devolved company structure created a space between constitutional principles and employment practices in which local managers operated. Branch recruiting officers had significant power in decision making, as did department managers, who rated performance for pay reviews and assessing promotion potential; we can recognize the application process as another 'border' that Black prospective Partners had to try to cross.[48] Despite Spedan Lewis' insistence that there was no colour bar in the Partnership, he appeared to accept that too many applications from 'British citizens with coloured skins' would present a problem, a formulation that is notable for isolating racialization from migrant identity and legal status. Striking now, the term 'migrant' or 'immigrant' is almost completely absent from Partnership journalism and memoranda when referring to people from the Commonwealth. Indeed, a *Gazette* cartoonist represented 'migrant labour' in 1962, during Edward Heath's negotiations for Britain's entry into the Common Market, as a flock of White workmen flying out over the cliffs of Dover, tool bags in hand.[49] Black Commonwealth arrivals raised, for Spedan Lewis, an issue of such import that, in 1954, he referred their recruitment to the Partnership's equivalent of the House of Commons; it was for the Central Council to debate whether such applicants are to be 'admitted ... at all and, if so, to what extent and that limit will have to be maintained'.[50] Constitutional principles were not to determine recruitment policy alone, rather, the latter was the outcome of a necessary deliberative process – subject to many influences, considerations and concerns – whereby those principles would be translated into administrative rules.

Seeing colour on and off the shop floor

In 1960, the Oxford Street store, destroyed by an incendiary bomb during the Blitz, was reopened: a symbolic moment in the company's postwar recovery. Six new Waitrose grocery shops had opened since the war. The percentage of pay dispensed as Partnership Bonus – an annual distribution among all Partners as co-owners – had been growing following a five-year pause; in 1959/1960, the rate had jumped from 7 to 13 per cent. 'Certainly we have grown and thrived', observed the General Editor of the *Gazette*, in an essay-length reflection on the upcoming thirtieth anniversary of the First Trust Settlement that created the Partnership, 'but not more quickly than other "ordinary" businesses. We have doubled our numbers and multiplied our Branches in a shortish span of years, but so have other people'.[51] This circumspect appraisal of the company's fortunes spoke, among other things, to difficulties in the recruitment and retention of staff as the retail sector expanded. 'Our experience appears to be shared by the manufacturing and retail industries', commented the Director of Personnel in July 1960, reporting a poor response to the latest round of advertisements and informing senior colleagues of the 100,000 registered vacancies in the London region on the latest Ministry of Labour return against a total unemployed figure of 48,600.[52] Alongside selling staff, JLP found drivers, porters, clerks and typists difficult to find and retain.

The displacement and migration of people from Europe and the former Empire in the decades after the Second World War created new pools of potential applicants for the expanding Partnership and particular challenges for the company's recruitment procedures. There was a matter of due process: how do people who have left their countries of birth provide satisfactory references from, or even traceable contact details for, their former employers? Marcus Collins explored the difficulties West Indian men faced in providing certification of their skills; in the context of the Partnership, such verification was only the start.[53] Checking references – testimonials of prospective Partners' character and conduct – was essential as joining the JLP community brought an entitlement to all the benefits of membership as well as the obligation to act in the collective interest. As a consequence, engaging a new Partner without references demanded the attention of top-level management. In 1956, for example, when the Partnership stood at almost 12,500 members, the Chief Registrar issued a memorandum requiring all decisions on employing Hungarian refugees without references to be submitted for her personal attention – a striking example of branch-level recruitment being subject to central scrutiny.[54]

Being qualified to work and suitable for membership were separate matters and it is here that we can start to unpick the assumptions inflecting the company's recruitment practices. In the case of Hungarian refugees, the importance of 'intelligibility' between customer and sales assistant may have meant that the selling side 'is not necessarily the ideal field into which to attempt to absorb these unhappy people' – but their (uncredentialled) admissibility to the Partnership was not in question. For the Chief Registrar, Commonwealth Partners were 'not in the same class as political exiles. ... Sooner or later one must complete [their] references'. Should documentation not be forthcoming, termination may be 'in many cases' the preferred option.[55] Unspoken here, but revealed in other records, are the racialized ways in which notions of suitability were framed.

The prompt for JLP to create an explicit policy on Commonwealth recruitment was Mervyn Jones' three-part investigation in the *Observer*, published in 1961. The first instalment – 'Second-class citizens?' – dealt with finding employment and included a section on the retail sector subtitled 'We have to study our customers'. An unnamed John Lewis representative was quoted as saying 'You see coloured railwaymen because the traveller is required to give up his ticket, but nobody is required to buy here', before asserting: 'We have a duty to people we employ – a duty not to expose them to unpleasantness'.[56] In his article, Jones mentioned Glass' findings on the downgrading of occupational status experienced by West Indian arrivals.

Glass had found that this effect was pronounced in the case of non-manual workers, which included the sub-category of shopkeepers and assistants and salesmen. Five per cent of men and 16 per cent of women had been employed in this sub-category prior to their departure for Britain. Not a single person in her sample had found an equivalent job in London.[57] She also observed that those employers who did operate a colour bar justified their policy by shifting the blame; they pointed to the potential objections of White workers, disapproval of customers or effect on company reputation. The Partnership may have claimed to reject a colour bar, but managers believed that the reactions of staff and the public were serious considerations in their hiring of Commonwealth applicants.

The publication of Jones' article prompted a Partner to write to the *Gazette* under the pseudonym Quo Vadis to query why 'your "coloured" employees ... are not for the Selling Side', only finding roles in 'hidden warehouses and stockrooms'. The reply, printed with the letter, indicated that executives had already begun to position the Constitution at the centre of a new statement, which balanced equity in principle with due regard for 'the views of customers ... in assessing the suitability of candidates for work that involves personal dealings with customers'.[58] The imagined (White) customer plays a dual role in this emerging policy. Her views – the John Lewis shopper was routinely referred to as 'she' – were at once valued contributions to a legitimate conversation about shop-floor service and a potential source of offence and insult to Black Partners.[59] The apparent dilemma she created for the company was not a new one. Seven years earlier, in 1954, another *Observer* journalist had investigated an allegation from an Indian student that he and two others were told only shop-floor work was available and he 'might be exposed to rudeness from customers'. Their applications were therefore being rejected 'for their own sakes'.[60]

This paternalistic 'solicitude for the coloured man's feelings' (to borrow Jones' phrase) can been seen as a form of Glass' 'camouflage', a refashioning of prejudice – held by both staff and customers – in images conducive to those audiences. I use the term 'audiences' consciously. It is, of course, far from neutral; imagining an audience involves (at least implicit) judgements about power, accountability and entitlement: to whom do we address ourselves? Whose appraisal of us matters? The racial conditionality of JLP's audiences is perhaps best drawn out by reference to the BBC. In the late 1950s and 1960s, the Corporation covered Commonwealth migration and race relations in a range of programming to fulfil its charter to inform, educate and entertain. At the same time, White viewers' responses to content featuring Black characters were anxiously monitored in audience surveys.[61] That Partners had the right to challenge and scrutinize company policy through the *Gazette* fits well with the notion of an audience whose opinions and preferences required careful handling. By understanding majority-White staff and customer groups as (preferred, privileged) audiences, we can tune in to the silences and the muted notes of the Black presence in retailing.

White audiences – Partners and customers – were in the foreground as JLP debated its approach to Commonwealth recruitment over the course of 1961. Commenting on a census of 'coloured workers in the Partnership', the Director of Personnel saw 'remarkably little trouble which could be said to be directly attributable to colour prejudice', drawing attention instead to a wider 'hardening of opinion' against 'the rise in the numbers of them entering the country, which is tied up with a very real feeling that the coloured people (and of course by this are meant West Indians and Africans) may become a dominating force in some districts and some fields of labour'. In this context, 'colour prejudice' followed 'quite naturally' from this kind of thinking, he argued: 'I would suggest that we do not attempt to move in this matter in advance of public opinion.'[62]

'Public opinion' served, for the Partnership, to shape and constrain the company's experimental approach to Commonwealth recruitment.[63] But how could such an elusive, fragmented and discordant entity as public opinion be reconciled with the Constitution, which specified that an individual would be assessed only for their contribution to the efficiency of the business? The nine London-area branches surveyed for the census employed 180 'Coloured' workers, the majority in portering, maintenance, stockrooms and catering, plus a small number in clerical roles. Only ten (all 'Asiatics') worked on the selling side.[64] Even with access to individual personnel files, we cannot know if Glass' findings about the difficulties for West Indian shopworkers finding equivalent roles in the United Kingdom were reflected in John Lewis' hiring patterns. It is nonetheless striking that of the 71 West Indians, none was employed in a selling job, particularly as it was the shop floor where expansion in Partner numbers was happening.[65] We can perhaps see here how a distinctive form of Jones' 'solicitude' acted to modulate managers' interpretations of the constitutional principle on the ground. Protecting Black employees from hostility and prejudice in public-facing roles reframed the hidden work of moving goods and typing memos as 'work that suits them best'.[66] If the suitability of these Partners was understood as primarily a matter of context – where they worked and with whom, rather than the kind of work their qualifications and prior experience equipped them to do – then we can start to discern the practices that affected the experiences and opportunities of Black Partners.

That is not to say that work contexts could be neatly divided into public and private, shop floor and back office, in JLP or in other large retailers. Drivers, for example, occupied a liminal space. They belonged to those hidden warehouse operations less popular with White applicants, but also entered customers' houses in the company's name to deliver or repair items (an inconsistency Quo Vadis' letter had pointed out: 'Is there any difference between serving the customers in their homes and in the shop?').[67] Here was an occupation in demand where the supply was largely drawn from a growing West Indian community. 'Do we know from experience that customers object to coloured drivers or are we just assuming they would?' queried the Registrar of Bon Marché, a department store in Brixton acquired by the Partnership in 1940. She was concerned that inadequate references would mean discharging a newly appointed driver: 'Have the Central Council ever discussed it or is it too dangerous a subject?'[68] Drivers and porters were, indeed, recognized centrally as something of a special case. Encountering Commonwealth newcomers employed in public transport 'must increasingly condition customers to accepting them on commercial vans' was the explanation offered in the Partnership's policy statement.[69]

Within the business, the many amenities available to members also created complexities of context. In the leisure and residential clubs run by the Partnership for its members (such as the Odney estate, where the Heritage Centre and Archives is now located) Partners became customers; they were served by their peers. But it was in the branch canteen that this shift from providing to receiving service was routinized; though behind the scenes and far from potential public disapprobation, it was nonetheless a customer-facing context. The Bon Marché restaurant manageress complained to the branch Registrar in 1960, after a Nigerian member had left to have a baby, about recruiting Black Partners to the kitchen in future, claiming 'she cannot ask them, as she would ask any other partner, regardless of her theoretical duties, to serve at the counter. She says that partners [presumably White colleagues eating in the dining room] would consider them dirty'.[70] These assertions speak to the 'gendered terms of racialization that Black migrant workers encountered'; poor personal hygiene was just one of faults attributed to Black women, along with being 'slow, touchy, unadaptable, choosy, hypochondriac, and lacking in stamina'.[71] The Registrar, in her role as the branch's nervous system, was 'bothered by the [manageress'] attitude' and, should another Black member join the team, she would 'see [any] complaining partner'.[72] It is not clear from the document whether the registrar intended in such a meeting to confront complaints and support the Black Partner's continued employment in the dining room or move her to other work (and so ostensibly away from potential sources of offence). Yet it is the very lack of clarity or consistency in these examples that calls for attention; they show the importance of looking at between and behind-the-scenes work settings, where everyday encounters played out away from the stage of the shop floor.

Conclusion

For the John Lewis Partnership, recruitment policy turned on the fundamental question of 'who belongs?' Making a judgement on whether a candidate was likely to contribute to the efficient conduct of the business was not just about their aptitude for a specific job but also about how well they would discharge the duties of citizenship and community at all levels: among fellow Partners; in their engagements with the shopping public; and as a member of a democratic 'state within a state'. For this reason, attributes such as race – but also, as we saw in the Constitution, gender, class and political conviction, among others – were part of the lexicon in which internal policy debates were conducted, more than a decade before a long process of legislative interventions sought to curb discriminatory practices in employment, housing and other areas. Presenting the encounter with a changing environment as an experiment fitted with the company ethos and so created some space for testing and translating the Constitution into rules for recruitment on the ground. The story of the policy on Commonwealth workers is just one thread in a complex emerging pattern weaving together – sometimes unevenly or in jarring colours – principles and practices, ideas about citizenship and the realities of daily work.

This chapter sought to demonstrate the value of using companies (and their archives) as ways into thinking through how we can gain some critical, historical purchase on the ways race, identity and belonging were handled within organizations and by groups of people at a granular level. Retail is a useful sector on which to focus because the shop is a space premised on display: the window-dressing, the arrangement of goods or the conduct and appearance of selling staff – a quality that brings into sharp relief images of acceptable, respectable service and consumption.[73] It is also a sector of hidden labour, allowing us to work across the apparent public/private divides of shop floor and back office to understand with more nuance how questions of colour were processed within companies. These business histories are vital to a larger project of noticing race and attending to processes of racialization. If we are to integrate race seriously and systematically into accounts of modern Britain, then historians of business and organization must engage. Without the private sector, we lose access to a whole series of settings in which – despite the beliefs reported to Glass – colour was very much seen and Black British citizens led working lives too long out of historical eyeshot.

Acknowledgements
I am grateful to Judy Faraday, former Heritage Services Manager at the John Lewis Partnership Heritage Centre and Archives, and her colleagues for their openness, generosity and engagement over many years of collaboration. Thank you also to Katharine Carter, Company Archivist at Marks & Spencer,

for sharing details of its contemporary recruitment policy, and to Shirin Hirsch and Essex colleagues, especially Tracey Loughran and Lisa Smith, for offering support and encouragement as well as incisive and helpful feedback.

Notes

1   'The Partnership's Policy in the Employment of Coloured Workers', Memorandum 8102, Chairman to Director of Personnel, 28/11/1961, box 650, 24.

2   M. Jones, 'Second-class citizens?', *Observer*, 26/02/1961.

3   'The Partnership's Policy in the Employment of Coloured Workers', Memorandum 17140, Director to Personnel to all Heads of Branches and Directors of Buying, 29/11/1961, box 2524(a). The written Constitution is an evolving document which sets out the company's governance system, principles and rules. The current version is publicly available: https://www.johnlewispartnership.co.uk/content/dam/cws/pdfs/Juniper/jlp-constitution.pdf (accessed 18/06/2021).

4   'The Partnership's Policy in the Employment of Coloured Workers' Memorandum 8102.

5   Memorandum 16,756. Director of Personnel to Chairman, 10/11/1961, box 650, 24.

6   S. Decker, 'The silence of the archives: business history, post-colonialism and archival ethnography', *Management & Organizational History*, 8:2 (2013), 155–173.

7   See, for example, Royal Historical Society, *Race, Ethnicity & Equality in UK History: A Report and Resource for Change* (2018).

8   D. Dean, 'The Conservative government and the 1961 Commonwealth Immigration Act: the inside story', *Race & Class*, 35:2 (1993), 57–74.

9   K. Hammond Perry, ' "Little Rock" in Britain: Jim Crow's transatlantic topographies', *Journal of British Studies*, 51:1 (2012), 157.

10 While the Act itself prefers the passive construction of a Commonwealth citizen 'taking employment' (see Part I, Section 2, paragraph 3(c)), the preceding parliamentary debates gave prominence to the role of employers. In terms of process, the employer would both apply for and then remit the voucher to the chosen employee. See, for example, *Hansard* HC Deb vol 654 (22/02/1962) 'Clause 2—(Refusal Of Admission And Conditional Admission)'.

11 N.T. Duncan, *Immigration Policymaking in the Global Era: In Pursuit of Global Tale* (New York: Palgrave Macmillan, 2012), 94; Home Office, 'Controlling our borders: making migration work for Britain. Five year strategy for asylum and immigration', Cm 6472 (London: HMSO, 2005).

12 K. Hammond Perry, *London is the Place for Me: Black Britons, Citizenship, and the Politics of Race* (Oxford University Press, 2015), 54.

13 N. El-Enany, *(B)ordering Britain: Law, Race and Empire* (Manchester University Press, 2020), 95, 86.

14 R. Glass, *Newcomers: The West Indians in London*, vol 1 (London: Centre for Urban Studies, 1960), note to Table 10, 30.

15 Glass, *Newcomers*, 216–219.

16 It is impossible to capture the work of scholars or do justice to the wider fields of enquiry to which they belong. As an all-too-brief selection: M. Banton, *White and Coloured: The Behavior of British People Towards Coloured Immigrants* (London: J. Cape, 1959); S. Patterson, *Dark Strangers: A Sociological Study of the Absorption of a Recent West Indian Migrant Group in Brixton, South London* (London: Tavistock Publications, 1963); S. Hall et al, *Policing the Crisis: Mugging, the State, and Law and Order* (Basingstoke: Macmillan, 1978); S. Hall, 'Minimal selves', in H. Baker, M. Diawara and R. Lindeborg (eds), *Black British Cultural Studies: A Reader* (University of Chicago Press, 1987), 114–119; University of Birmingham Centre for Contemporary Cultural Studies, *The Empire Strikes Back Race and Racism in 70s*

Britain (London: Hutchinson, 1982); B. Schwarz, '"The only white man in there": the re-racialisation of England, 1956–1968', *Race & Class*, 38:1 (1996), 65–78; W. Webster, *Imagining Home: Gender, Race, and National Identity, 1945–64* (London: UCL Press, 1998); C. Waters, '"Dark strangers" in our midst: discourses of race and nation in Britain, 1947–1963', *Journal of British Studies*, 36:2 (1997), 207–238.

17   G. Eley, *A Crooked Line: From Cultural History to the History of Society* (Ann Arbor: University of Michigan Press, 2005), 133–148.

18   Hammond Perry, *London is the Place for Me*; M. Grant, 'Historicizing citizenship in post-war Britain', *The Historical Journal*, 59:4 (2016), 1187–1206; D. Newton, *Paving the Empire Road: BBC Television and Black Britons* (Manchester University Press, 2013); D. Olusoga, *Black and British: A Forgotten History* (London: Pan Macmillan, 2016).

19   M. Matera, R. Natarajan, K. Hammond Perry, C. Schofield and R. Waters, 'Introduction: marking race in twentieth century British history', *Twentieth Century British History*, 34:3 (2023), 407–414.

20   Commons Debate, 14/06/2018, https://hansard.parliament.uk/Commons/2018-06-14/debates/0661DB22-68A9-4F6C-9C69-4F42C9837511/Windrush70ThAnniversary, https://www.bl.uk/windrush/articles/windrush-generations-1000-londoners, https://www.museumsassociation.org/museums-journal/news/2020/06/22062020-museums-mark-windrush-day/# (accessed 15/09/2020).

21   See, for example, https://windrushfoundation.com/windrush-70/ (accessed 15/09/2020).

22   See, for example, T. Harris (ed), *Windrush (1948) and Rivers of Blood (1968): Legacy and Assessment* (Abingdon: Routledge, 2019); El-Enany, *(B)ordering Britain*.

23   L. McDowell, *Working Lives: Gender, Migration and Employment in Britain, 1945–2007* (Chichester: Wiley, 2013).

24   See, for example, S. Virdee, 'Racism and resistance in British trade unions, 1948–79', in P. Alexander and R. Halpern (eds), *Racializing Class, Classifying Race: Labour and Difference in Britain, the USA and Africa* (New York: St Martin's, 2000), 122–149; F. Lindop, 'Racism and the working class: strikes in support of Enoch Powell in 1968', *Labour History Review*, 66:1 (2001), 79–100; L. McDowell, S. Anitha and R. Pearson, 'Striking narratives: class, gender and ethnicity in the "Great Grunwick Strike", London, UK, 1976–1978', *Women's History Review* 23:4 (2014), 595–619.

25   See also P. Cox and A. Hobley, *Shopgirls: The True Story of Life Behind the Counter* (London: Hutchinson, 2014), 228–229.

26   J. Rex and S. Tomlinson, *Colonial Immigrants in a British City: A Class Analysis* (London: Routledge & K. Paul, 1979), 107.

27   A. Greenwood and H. Ingram, 'Sources and resources. "The people's chemists": The Walgreens Boots Alliance Archive', *Social History of Medicine*, 26 (2018), 857–869.

28   A.R. Green and E. Lee, 'From transaction to collaboration: redefining the academic-archivist relationship in business collections', *Archives and Records* 41:1 (2020), 32–51.

29   J.S. Lewis, *Partnership for All* (London: Kerr-Cros Publishing Co., 1948), 192.

30   Indeed, 'the happiness of all its members' was, and is, defined as the 'ultimate purpose' of the Partnership, enshrined in Principle 1 of the Constitution.

31   Lewis, *Partnership for All*, 209–210. I discuss the implications of Spedan Lewis' (henceforth in notes JSL) notion of the 'state within a state' in terms of pay policy in A.R. Green, '"Secret lists and sanctions": the blacklisting of the John Lewis Partnership and the politics of pay in 1970s Britain', *Twentieth Century British History*, 30:2 (2019), 205–230.

32   Lewis, *Partnership for All*, 209. 'Member' is synonymous with 'Partner' as in 'member of the Partnership'.

33   E. Bleich, *Race Politics in Britain and France: Ideas and Policymaking since the 1960s* (Cambridge University Press, 2003).

[34] 'The Founder's further attempt to enlighten the Partnership', *Gazette*, 23/07/1960, 595. JSL stood down as Chairman in 1955 and was thereafter accorded the title of 'Founder'. JSL's conception of team-work accords with Ussishkin's discussion of 'team-spirit' in British industry as an expression of and response to the collective mobilization of the Second World War: *Morale: A Modern British History* (Oxford University Press, 2017), 122–123.

[35] *Personnel and Welfare Manual*, box Q/Q1/3/1, The M&S Company Archive.

[36] 'The Founder's further attempt to enlighten the Partnership', *Gazette*, 23/07/1960, 595.

[37] Lewis, *Partnership for All*, 428–430.

[38] 'The Founder's further attempt to enlighten the Partnership', *Gazette*, 23/07/1960, 595.

[39] T. Kushner, 'Racialization and White European immigration to Britain', in K. Murji and J. Solomos (eds), *Racialization: Studies in Theory and Practice* (Oxford University Press, 2005), 207–225.

[40] JSL's conception of Jewish traits and of Jews as inherently 'alien' was by no means exceptional. See T. Kushner, *The Persistence of Prejudice: Antisemitism in British Society during the Second World War* (Manchester University Press, 1989) for widespread wartime antipathy to Jews, including as shadowy financiers, and its deep historical roots in Britain.

[41] *Gazette*, 15/07/1944, 293.

[42] Waters, ' "Dark strangers" in our midst', 220. On race relations in Britain, see: M. Matera, 'The African grounds of race relations in Britain', *Twentieth Century British History*, 34:3 (2023), 415–439.

[43] *Gazette*, 03/07/1954, 435.

[44] 'Commonwealth Day', *Chronicle for John Lewis*, 26/05/1956, box Acc/2018/107/6.

[45] On paying for brains: Lewis, *Partnership for All*, 228–229. 'Rank and file' was an official term in JLP at this time.

[46] The article describes these Partners as 'a floating part of our Partnership'; of the ten short 'portraits' of Commonwealth Partners that follow, seven refer to potential return to home countries: 'Commonwealth Day', *Chronicle for John Lewis*, 26/05/1956, box Acc/2018/107/6.

[47] See, for example, 'From bad to worse', *Times*, 17/11/1961, 15 (the paper was an insistent critic of the Bill).

[48] For example: 'Apart from coloured workers, [the advertisement] produced one suitable applicant': Routine report from Clearings Registrar, 05/12/1959, box 472/y. Clearings was the branch handling despatch, distribution, stockrooms and workrooms.

[49] 'Fresh air from Europe', *Gazette*, 03/03/1962, 108–109.

[50] *Gazette*, 03/07/1954, 436.

[51] 'What story has the Partnership to tell?', *Gazette*, 15/11/1958, 975–979.

[52] 'The Chairman's Conference', *Gazette*, 16/07/1960, 570.

[53] M. Collins, 'Pride and prejudice: West Indian men in mid-twentieth-century Britain', *Journal of British Studies*, 40:3 (2001), 402.

[54] 'Employment of Hungarians', Memorandum 26,390 Chief Registrar to all Registrars, 21/12/1956, box 2524(a).

[55] 'Employment of Pakistanis', Memorandum 29,910 Chief Registrar to Director of Personnel, 23/09/1958, box 2524(a).

[56] M. Jones, 'Second-class citizens?', *Observer*, 26/02/1961. The second part concerned housing ('The subtle barriers on the doorstep', 05/03/1961) and the third, living in multi-racial societies ('A cold co-existence', 12/03/1961).

[57] Glass, *Newcomers*, 30.

[58] *Gazette*, 18/03/1961, 149; internal memoranda also indicate that managers were starting to position the Constitution as part of an emerging policy on Commonwealth recruitment: 'Extract from Minutes of the 149th Meeting of the Chairman's Conference,

held 28th February 1961', box 650/24; Memorandum 12460 'The Employment of Coloured People', Director of Personnel to Chairman, 01/03/1961, box 650/24.

59 On women as consumers, see: M. Hilton, 'The female consumer and the politics of consumption in twentieth-century Britain', *The Historical Journal*, 45:1 (2002), 103–128. The ways in which race and gender (and, indeed, race and class) are entwined in the shopper/shopworker relationship here cannot be explored in this short chapter but would be an interesting area for future exploration. On race and class, Waters has shown how the absorption of the working class into the national community in the 1930s and 1940s allowed Black migrants to be positioned as the new, threatening 'other': Waters, ' "Dark strangers" in our midst', 212.

60 'Employment of Coloured People', Memorandum 78,183, Director of Personnel to Chairman, 12/07/1954, box 650/24. The *Observer* does not seem to have actually published anything on the case.

61 Audience research for TV began in 1949; for a detailed discussion, see Newton, *Paving the Empire Road*. See also C. Grandy, ' "The show is not about race": custom, screen culture, and *The Black and White Minstrel Show*', *Journal of British Studies*, 59:4 (2020), 857–884; G. Schaffer, *The Vision of a Nation: Making Multiculturalism on British Television, 1960–80* (London: Palgrave Macmillan, 2014). These were also increasingly powerful audiences: as Schaffer notes, TV ownership went from under 10 per cent in 1951 to 75 per cent in 1961, as households with more discretionary spending power created demand for consumer goods: B. Harrison, *Seeking a Role: The United Kingdom 1951–1970* (Oxford University Press, 2009). On the anxiety-inducing intersection of TV-watching and consumer audiences, advertising, see P. Gurney, *The Making of Consumer Culture in Modern Britain* (London: Bloomsbury Publishing, 2017), 167–169.

62 'Employment of Coloured Workers in the Partnership'.

63 'Employment of Coloured Workers in the Partnership'. The 'experiment' was a long-standing John Lewis approach. Indeed, JSL saw the Partnership itself as 'an experiment in industrial democracy'. Managers were given significant independence of initiative to test proposals that may help the company fulfil its aims and purposes. See Green, 'Secret lists and sanctions'.

64 The term 'Asiatics' was not defined and appears to have been used interchangeably with 'Asians', also undefined.

65 The full annual census for 1961 indicates that total numbers increased by 1,006 (7.3 per cent) from 1960, with all of that increase falling on the selling side. John Lewis Oxford Street, part of the nine-branch survey discussed here, appointed 204 of those additional selling staff: *Gazette*, 15/07/1961, 549–551.

66 A phrase used by the Director of Personnel in response to 'Quo Vadis' letter and in his letter to the Nottingham Council of Social Service, which had asked the company to consider employing some temporary West Indian workers over the Christmas period: 26/06/1961, box 650/24.

67 *Gazette*, 18/03/1961, 149. Kreydatus has pointed out with reference to segregated department stores in the United States that Black retail workers were largely expected to be invisible; elevator operators and delivery drivers were among those were visible but it was a visibility that demanded deference and extreme courtesy: B. Kreydatus, ' "You are a part of all of us": black department store employees in Jim Crow Richmond', *Journal of Historical Research in Marketing*, 2:1 (2010) 109.

68 'Registry Report – April 1961', Extract from Memorandum 3034, Registrar Bon Marché to Chief Registrar, 05/05/1961, box 650/24. The Registrar comments here that there are 'plenty of coloured men (drivers) on the Ministry of Labour's books'.

69 'The Partnership's Policy in the Employment of Coloured Workers'. The Bristol Omnibus colour bar dispute, first exposed in 1961 but hitting headlines in the boycott of 1963,

shows that public transport was not as open to Black workers as may have been assumed within JLP: M. Dresser, *Black and White on the Buses: The 1963 Colour Bar Dispute in Bristol* (Bristol: Broadsides, 1986). Dresser points to the division between public-facing 'on the buses' work and behind the scenes garage work.

[70] Memorandum 2671, Registrar Bon Marché to Chief Registrar, 06/04/1960, box 472:E.

[71] Hammond Perry, *London is the Place for Me*, 86–87. Hammond Perry cites Sheila Patterson's survey of White employers' impressions of West Indian workers, conducted in Brixton in the late 1950s. She quotes a labour exchange official, who reported that White women objected to working alongside Black women for 'personal hygienic reasons'. Patterson, *Dark Strangers*, 135–136.

[72] Memorandum 2734, Registrar Bon Marché to Chief Registrar, 26/05/1960, box 472:E.

[73] On the racialized 'reading' of professional behaviour, see: D. Payling, '"The people who write to us are the people who don't like us": class, gender, and citizenship in the survey of sickness, 1943–1952', *Journal of British Studies* 59:2 (2020), 315–342. On retail as a 'compelling site to study' for historians of many kinds: T. Deutsch, 'Exploring new insights into retail history', *Journal of Historical Research in Marketing*, 2:1 (2010), 136.

11

Encounters at the Counter: Race, Class and Belonging in the British Asian Corner Shop

Harshad Keval

Introduction

There is a constant in the conundrums that may present themselves to White, British people and which many of us who 'wear our passports on our faces'[1] have been either deflecting, ignoring, answering or contesting for many decades. That constant is the question, "But where are you *really* from?".[2] In November 2022, the founder of the charity Sistah Space, Ngozi Fulani, was repeatedly asked by the Queen's former Lady-in-Waiting, "But where are you *really* from?". The question prompted the continuation of discussion and debate about issues long haunting the sceptred isle, namely, *foreignness*. The question is apparently an innocent interactional quizzing, a polite and interested request to know more about this *other* person (who *always* stands in to represent a larger group). But as many writers have shown, such questions are far from innocent, regardless of apparent intentions.[3] This question forms the background and foreground to so many of the socioeconomic, cultural and political questions about race, racial differences, ethnicity, multiculturalism, and the many complex and interconnected forms of racism which many of us have lived, and continue to live through. Whether it is migrants and migration, Brexit, pressures on education, housing and healthcare, or the persistent anger and unease at the felt marginalization of 'indigenous' British folk, the constant target has always been the obvious one, the *racialized other*. Into this complicated and troubling setting, this chapter opens sociohistorical and sociological doors to the significance of this racialized context, by exploring the British Asian corner shop. It seeks to unravel the ongoing production of the people who lived and worked there, often fully embedded within White, working-class British communities, and who are integral components of living, local and global history.

In this chapter, my aim is to unpack a network of interconnected narratives, mythologies and empirical realities of what is known as the Asian corner shop. Racial and racist stereotyping, such as the children's author David Walliams' characterization of *Raj* – ostensibly a British, South Asian shopkeeper appearing in a number of books and film adaptions, oversimplify the rich, complex ethno-religious, linguistic and cultural systems from different parts of the world, with distinct but connected histories of migration and diasporic movement. I situate race-critical sociological and historiographical questions to ask what the *encounter at the (shop) counter* has come to mean. I argue that the British Asian (BrAsian) shopkeeper, the raciologically imagined one, performs a series of functions in representation and in material reality that allow fantasies of quotidian tolerance to be played out against the backdrop of the United Kingdom's turbulent, racial and classed colonial landscape.[4] I argue the shop is a site where *semi-strange* others can be fixed in racial imaginations, often infused with notions of national belonging. The reality is that this *fixing* cannot work in a culturally fluid social world, as identities and ways of living merge, clash, hybridize and reflect what it means to be British.

I begin with a contextual self-location of myself as author, and weave my biography and analysis together as part of the history of Asian shops. Knowing and learning about people, places, ideas and beliefs that are different from us often happens through representations in media, television, film and news. In this section I outline how the figure of the Asian shopkeeper has been a feature of Britain's relationship to race. This is followed by a short history that problematizes the notion of the *presence* of Asians in the United Kingdom through tracing their colonial journeys into postcolonial lives. Finally, I discuss the physical and symbolic complexities of space and place in *encounters at the counter*. In terms of the physical borders of what a shop represents, there is something interesting about the inside and outside of the social relational field occupied here that signposts intimacies, anxieties, identities and a constant negotiation of strange encounters that both reflects wider issues and produces its own navigable intimacies on an everyday stage. After all, buying breakfast things, medicines, gifts, or contraceptives, are fundamentally everyday intimacies shared at the counter, among otherwise strangers, and are part of a wider context of the racial contours of Britishness. Such analyses can facilitate complex and nuanced discussions about the social embeddedness of retail in Britain as a connection to wider global histories. Ultimately, answering the question "Where are you *really* from?" is about the interrogator's collusion in Whiteness and racialized colonial history. The shop becomes a vehicle to begin understanding these complexities.

Really from here

Growing up in 1970s Lancashire, I had little interest or knowledge about *why* racist corner shop jokes were so powerful and damaging (for example, a schoolyard joke often heard in the 1980s: "Why did the Romans build straight roads? To stop 'Pakis' building corner shops"). I knew their performance was a hailing moment, a powerful articulation of race, racism, nation and unbelonging that often preceded violence in the schoolyard, on the street, in the classroom and in the mind. Physically fighting racism is connected but also *different to* the battles that rage in institutions, employment and the sites of intellectual knowledge production – universities. How we normalize specific forms of knowledge as legitimate and necessary is often a result of power relations – epistemic privilege.[5] I make these points because my identity as a writer and educator in race, racism, postcolonial and decolonial theory is fundamentally tied to my multiple identities generated in the heart of a working–class, White English, industrial town in Lancashire *and* as someone whose identity is also part of the BrAsian, African, Gujerati diaspora that was produced in the retail corner shop arena. My racial, class, ethnic and cultural identity is formed in and through the connection and layering of multiple sites of social and economic production. Receiving and hearing racist jokes was an everyday matter and were normalities produced by the architecture of racial and racist landscapes, occupied by people who simply could not find any other way to articulate *strange-ness* around them. There is a long history that undergirds the existence and placement of the Asian corner shop, that speaks to a silenced history of what Nasreen Ali, Virinder S. Kalra and Salman Sayyid call a 'postcolonial people'.[6] I grew up in the heart of a northern mill town in Lancashire, known for its cotton spinning and processing factories. The 'paki shop' was located at a psycho-social, racial ley line, intersected by colonial, postcolonial and capitalist relations. Historical centres of the *stories of* the British industrial revolution are often understood to exist outside of Global Southern countries and peoples, and yet would not exist without the cotton, spices, labour and centuries-long oppression of those people and places through colonial power.[7]

Representations of Asian shopkeepers – familiar strangers

The Asian shopkeeper emerged in the representational machinery of television throughout the 1970s. These images and representations partly shaped how people came to learn, think and know about the semi-strange, familiar yet unfamiliar strangers who provide services and products. It is both deeply unfortunate but also logical that these representations were racist, often reducing the rich migratory journeys and historical connectedness to British history to accents and negative caricatures. British media has a long and dark history in perpetuating racist stereotypes.[8] These representations enable, steer and reconstruct dominant versions of the shopkeeper as miserly, unfeeling, uncaring and unable to integrate fully into the social and cultural fabric of what comes to be understood as *the community*. We see this version of the stranger appearing time and again in 1970s sitcoms such as *Till Death Do Us Part*, and the intermittent absent presence of Arkwright's rival in *Open All Hours*.[9] Of course, these tropes are not limited to the United Kingdom, and the hit US animated series *The Simpsons* had Apu, replete with accent, accented wife, Hindu religious statues, extra-large family of children, and of course the financial extractionist ethic. Raj in David Walliams' series of books performs a similar function, reinforcing multiple stereotypes and the focus of much media attention, as well as complaints from Muslim rights groups and anti-racist campaigners.[10] The character is heavily accented in film adaptations and is reduced and defined solely through his one-dimensional, financial transactionary nature. The stranger is a figure that is accepted as neither self nor other and therefore generates anxieties on the part of the onlooker. In other words, he (always a male) sits in a no-man's land of belonging, and is both inside a given community, and at the same time outside of it due to his racial *foreignness*. Television, film and literary representation played a damaging role fixing the British–Asian shopkeeper in a particular representational space, mapped partly by pre-existing stereotypes in national consciousness and renewed as new forms of race–nation–migrant complications.[11]

The South Asian shopkeeper occupies a particular space in the racial imaginary that straddles the 'strange space', where goods transactions are necessary. In the same way that borders and boundaries between social groups are not naturally occurring and need to be constructed, so the borders of identity and its negotiation are produced in and around the shop.[12] These others are part of the raced representational economy of consuming the other. Consuming race occurs across several social, political, cultural and capital intersections, and often mediates how race works.[13] The South Asian shopkeeper occupies a *representational circuit*, showing us how chains of connection are re-enacted through colonial and imperial fantasies of subservience or subversion. Under the fantasy of these stereotypes, the realities of British colonial power, so intimately connected to immigrant and migrant communities, can be ignored.[14] These *raciological imaginations* are forms of systemic, psycho-social longings to distil complex lives into simplistic, insular and reduced versions.

'Presence' of empire's children …

Popular and cultural consciousness unfolds then freezes migration from the Indian subcontinent in specific, post–Indian independence time frames, but the reality is more complex. The chronology of Asians in Britain starts with the East India Company's trade agreements and then monopolies in South Asia and moves through a series of phases, from pre-colonial to proto-colonial, colonial and postcolonial.[15] With each of these phases, the relationship between Britain's imperial power base and the subject countries and people changes. As Nasreen Ali neatly summarizes, each change generates movements of populations,[16] from the Ayas and Lascars (Indian Seamen) arriving in the 1600s in Britain, through Victoria's reign as Empress of India, and the postcolonial configurations of decolonial diasporic existence post 1947.[17] Such changes brought South Asians into Britain, and embedded them within the social, economic and labour market processes, inseparable from Britain's growth and a growing and incontestable demonstration of the changing nature of what it meant to be British or 'Brit(ish)', as Afua Hirsch insightfully phrased it.[18]

Everyday difference

The communities in which shops are situated might be multicultural, liberal, ethnically diverse and plural in many ways. The most ethnically diverse areas in the United Kingdom have landscapes that may reflect versions of what I present here, within which the Asian corner shop is an extension of the other components of social and cultural mixing that Paul Gilroy called 'convivial multiculture'.[19] This is the everydayness of culture, as differences rub up alongside and against sameness – in all their manifestations. As Rozina Visram tells us, South Asian presence has been well documented for over 400 years.[20] The *presence* (an interesting term, as one would only use this term when referring to an object that would ordinarily be seen as out of place) of Asians in Britain is a story that intersects the narrative of this chapter. Where have they come from? What journeys, situations and diasporic processes – political, transnational, economic, social and cultural – have brought these people to places where they felt compelled to open a small business – often on a corner? From the beginnings of trade, war and imperial and colonial extraction of profit in South Asian countries, the interconnectedness of White Britain with its dark Others has been beyond question. Yet the ever-present boundaries of belonging continue to be fortified using populist yearnings for racial and ethnic purity. While the scope of this wide view is beyond this chapter, it serves to situate what it means to observe and identify Asians in the United Kingdom, especially in the shop.

The term Asian or South Asian masks a multitude of linguistic, ethno-religious, social and cultural differences and crossovers, but like most hierarchical categories comes from power relations, and functions to simplify, reduce and essentialize. It was only in the early 1970s, with the crisis of

Idi Amin's expulsion of all Ugandan Asians, that the British government needed to substitute British Indian for the term 'Asian'. The requirements of policy and governance necessitated terms and labels for the groups arriving in the United Kingdom. As Singh reminds us: '[T]he sum population of the geographical region of South Asia is almost 2 billion people. And the land mass is roughly 22 times the size of Britain. There are about 30 major languages in South Asia, written in 16 different scripts.'[21] Logical, conceptual and statistical validity is thrown to the wind in exchange for ideological simplicity.

The Indian subcontinent and diaspora have multiple, bloody and traumatic connections to Britain beyond the popular Raj discourse, or the cinematically convenient representations of Mahatma Gandhi and Lord Mountbatten entering into civil conversations about India's request to leave the empire.[22] The trade connections that existed on the silk roads and within the subcontinent pre-existed the Royal East Indian Company (the largest and most profitable corporation in the history of the world).[23] The opportunities for exploitation and extraction of profit that lay ahead were clear and so began the long, bloody and ever-present Britain–India/South Asian connection. Indian gross domestic product was 25 per cent of the world economy in the 17th century and 2 per cent in 1947.[24] Shorn of its Platinum Jubilee and Commonwealth camaraderie, the empire was an advanced, profit-generating colonial slavery system.

Displacement

The British Asian shopkeeper did not magically appear in the heart of White, British communities, ready to serve (and be represented in racist television comedies). Rather, they had travelled long and far, via multiple migratory routes, across several continents, surviving complex traumas and experiences that brought them to this particular location.[25] Over the course of some 300 years, generations of South Asians made journeys to many different locations across the globe – as diasporic, and often displaced groups do, from the United States, Canada, Singapore and many African countries. Indian migrants who were brought into the African continent as indentured labour in the 1860s and 1890s were part of the tiered extraction of labour to build infrastructures that would service the new capitalist worlds of colonial rulers. Slavery was abolished in 1834, with compensation paid to former slave owners for loss of property and capital, and British celebrations of the new liberal ethical spirit were under way.[26] This newly emergent gap in the 'labour market' – such euphemisms are common – was quickly filled with new *dark foreigners* from Britain's imperial jewels, India, South Asia and China and the Pacific.[27] Caught in indentured labour systems that would see them as the targets of profit extraction – with legally binding contracts for *bonded labour* that did little more than justify barely human treatment – they were shipped all over the globe to build Empire's new world.[28]

The British Empire exported 30,000 Indian labourers to the eastern seaboard of Africa in order to build the railway system for that region.[29] This area of Eastern Africa boasts the Tazara railway, as well as Zambian Railways, and the notorious Uganda Railway was nicknamed the 'lunatic railway' for its appetite for Indian labourers' lives. By 1903, 2,500 Indian labourers had died since the construction began and although many thousands were allowed passage back to India, others stayed to build on the small holdings, stores and goods huts that they had started during their experience with the railways.[30] The heritage East African Indians brought to the United Kingdom was not solely entrepreneurial, but also borne of much tragedy and displacement.

In the 1970s, Idi Amin's vision of Uganda excluded Asians; 80,000 were exiled in a whirlwind of violence, abuse and diasporic dispossession. It is therefore vital that we situate the experience of Asian shopkeepers in the United Kingdom who migrated from Africa, as exiled from often ideal lives into the United Kingdom's turbulent, violent racial hostilities *and* acknowledge the truths of their own hierarchical context. African Indians were caught in a system where they were both subjects and agents of colonial domination. The dynamics of rapid and sudden downward mobility from potentially being subordinate ruling classes to a subjugated racialized class are part of this complexity.[31] Many Asian shopkeepers were part of this complex picture.

Troubled hierarchies

The tendency to binarize the East African Asian migrant's experience as emanating solely from the expulsion experience needs to be treated delicately. A high proportion were Ugandan and Kenyan Asians, expelled due to the culmination of Africanization and newly decolonized African regimes that sought to regain economic control of their countries. So it is tempting to situate these migrant experiences as the straightforward outcome of East African leaders violating their rights and exacting revenge for colonial dispossession. The expulsion of African Asians was a fundamental dislocating trauma for them, their families, *but* it is also important to locate the action within a wider, East African perspective. For the Black East African populations, already experiencing cultural, economic, physical and social decimation and oppression through capitalist, colonial extraction from Europe, Asian presence meant another form of colonizing. As Sharma writes, the dispossession of East African Asians was traumatic, violent, and disrupted forms of ideal life in their countries.[32] For Black Africans, however, it represented a form of reparation and restitution. This does not discount the fact that thousands of Asians had been forcibly exiled and removed from Uganda, without proper home, citizenship or means to earn a living. However, the picture rendered of life lived in Africa by many East African Asians is paradoxically one which erases both Black African lives and their exclusion and oppression in their own country. As Sharma explains, 'my cousins enjoyed a comfortable standard of living. A cleaner took care of all the household chores so my aunt could concentrate on raising five children'.[33] The question that begs to be asked is who was the cleaner, and what was their life like? And what kinds of systemic colourism and racism were cascaded down through the Asian middle classes that locked Black people in the lowest orders in society? These questions do not negate the established and documented histories of East African Asian experiences of violent racism and consistent institutional disadvantage in the United Kingdom. Rather, these questions provide for us a more nuanced appreciation of contradictions and paradoxes of multicultural British society.

The logic of coloniality worked to demarcate populations on various hierarchies of legitimacy and the racialized power mechanisms worked within government policies structuring immigration and citizenship accordingly. Britain's colonial brothers and sisters became unwanted, unliked and unwelcome.[34] Hostile environments, rebranded by Theresa May's Conservative government in 2013, have a long British pedigree, rooted even in Elizabeth I's hostility to, then expulsion of, Jewish and Moorish communities in the 16th century.[35] Race is, as Alana Lentin cogently reminds us, a technology of power and is utilized flexibly depending on the desires and economic needs of a civic and institutional framework, and it is also a fundamental component in demarcating sub-humanity.[36] Hostile environments are nothing new in the United Kingdom.

End of empire as a chronological metonym signposts a symbolic and material process that fundamentally racialized people according to the variegated needs of the nation's journey. We have seen a similar tragedy unfolding in the brutality meted out to the Windrush generation of Caribbean migrants who arrived in the United Kingdom on the *Empire Windrush*, at the invitation of the government to help build the National Health Service and other vital infrastructures in need of support in post-war regeneration. As journalist and writer Amelia Gentleman reported, hundreds of Black, Caribbean people who had settled here for over half a century, with families, communities, jobs and networks, were targeted for removal and expulsion.[37] The scandal caused much harm to communities, lives and livelihoods, and the increasing sense of alienation felt by many communities of colour and many non-White residents long established in Britain, especially as the European Union referendum decision in 2016 continues to have effect.[38] As Alix Green pointed out in the previous chapter, the fundamental race-immigration exclusions to national citizenship have been a long process, steeped in political manoeuvres and legislation that works its way into many aspects of society. The everyday, taken-for-granted location of the Asian shop has its roots in this very colonial history.

Entrepreneurial spirit or brutal necessity?

The Asian shopkeeper standing at the till (cash register), often on his or her own, providing a gentle, useful service in practical terms for local residents, but also functioning as part of the everyday conviviality that multicultural realities allow, is a deceptively and easily oversimplified entity.[39] The realities of setting up and operating small businesses in the 1970s and 1980s, meant risk, sacrifice, long hours of manual work by family members, and potential isolation. The task was accepted wholeheartedly, when confronted with the alternative routes to settlement, taken and suffered by many. Explanations for why BrAsians often opted for the entrepreneurial routes to self-dependency focus on positive attributes and negative experiences that drive people to adopt self-determination strategies.[40] There is a need for realism here, given the discriminatory structures in the labour market. As Shinder Thandi succinctly summarized, the explanatory models for South Asian small business success range from the culturalist to the structural environmental.[41] However, more nuanced and interactive exchange models furnish a richer, contextual explanation for what people might be experiencing. These may indicate the ways in which 'business success in ethnic neighbourhoods is not simply the aggregate sum of the attributes of individual businessmen but is a tangible outcome of social capital created in such communities'.[42] Roger Waldinger's interactive model provides a more robust way of thinking about the overlapping, connecting and often conflicting threads leading to owning and running a shop.[43] Opportunity structures, group characteristics, access to ownership, resource mobilization, market conditions and motivating factors are some of the core elements of this model and demonstrate some of the complexity behind the overt simplicity of being a corner shopkeeper.

There are limitations to Waldinger's model, such as the need for more intersectional detail to explore the role gender, race, class and even caste play. Thandi emphasized that a one-dimensional account of the nature of this labour is not sufficient, since there is always a combination of formal and informal labour structures in operation.[44] Given the stark reality of small business survival it is interesting to note that 'life on the margins [attempting to run a small business such as a shop] is better than subjecting oneself to the humiliation and drudgery associated with working low paid, dead-end jobs'.[45] The contradictions inherent in the selective rejection and acceptance of racialized minorities is ample demonstration of Stuart Hall's articulation of race as a 'floating signifier'.[46] A signification of good/bad strangers is at play; their position, and the processing of this difference in the social, economic and cultural consciousness determines what race looks like in a given moment. The hierarchical and contradictory splitting of racialized minorities in the United Kingdom has been part of this division-making process. As Virdee points out, the Labour government's Race Relations Act 1965 was double-sided, given its insistence on supporting racist immigration controls.[47]

A nation of (Asian) shopkeepers ...

The marked Conservative shift in the United Kingdom in 1979 under Margaret Thatcher, closely connected to corresponding neoliberal developments in the United States, manifested partly in the ability to buy one's own house and self-generated wealth. This could be seen as the gateway for many BrAsian people to escape the oppression and poverty of the previous decades and also acquire the economic prosperity promised to everyone else. The conditional exchange in this relationship was of course driven by the currency of hard work, long hours and sacrifice. Something that was born out of a series of historical, political and migratory processes was constructed as an inherent, cultural trait: *the Indian work ethic.* BrAsian shopkeepers may have also played a role in organizations such as the Indian Workers Association, or community anti-racism and resistance groups, but it is more likely that the new neoliberal capitalist fantasies of economic security and protection became fused onto older insecurities about cultural and ethnic reproduction, alienation, marginalization, and the constant shifting landscape of Britain's race problem. Being a shopkeeper, performing the multiple functions they did, it was possible to be disjointed from those larger structural, international labour and race struggles, but still play vital status roles within one's cultural and physical space and community, via the vehicle of the shop.

A new race-class formation was birthed just as the economic problems of the 1970s gave way to the new decades of global capitalism, which also heralded the slow demise of small shops and businesses, like the Asian corner shop. There are multiple ways in which BrAsian classed identities are seen as forms of middle-class 'good immigrant' constructions. Here, the nature of entrepreneurial connections to Conservative ideologies in the United Kingdom become complicated through the intersections of ethnicity and class. The middle-classing of BrAsian groups through their presence in business ventures, specifically in the retail shop unit, is tensioned. As Rina Saini explained, British Indian Hindu groups are seen as model minorities, feeding into existing notions of cultural exceptionality, rooted in a sanitized and imagined colonial past, which 'aligns with normatively bound "British values" of hard work, traditionalism and family stability and strongly underpin conservative political ideologies'.[48]

The encounter in the shop exists in circumstances that are complex, historical and interconnected with the histories of those who may not always welcome this corner existing.

Adam Smith popularized 18th-century economic discourse that emphasized interconnections between shopkeeping, nation and empire building. This discourse demands another question – what of colonization, racial capitalism and the bourgeoisie grouping?[49] As Sita Balani indicated, the era of liberal individualism and John Locke's predictions of private property (so forcefully mobilized by Margaret Thatcher) was truly in place in the shopkeeping culture.[50] Balani reminds us: 'The figure of the shopkeeper was analogous to the nation in the early years of the empire.'[51] If the relationship between Britishness, Empire and shopkeeping is significant enough to warrant an analytical integration into 18th-century economic discourse, then it must equally be central to ask: Who are these shopkeepers over time and what do they symbolize and signify? The Asian shopkeeper as ideal type performs the function of fixing national racial stereotypes inside a neatly compartmentalized version of the 'stranger'. It also tallies with the narrowly defined categories of working-class, labour and exploitation in the fabric of British class systems, constructed to be fundamentally White and born of European capitalist ideations.[52]

The separation of racialized oppression from classed oppression was a common feature of much sociological and class analysis that organizations such as the Institute of Race Relations, under Ambilavaner Sivanandan and colleagues, attended to and resisted. W.W. Daniel's 1968 study showed the proletarianizing trend undergone by racialized migrants in the United Kingdom.[53] Seventy-two per cent of those previously working as white-collar professionals were forced into industrial manufacturing. Accumulatively there was an additional layer of racism that worked to disadvantage these workers, with discrimination ranging from 'massive to the substantial'.[54] While political responses to Powell's 'Rivers of Blood' speech were robust – he was fired the next day – working-class support was still widespread.[55] F. Lindop described race strikes of tens of thousands of White workers, supported by their unions, in defence of Enoch Powell.[56] Certainly, Enoch Powell's racism was different to the racism that confidently undergirded imperial and colonial extractionism. This was a racism that outwardly quivered with anger and sought only one outcome: to be rid of this strange, dark presence that blighted the otherwise pure, White, British landscape. Raciological imaginaries drove the sociopolitical contexts which any South Asian migrant family in the United Kingdom would have had to contend with and negotiate to survive. The corner shop was born from self-determination and a self-defensive urge. The cyclical nature of how the United Kingdom processes its ambivalently violent relationship with its colonial and postcolonial others is implicated in the history of shopkeeping.

We are here because you were there ...

The process of Asians appearing in Britain began long before the migration waves now fixed in modern popular consciousness.[57] The end of empire is often regarded as a driving factor for migration but this overlooks that the end part of the process necessitates a beginning and signifies a temporal, material and social continuum. It is this continuum that connects the presence of those who were *not present* and those who demand their legitimacies as *always here*. As imperial soldiers, euphemistically termed 'traders' and 'adventurers', returned from their exploits back to the home country, so did the abjected subjects of this relationship, like imperial possessions – servants and nannies to the crown.[58]

As Nasreen Ali explained, while migration flows from South Asian peaked between 1962 and 1975, the governmental approach to curbing this 'tide' put into place the roots of racialized immigrant control that we now see in contemporary landscapes of border control. The peaks and troughs of immigration are only segments of the historical connections between the United Kingdom and South Asian countries. The postcolonial phase from 1947 onwards saw Britain's industrial urban landscapes in dire need of help to rebuild a country bombed and destroyed. Immigrants arrived just in time for new economic investments from the government and a newly emergent ethos of liberal individualism that regaled the older traditions of self-reliance, private property and commerce-driven middle-class aspirations. As geopolitical decolonization forced the Empire to relinquish formal control and post-industrialization preceded the service industries, '[t]he British Asian shopkeeper becomes a visible and anxious node in the national imagination'.[59] In these contexts, the corner shop became the 'paki-shop', the beloved phrasing so popular in everyday discourse – even in television sitcoms such as *Only Fools and Horses*. The shop was a paki-shop, the people inside, *produced relationally* as 'pakis', and yet at the same time, the man, woman or child behind the counter was also the person who provided everything you would need for the evening meal, the week, the morning, the children. The shop stocked everything one might need, even when one didn't know what one needed. In those moments they did not *cease to be pakis*, this layer simply subsided for a while, as new demands for cooperation and conviviality took priority. The propensity to hold competing, jarring versions of the *other* are complex but real components in racism.

The drive to secure independence in income and financial security is also about the maintenance and cultural reproduction of securities, in precarious social and economic positions for people of colour. To begin the journey of securing financial, property and belonging is also to assume the intention of passing this responsibility and drive to subsequent generations. Small Asian businesses in the United Kingdom utilize family labour, and although this is no different to any family-based enterprise, where the reproduction of property, finance and material heredity is a concern, for diasporic groups there is always an added issue of continuity that transcends everyday issues. In a landscape where one's difference is marked by racial, ethnic, cultural and linguistic coding, the ever-present sense of temporary-ness is difficult to escape. In such a space reserved for the historical continuities of belonging afforded to groups who claim legitimacy in origin, soil and blood, citizenship itself was, and still is, a contested parameter of equality.

Colonial space (inv)Asians – the postcolonial encounter at the counter

The social relational encounter in the shop was, and is, a complicated nexus of delicate cultural and racial negotiations of identity, with the ever present risk of the shop owners being regarded as foreign bodies, what Puwar so eloquently called 'Space Invaders'.[60] Such everyday negotiations show us just how fragile the layers of social relations can be when it comes to processing racial and ethnic difference, but also how nuanced and fluidly these interactions can flow in order for successful interaction to result. In the theatre of *good/bad migrant* politics, the BrAsian shopkeeper plays a tricky identity role as both *part-of* and *part-against* the worst excesses of the British racial state and its turbulent and inconsistent handling of multicultural realities. The tensions in this plot are multiple, layered and held together by Britain's postcolonial encounter with its wanted and unwanted guests. Britain's colonial history is intimately tied into its flexible and selective notions of citizenship and belonging when it comes to the presence of what came to be defined as foreign populations.[61]

The interplay of race and classed lives is important. As Stuart Hall reminded us: 'Race is the modality in which class is lived.'[62] If race and class are not simply accumulatively layered, but co-constituted, then what does this tell us about the *situated labour* of shopkeeping? The community space – concrete pavement space there to be consumed by passers-by, passers-through and, crucially, those other co-constituents of that space – indicate intimate links. As Pierre Bourdieu explained, *space is a relational* thing.[63] Any given space and place will hold multiple meanings simultaneously, for different people, but crucially these meanings will cross over, clash and interconnect at the same time, depending on power relations.

The doorway into the corner shop was a threshold device, a control that provided a symbolic and often real security measure to keep unwanted (unpaying) people out, financial security within, and the possibility of an open doorway for convivial multiculture to exist and even thrive. It was also a mediating factor that opens the family up to vulnerabilities of attack, and the insecurities of whatever vicissitudes the market may produce. Adaptability then becomes a key component of survival, since 'small interactional and sensuous details of racialised differences are produced, transacted and confronted in our daily lives'.[64] The shop counter was the space and physical point where interactional exchange of goods, service and money take place. This seemingly straightforward apparatus furnishes not only the physicality of the exchanges, but also allows for a symbolic structure that doubles as both defence and border against hostility and an interactional shared space where *others* can come together. In the early days of the United Kingdom's newly formed BrAsian shopkeeper class, where multicultural relations and tolerances were fragile, the physical negotiating space was necessary. Such *counter-measures* provided the shopkeeper with a degree of protection against attack, but also a form of negotiated counter-culture where they could be more or less welcoming, depending on the needs of the interaction. I argue that in this way, the shop, the agents within the shop and the customers passing in and out, were and are part of a constantly played out stream of social and political negotiations about ambivalent belongings. The shop was and is a *holding* mechanism to contain the dialectical turbulence of tolerance, anxiety, ambivalence and active intolerance.

The physical and symbolic location of retail units in the heart of communities provides a possibility to view this encounter through a service-control contingency lens. By this I mean that both shopkeeper and customer arrived at the encounter with needs and requirements that must be fulfilled, and both hold various modalities of power – one the power to provide/withhold goods, services and custom, the other their patronage as an ongoing relation that was always held in some form of tension. In contemporary raced landscapes the shop remains a contested interactionally raced order.

The Asian-owned corner shop is at the crossroads of multiple sociocultural, economic, racial and political ley lines, and therefore should be read as such: a complex network of historical, cultural, embodied forces. The physical space occupied by the shop is also the physical space taken up by the people in the shop – the mothers, fathers, sons and daughters, whose lives are as equally complex as those lives that sit outside of these boundaries. The shop is a *processual context*, always changing in relation to other factors, a physical and social space that mediates this troubled negotiation, through everyday goods and services. Here, at the counter, in the aisles, on the spaces between shelves stocked with the things that people know they need, and the items they often did not even realize they needed, we can start to knit together a more nuanced understanding of lives lived, battles fought, journeys taken, rejections and acceptances felt.

In between the spaces that belong to White British communities and that space indoors that belongs to those who occupy contested identities (and who slip in and out of being *foreign*), the doorway becomes a simple, undiscussed but powerful tool for leveraging acceptance, power, authority and belonging, that far transcends economic and material gain. Positions that provide service, engage in interaction, give advice and ultimately form mediated friendships are a currency whose value still exists today in shops all over Britain, owned and run by those who were once owners of 'paki' shops, but are now termed Asian businesses. The porous layers of identity that clash or come together on the site of the shop are 'contact zones'.[65] Sita Balani sharply addresses the racial–imperial–colonial crux: 'This contact zone is one in which "native" and "settler" interact in seemingly banal ways that may nonetheless be fraught with the tensions and connections that characterise multicultural Britain.'[66] The differences between people, fundamental to the processing of the other, fluctuate, recede or get pushed to the foreground of contact in different ways at different times. What occurs then in the daily postcolonial *encounter at the counter* is precisely the intimate and intricate working out of this difference.

The shop is also a living, working, sleeping, family place where cooking, eating, washing, studying and talking also take place. There is something fundamentally vulnerable, as Sharma and others have pointed out, about the same space being partially occupied by customers/strangers.[67] Here the raciological imaginary of the *foreign* stranger occupying *pure* space that is otherwise the refuge of the native is *inverted*. The entrance of the customer into the space owned by the Asian shopkeeper is regulated and controlled by them and represents a negotiation of both service provision and protection of vulnerable, private family space. Shop counters that are placed at the rear of the store can be seen as guarded entrances to the family home space, where culture, religion, food and life happen away from the cognition of incoming custom. Such boundaries are tested and contested in various ways, such as cooking smells, given Britain's perverse and selective love–hate relationship with aspects of foreign-ness. Growing up in the 1970s, a frequent racist insult directed at Asian children in school, but also commonly on the street, was charges of 'smelling like a paki'. An interesting feature of Britishness, since South Asian food has since become part of the island's celebrated identity, even among the staunchest of racists. For some, the smells invoked curiosity, learning and taste, while for others, barely acknowledged semi-conscious resentments rise and attack the vulnerable targets. I argue these are thin, fragile veneers that mark the sensuous, fleshy, embodied multicultural spaces forming the encounter at the counter, while the everyday exchange-interactions circulate within and outside of this. The entanglement of histories, spaces, privacies and sensuous locations are complex, nuanced and only ever precarious, despite this being a nation of shopkeepers and customers.

Conclusion

In this chapter, I have presented the Asian corner shop as a historical and contemporary site for a critical analysis of Britain's long and troubled relationship to race and colonial power. It unpacks how everyday normalcies can gloss over the complicated journeys of migration that lead to people living within communities and serving populations. The dynamic nature of racial categories intersects with the ambivalent, troubling and necessarily desired presence of the shopkeeper. At times racial, at times ethnic, cultural, and oftentimes just the 'paki' who runs the corner shop, the British South Asian shopkeeper was *never* British in the raciological imagination, nor a figure of explicit, outright rejection, categorized as the racial other as other people and groups are.

The shopkeeper *slips in and out* of *race*, because of the necessary exchange value of their presence; the interactional relation (that is, you cannot enter into the exchange of goods, money and services *without* some form of relationship); the wider, historical, sociopolitical arena of race and ethnic relations and the inevitability of difference that multicultural reality produces. The BrAsian shop is always in production, as an interplay of migration histories, societal changes, and contemporary cultural community processes. The multiple ways in which foreign others appear in the British national consciousness is contingent on the social and political relations that mark exchange and interaction. *How* race is played out, and *what* race is at any given moment, flits between skin colour, accent, appearance, perceived smells and sounds, class location, and the degree of interdependence involved in goods, monetary exchange and services. The innocuous, fixed-ethnic-stereotype multicultural figure, so beloved of British humour, as we see in *Raj* and others, is a reminder of the connected histories rendered invisible among the pints of milk, loaves of bread and packets of cigarettes that line shelves and furnish everyday lives.

Neither Asian shops, nor the multitude of other minority ethnic retail or wholesale businesses that have emerged in the last six decades, are going to fade away anytime soon. This is especially the case in a time and arena where the presence of semi-strange others is mediated by consumer media capital relations and the consistent redrawing of ideas about who belongs where, and why. All the more reason to situate the messy, entangled and connected histories of people – shopkeeper and customer alike – as being wholly implicated in each other through race, class, gender and colonial processes, always in production. These analyses and histories are always without guarantees.[68] They are always in motion – like the dynamic encounter at the counter.

Acknowledgements

I would like to thank the editors of this collection for their constructive insights and patient support in the writing of this.

Notes

[1] A. Sivanandan, *Catching History on the Wing: Race, Culture and Globalisation* (London: Pluto Press, 2008), xv.

[2] K. Sahota, 'In Buckingham Palace and outside it, we know what it means when people ask "where are you from"', *The Guardian*, 30/11/22, https://www.theguardian.com/commentisfree/2022/nov/30/buckingham-palace-where-are-you-from-black-british (accessed 11/02/2024).

3 A. Hirsch, *Brit(ish): On Race, Identity and Belonging* (London: Vintage, 2018).

4 BrAsian – a term referring to processes, ideas and practices that rely on uncritical and unquestioned uses of race as an objective entity. Coined in N. Ali, V.S. Kalra and S. Sayyid, *A Postcolonial People: South Asians in Britain* (New York: Columbia University Press, 2008).

5 H. Keval, '"Merit", "success" and the epistemic logics of whiteness in racialised education systems', in D.S.P. Thomas and J. Arday (eds), *Doing Equity and Diversity for Success in Higher Education: Redressing Structural Inequalities in the Academy* (Cham: Palgrave Macmillan, 2021), 127–137.

6 Ali et al, *A Postcolonial People*.

7 G. Bhambra, 'Undoing the epistemic disavowal of the Haitian revolution: a contribution to global social thought', *Journal of Intercultural Studies*, 3 (2016), 1–16.

8 L. Young, *Fear of the Dark: 'Race', Gender and Sexuality in the Cinema* (London: Routledge, 2006).

9 Z. Bauman, 'Making and unmaking of strangers', *Thesis Eleven* 43:1 (1995), 1–16.

10 J. Selby, 'David Walliams accused of racism over "penny pinching" Indian shopkeeper Raj in TV adaptation of his books', *inews*, 30/12/2018, https://inews.co.uk/culture/books/david-walliams-racism-childrens-book-character-raj-indian-shopkeeper-midnight-gang-240641 (accessed 11/02/2024).

11 M. Goodfellow, *Hostile Environment: How Immigrants Became Scapegoats* (London: Verso Books, 2020).

12 Bauman, 'Making and unmaking of strangers'.

13 B. Pitcher, *Consuming Race* (New York: Routledge, 2014).

14 G. Bhambra, *Connected Sociologies* (London: Bloomsbury Academic, 2014).

15 Ali et al, *A Postcolonial People*.

16 Ali et al, *A Postcolonial People*.

17 R. Visram, *Ayahs, Lascars and Princes: Indians in Britain (1700–1947)* (London: Pluto Press, 1986).

18 Hirsch, *Brit(ish)*.

19 P. Gilroy, *After Empire: Melancholia or Convivial Culture?* (London: Routledge, 2004).

20 R. Visram, *Asians in Britain: 400 Years of History* (London: Pluto Press, 2002).

21 G. Singh, 'What does it mean to be "South Asian" and when did we become "South Asians"?', *Asian Samachar*, 24/08/22, https://asiasamachar.com/2022/08/24/what-does-it-mean-to-be-south-asian-and-when-did-we-become-south-asians/ (accessed 11/02/2024).

22 S. Rushdie, *Imaginary Homelands: Essays and Criticism 1981–1991* (London: Granta, 1991); S. Tharoor, *Inglorious Empire: What the British did to India* (London: Penguin, 2018).

23 A. Sen, 'Illusions of empire: Amartya Sen on what British rule really did for India', *The Guardian*, 29/06/2021, https://www.theguardian.com/world/2021/jun/29/british-empire-india-amartya-sen (accessed 11/02/2024).

24 Tharoor, *Inglorious Empire*.

25 P. Bachu, *Twice Migrants: East African Sikh Settlers in Britain* (London: Tavistock Publications, 1985); D. Hiro, *Black British, White British: A History of Race Relations in Britain* (London: Grafton Books, 1991).

26 D. Olusoga, *Black and British: A Forgotten History* (London: Palgrave Macmillan, 2018).

27 T. Mahmud, 'Cheaper than a slave: indentured labor, colonialism and capitalism', *Whittier Law Review*, 34:2 (2013), 215–243.

28 'Indentured labour from South Asia (1834–1917)', *Striking Women*, https://www.striking-women.org/module/map-major-south-asian-migration-flows/indentured-labour-south-asia-1834-1917 (accessed 11/02/2024).

29 M. Mamdani, 'The Asian question: Mahmood Mamdani writes about the expulsion from Uganda', *London Review of Books*, 44:19, 06/10/2022, https://www.lrb.co.uk/the-paper/v44/n19/mahmood-mamdani/the-asian-question (accessed 11/02/2024).

30   M. Dabas, 'A railway line in Kenya is so "lunatic", it took lives of 2500 Indians during its construction', *India Times*, 24/06/2018, https://www.indiatimes.com/news/india/a-railway-line-in-kenya-is-so-lunatic-it-took-lives-of-2500-indians-during-its-construction-347711.html (accessed 11/02/2024).

31   S. Mahtani, 'It's time to confront anti-Blackness in Asian-African communities', *African Arguments*, 05/08/2020, https://africanarguments.org/2020/08/its-time-to-confront-anti-blackness-in-asian-african-communities/ (accessed 11/02/2024).

32   B. Sharma, *The Corner Shop: Shopkeepers, the Sharmas and the Making of Modern Britain* (London: Two Roads, 2019).

33   Sharma, *The Corner Shop*, 31.

34   Olusoga, *Black and British*.

35   H. Jones, Y. Gunaratnam, G. Bhattacharyya, W. Davies, S. Dhaliwal, K. Forkert, E. Jackson and R. Saltus, *Go Home? The Politics of Immigration Controversies* (Manchester University Press, 2017); M. Boatcă, *Global Inequalities Beyond Occidentalism* (Florence: Taylor & Francis, 2016).

36   A. Lentin, *Why Race Still Matters* (Cambridge, MA: Polity Press, 2020).

37   A. Gentleman, *The Windrush Betrayal: Exposing the Hostile Environment* (London: Faber & Faber, 2019).

38   D. Dorling, *Rule Britannia: Brexit and the End of Empire* (London: Biteback Publishing, 2019).

39   Gilroy, *After Empire*.

40   S.S. Thandi, 'Brown economy: enterprise and employment', in N. Ali, V.S. Kalra and S. Sayyid, *A Postcolonial People: South Asians in Britain* (New York: Columbia University Press, 2008).

41   Thandi, 'Brown economy'.

42   Thandi, 'Brown economy'.

43   R. Waldinger, *Ethnic Entrepreneurs: Immigrant Business in Industrial Society* (Newbury Park: SAGE, 1990).

44   Thandi, 'Brown economy'.

45   Thandi, 'Brown economy'.

46   S. Hall, *The Fateful Triangle* (Cambridge, MA: Harvard University Press, 2017).

47   S. Virdee, *Racism, Class and the Racialized Outsider* (London: Bloomsbury Publishing, 2014).

48   R. Saini, 'The racialised "second existence" of class: class identification and (de-/re-) construction across the British South Asian middle classes', *Cultural Sociology*, 17:2 (2022), 277–296; R. Saini, 'The racialisation of class and the racialisation of the nation: ethnic minority identity formation across the British South Asian middle classes', *South Asian Diaspora*, 14:2 (2022), 109–125.

49   C. Robinson, *Black Marxism* (London: Penguin Classics, 2021).

50   J. Trafford, *The Empire at Home: Internal Colonies and the End of Britain* (London: Pluto, 2020); S. Balani, 'Britain: a history of shopkeeping, empire and racial tensions', *Media Diversified*, 07/10/2013, https://mediadiversified.org/2013/10/07/a-nation-of-shopkeepers/ (accessed 11/02/2024).

51   Balani, 'Britain'.

52   G. Bhambra and J. Holmwood, 'Colonialism, postcolonialism and the liberal welfare state', *New Political Economy*, 23:5 (2018), 574–587.

53   W.W. Daniel, *Racial Discrimination in England* (London: Penguin, 1968), 209, cited in Virdee, *Racism, Class*.

54   Daniel, *Racial Discrimination in England*.

55   Olusoga, *Black and British*.

56   F. Lindop, 'Racism and the working class: strikes in support of Enoch Powell in 1968', *Labour History Review*, 66:1 (2001), 79–100.

57   Ali et al, *A Postcolonial People*; Visram, *Asians in Britain*.

58 Ali et al, *A Postcolonial People*, 158.

59 Balani, 'Britain'.

60 N. Puwar, *Space Invaders: Race, Gender and Bodies Out of Place* (Oxford: Berg, 2004).

61 R. Shilliam, *Race and the Undeserving Poor: From Abolition to Brexit* (Newcastle upon Tyne: Agenda Publishing, 2018).

62 S. Hall, C. Critcher, T. Jefferson, J.N. Clarke and B. Roberts, *Policing the Crisis: Mugging, the State, and Law and Order* (London: Macmillan, 1978), 394.

63 P. Bourdieu, *In Other Words: Essays Towards a Reflexive Sociology* (Stanford University Press, 1990).

64 Balani, 'Britain'.

65 M.L. Pratt, 'Arts of the contact zone', *Profession* (1991), 33–40.

66 Balani, 'Britain'.

67 Sharma, *The Corner Shop*.

68 S. Hall, 'For a Marxism without guarantees', 1983, reproduced in *Salvage*, 13/08/2022, https://salvage.zone/for-a-marxism-without-guarantees/ (accessed 11/02/2024).

12

'The Grocer Carried Me for Three Months': Retail Support for Workers Involved in Extended Industrial Disputes

Grace Millar, Ben Curtis, Keith Gildart and Andrew Perchard

Introduction

Throughout the 1984/1985 Miners' Strike, the Morrisons supermarket in Staveley, Derbyshire donated food to the strike centre to be distributed to striking miners. Historians of working-class retail (and industrial disputes) in the early 20th century have often noted the importance of support from food retailers in working-class areas during strikes and lockouts. This example suggests that the practice of support continued into the later decades of the 20th century, even though food retailing in working-class communities changed dramatically. Retail support during industrial disputes will be explored using two case studies: the 1984/1985 British Miners' Strike and the 1951 New Zealand waterfront dispute. Both were protracted industrial disputes that involved a significant proportion of the population and were treated as important historical events, particularly by participants and supporters. In both cases there is considerable evidence of local retailers' support for their customers during the dispute.

This chapter addresses all three of the themes of this collection. New Zealand in the 1950s was still entangled in the British world, as the New Zealand case study shows. The approach of this chapter is primarily comparative. It uses case studies of two separate, but connected, societies to makes its core argument that the consistency of support from retailers in working-class communities during strikes and lockouts demonstrates the socially embedded nature of their business. Two of the case studies involve both co-operative and commercial retailers acting in similar ways, but rather than exploring the economic imperatives that shaped both, these examples show both co-operative and commercial retailers operating to actively support their communities. The final strand of the argument is that industrial disputes are a rich opportunity to understand working-class shopping, because everyday practices continued even though they were put under extreme stress. Understanding what changed and did not change under this stress can reveal aspects of everyday life that are usually taken for granted and therefore hard to access.

A few years after the Miners' Strike, Christopher Hosgood explored the economic and social relationship of small British shopkeepers in working-class areas from 1870 to 1914. Hosgood argued that there was a reciprocal, if complex, relationship between small shopkeepers and the communities their shops were located in. Alongside a clear economic relationship, shopkeepers were also socially located in the communities they were part of, particularly women's social networks.[1] When discussing Leicester shopkeepers' decisions during the 1895 shoe industry lockout, he argues that the efforts they made to support their customers were not just pragmatic, but that 'domestic shopkeepers' ideology incorporated an ingrained sense of social duty to their working-class constituency'.[2] Hosgood's argument is grounded in the particular time and place he is studying, but he also suggested that the reason that small shops still existed in the 1980s was because of their commitment to working-class communities. Other researchers have built on his work to learn more about the identities of these shopkeepers and their world.[3] Andrew Alexander and Simon Phillips argued that the social usefulness of small shopkeepers continued past the Second World War.[4] This chapter further demonstrates the power of the relationships that Hosgood described, by bringing together case studies far flung from his original area of focus, both geographically and temporally.

The exceptional nature of industrial disputes, and the trade union movement's political commitment to remembering them, can result in evidence about working-class shopping surviving that would not otherwise. This chapter brings together both documentary evidence and oral histories that were only created and saved because of the significance those involved gave to these industrial disputes. The union and police archival records used only mentioned retail because of the 1951 waterfront dispute. In addition, it uses Heather Wood's personal records during the 1984/1985 Miners' Strike that were only collected and deposited because of the value she and her community put on the work that they had done. The challenge of household provisioning and the disruption to local business presented by both disputes meant that aspects of working-class retailing were caught in the archival record that would normally have been lost. In the same way, the recording of oral histories has been influenced by the importance people put on the dispute. All the oral histories used in one case study were recorded specifically to capture memories of the dispute. Oral history is invaluable for studying the nature of relationships between retailers and working-class communities, because as well as describing what retailers did, participants reveal the meaning that they gave to that interaction. Alessandro Portelli identified the ability of oral history to capture meaning as one of its peculiarities.[5] This peculiarity is particularly useful when trying to explore the social and relational elements of economic transactions. This chapter can be written because both disputes have been fiercely remembered by the communities that were part of them, and that remembering has shaped the archival and oral history record.

Supermarket chains support the miners

The 1984/1985 Miners' Strike is particularly significant to a study of support during industrial disputes because of the scale of both wages lost and the relief effort. More than 100,000 miners were on strike for over a year in order to fight pit closures.[6] Striking miners received no social security, as the Thatcher government legislated to restrict locked-out and striking workers' access to benefits prior to the strike.[7] In response, substantive local, national and international solidarity campaigns were set up. These campaigns have received some academic attention, with an excellent recent contribution by Diarmaid Kelliher on support for the Miners' Strike in London.[8] The focus has been on national and international solidarity that has a political basis. However, a supermarket chain does not fit the image of miners' support in either academic or popular accounts of the strike. Local solidarity had a different set of complexities, including action that was not usually understood as political.

Tony Twibey was a miner at Prince of Wales in Pontefract. He shopped at G. T. Smiths, a small chain of outlets across the coalfield, and described the support he received during the 1984/1985 strike.

> G T Smiths in Knottingley were a big supermarket in them days. And they gave us a ten pound voucher four times in the strike and gave us a Christmas Hamper – yeah. They were really good to miners were G T Smiths.
>
> But it was smack in the middle of Pontefract, Castleford and Kellingley where the mines were. But – but – they knew who their customers were, but they didn't have to do that. They were really good to us.[9]

Twibey's description of the support he received from the G. T. Smiths supermarket chain 35 years later shows its importance to him.

G. T. Smiths was not the only supermarket chain that offered material support to miners during the 1984/1985 strike. John Walton described support in Derbyshire: 'In fact, Morrisons in Staveley the – see that was the – see Miners' Welfare and that's still open – just round the corner was a Morrisons supermarket and the manager there was very good and he used to – he used to supply the – the strike centre with food.'[10] Unlike G. T. Smiths, Morrisons was not a local chain. Although not as large as it would become, Morrisons had 33 stores in 1985.[11] Chain supermarkets offering crucial support to striking miners in 1984/1985 complicates both images of the Miners' Strike and discussions of the retail transition that took place over the second half of the 20th century.

Oral history allows access to how recipients saw support from supermarkets. Tony Twibey acknowledged the importance of miners as consumers to the supermarket chain he shopped at. He was clearly aware of the interest supermarkets had in both the economic survival of their customers, and the promotion of loyalty. He did not reduce the support to this economic interest, he acknowledged that the support of supermarkets was optional and his use of the phrase 'They were really good to us' emphasized a relationship with a moral element. John Walton also presented the donations of goods to Staveley Miners' Welfare in terms of morality and a relationship. They key difference is that Walton understood agency as lying with the local manager, rather than the corporation as a whole. Staveley Morrisons was (and as of publication still is) just a few hundred yards from the Staveley Miners' Welfare, which was a relief centre during the strike. Walton's mention of the closeness of the physical location suggested that existing as part of the same physical precinct and the relationships that built was important to the support Morrisons offered. Both Walton and Twibey discussed the support they received during the 1984/1985 dispute using a language of morality and emphasizing relationships.

Supporting striking miners does not fit the common image of a supermarket chain, just as a politically motivated person, rather than a supermarket chain, dominates popular images of miners' supporters in 1984/1985. 1985 was an interesting moment in a long transition in British food shopping; in the mid-1980s, supermarket chains outsold the Co-op and local stores for the first time.[12] The transition from independent or co-operative stores to self-service supermarket chains was a significant change in shopping practices and those researching that change have rightly emphasized the scale and importance of that transition.[13] One of the questions when understanding such a substantial shift in practice is what are the threads of continuity that survive the transition? Accounts of supermarkets supporting striking workers suggest a form of continuity, particularly when understood in the context of earlier forms of retail support from locked-out and striking workers, which primarily took the form of extended credit.

Labour historians and retail historians have both discussed the importance of retailers offering credit during strikes and lockouts. Labour historians have noted retail support in discussions of industrial disputes.[14] At times these accounts have revealed long-term relationships that would absolutely shape the lives of both retailers and their customers. Sue Bruley wrote that some families were still repaying debts from the 1926 miners' lockout in the 1970s.[15] Retail historians discussed credit during strikes and lockouts within the context of wider discussions of the role of retailers in their communities. Hosgood dedicated a page to discussion of retailers' responses to the 1895 lockout in Leicester.[16] Building on Hosgood's work, Erik Eklund explored the relationship between storekeepers and working-class communities in Australia entirely through the widespread evidence of support during strikes and lockouts.[17] Avram Taylor emphasized that the provision of credit provided shopkeepers power and distanced them from their communities, but still emphasized that industrial disputes were a particularly complex time for shopkeepers.[18] Supermarket support during the Miners' Strike is similar to long-standing practices of food retailers during strikes, and reveals hidden continuities during a time of significant change in food retailing.

The 1951 New Zealand Waterfront Lockout

The second case is the New Zealand 1951 Waterfront Lockout and supporting strikes, which began as a dispute over wages but became a wider battle for control over the vital role that shipping played in the New Zealand economy. The dispute lasted five months and involved 8,000 locked-out watersiders (the term used to describe dockers in New Zealand) and 7,000 seamen, miners, drivers and freezing workers (industrialized meat-processing workers), who joined supporting strikes. Initially a conflict between the New Zealand Waterside Workers Union (NZWWU) and ship owners, the government took over in the early days, ran the dispute, and was determined to crush the NZWWU.[19] In February 1951, the Cabinet passed a series of draconian emergency regulations, including a regulation that made it an offence to provide material support to workers involved in the dispute.[20] This regulation was never tested in court, but was widely believed to include providing food, or credit, to watersiders' families. After five months, the unions were defeated; workers returned to work on the government's terms. This section explores support from retailers, one aspect of how watersiders and their families survived for five months.

One shop that gave support to locked-out customers during the dispute was the Hutt Valley Consumer Co-operative (HVCC). The directors of HVCC felt the need to account for their actions supporting families of locked-out workers despite the law. In a fraught environment, they turned to ideals from the British world to justify their actions: 'When a major industrial upheaval of this nature occurs, it is necessary that an organisation such as ours, nurtured in the traditions of the British Co-operative Movement, should give consideration of the extent to which it can help the families of those likely to be affected.'[21] The police suspected HVCC was breaking the regulations with its support for the watersiders and undertook an investigation. The police files that touch on the investigation into HVCC include information from a member of parliament and a confidential informant. Retailers were risking surveillance and prosecution when they supported their customers, and willingness to accept the heightened risk provides insight into the nature of retail support during industrial disputes.

Despite criminalization, HVCC was not alone, and large number of retailers gave support to locked-out workers during the dispute. Retailers either gave essential goods on credit, or extended existing credit, even though payments could not be made. Debt comes up again and again in oral histories about the event. Ian Church, who was a child at the time of the dispute, described the situation in Port Chalmers, a port settlement close to a major town: 'Anyone in Port will tell you that the local grocer and butcher carried a lot of people through '51. So there were often quite large bills owing.'[22] In Wellington, Max Bollinger, a trade union activist, recalled that Maple, a furniture company, 'approached all their waterside and freezing works customers with hire purchase and told them that they weren't expected to make any payments until three months after they went back to work'.[23] These cases were not one-off examples; credit was central to how most families survived five months without wages. The Auckland branch of the NZWWU had 2,000 members, spread over a medium-sized city. They only discussed one grocer who was hostile to providing credit over five months.[24] In the final report, it was stated that members were living on credit.[25]

Why did so many small businesses offer extended credit during the dispute, putting themselves at legal and financial risk? The HVCC attributed the support it gave to the families of locked-out workers to its commitment to a wider ideal – that of the British co-operative movement discussed in Chapter 4. However, this presentation of its actions is challenged by how widespread they were. Grocers who provided credit to the families of locked-out and striking workers were offering essential material support for the dispute, which ran in contradiction to the political position of their national body. During the dispute, the New Zealand Master Grocers' Federation was opposed to all wage rises and actively criticized the NZWWU.[26]

The credit retailers offered during the dispute built on their practices under ordinary circumstances. In the case of hire purchase firms, credit had already been extended to watersiders' families, and the union successfully sought to avoid repossession. Grocers routinely offered short-term credit to customers in working-class communities. For example, Maureen Martin, the wife of a freezing worker, had previously always paid her grocer on time, and her grocer offered credit during the dispute and mentioned to her that he often granted credit to customers.[27] The practice of grocers providing credit to their customers continued (and expanded) during this industrial dispute, even though the circumstances were different.

Extending credit was part of grocers' economic model; there was a commercial advantage to the loyalty. During the dispute the economic motivations became more complex. Working with relief committees brought in direct business at a time when many customers were struggling. The NZWWU spent £150 a week at one Lower Hutt grocery store.[28] Co-operating with the freezing workers in particular was quite central to the HVCC's ability to open. There was a meat shortage due to the freezing-workers strike, and in the same annual report the directors note that they did not close and rarely experienced shortages during that time.[29] At the same time, the cost of credit grew, as families needed credit for longer and their ability to repay was threatened and retailers were operating under the threat of criminalization.

Oral history can provide access to the meanings that customers gave to credit that they received during strikes and lockouts. A story from Kevin Ford, who was a child at the time of the dispute, about how his father saw his grocer, showed the importance his father gave to the credit he was given:

> I do know once when the watersiders started their own sort of grocery shop up on the wharf in Bluff that had cheap groceries and that I brought a bagful home for Mum and that and Mum was delighted of course and she said 'oh that's good.' And Dad came home early one day and said 'oh the grocer's been early this week?' Because they usually come on Monday take an order and deliver on Thursday or Friday or whatever day it was. And Mum said no – no Kevin got these down the grocery store on the wharf. They're a lot cheaper than Charlie Denny – that was our grocer – and Dad took one look at me one look at my mother, picked them up and he said look at me – come follow me. I followed him out and he threw them in the rubbish tin and he said that if I bring anything home like again that I'll go in the rubbish tin and I'll be put out the gate. He said 'the grocer carried me for three years – three months and now – and half them bastards down there and they started a store up against him'. He says – he wasn't a very happy chappy.[30]

Kevin Ford's father placed a lot of value on loyalty to his grocer, after the grocer offered credit in 1951. The story Kevin Ford told took place at least ten years after the dispute, and the principle was still important enough that his father was paying more for food every week. Ford's father's action certainly suggested that the credit Charlie Denny extended during the dispute had an ongoing economic reward. While the strength of feeling in the story provides insight to the social and emotional aspects of Ford's father's relationship with Charlie Denny.

Maureen Martin's oral history also captured both her understanding of the economic factors for her grocer and the social and emotional aspects of their relationship. She quoted her grocer's response to her inability to pay:

> I want to tell you something, Mrs Martin, if it wasn't for people like you I could not keep open because your money is there every week and if there is anything you need at all don't worry about the money. Just wait till the strike is over and you're well and truly on your feet because it's customers like you who keep this shop open.[31]

Maureen Martin followed up her discussion of her grocer by saying, 'He was very, very kind to offer me the chance to get what I needed and it was good of him'.[32] The moral language she uses to understand his actions is illustrative. Both Martin and Ford clearly understand the economic incentive to the grocer for offering credit to their families, but they also articulated the relationship between their family and the grocer in more complex terms.

Comparison, change and continuity

The 1951 New Zealand waterfront dispute and the 1984/1985 British Miners' Strike were separated by half a world, decades and substantial changes in shopping practices, and yet there are key points of continuity between the way retailers acted during strikes. The form of support is different, as rather than extending credit supermarkets offered vouchers and hampers to miners and goods to relief committees. However, even in this change in form there is continuity. In both cases, food retailers extended their usual practice to support striking workers. When retailers offered credit on a day-to-day basis, they offered additional credit during strikes and lockouts; when retailers offered vouchers to customers on a day-to-day basis, they offered additional vouchers during strikes and lockouts. The change from grocers to supermarkets was a significant disruption, but industrial disputes reveal some hidden continuity. Supermarkets were still physically located in their community, and both the social and economic relationships embedded in that physical location were key to supermarkets offering support during industrial disputes.

There is also significant continuity in the way that interviewees talked about the support they received from retailers. These interviewees acknowledged the economic incentive retailers had for their support. Tony Twibey stated that the supermarket knew who their customers were and Maureen Martin remembered her grocer explaining how important her custom had been to him. Alongside the acknowledgement of the economic relationship, John Walton, Maureen Martin and Tony Twibey all used the language of firms being 'good' to them. This phrase is a weighted one. One of the strengths of oral history for understanding retailers' support during industrial action is that it allows access not just to what happened, but how people felt about it – and participants' language emphasizes relationships. Voluntary assistance is understood within an ethical framework of good community relationships which the narrators assume they share with the retailers.

The use of moral language by those talking about grocers and supermarkets suggests a moral economy may be one way of understanding this support. Of course, not the moral economy of the 18th-century crowd, as it would be stretching the specificities of E.P. Thompson's analysis to breaking point to suggest that level of continuity.[33] Thompson intended to make a narrow argument about a particular time and place that had long passed.[34] However, authors cannot control concepts they develop, and there has been widespread interdisciplinary use of moral economy.[35] A recent article asked 'do shopkeepers have a moral economy'? The author examined Greek shopkeepers through wars and economic crises from 1916 to 1945 and concluded that they did have a moral economy in a broad sense.[36] Broad concepts of a moral economy might help explain the shared worldview of customers and retailers – and the intertwined motivations of retailers. A final discussion of the Miners' Strike, from a single village in the North East, is revealing ground for exploring this possibility.

They shall not starve

A study of retail support within Easington Colliery, the name of both the pit and the village that it resided in, demonstrates the extent to which economic motivations of retailers, social relationships and a moral framework were intertwined. In 1984, Easington had a small Co-op and an array of other shops, all of which provided financial support for the strike. Peter Hetherington, a *Guardian* reporter who visited Easington in June 1984, described how retailers showed their support: '[T]he town's shopkeepers reassure the strikers that they will not go hungry. They display posters with a simple message of solidarity: "This shop is a member of the Chamber of Trade. We are giving support to the miners".'[37] The women's support group ran a canteen serving hot meals five days a week and also provided food parcels and used donations for both: potatoes from a fish and chip shop, mixed grills from a butcher, and groceries from the local Co-op. The Easington women's support group also received food from retailers who were further afield. A fruit and vegetable co-op in Durham provided leftover produce for the entire year. Heather Wood, one of the members of the women's support group, was explicit about how widespread the retail support was, and stated that every shop in Easington provided goods of some kind.[38] Wood's ability to name and remember the range of local retailers who provided goods three decades later shows how important these provisions were at the time.

Retail support did not stop at goods; the Easington women's support group also accessed retailers' facilities. Once a month one of the Easington fish and chip shops allowed the relief committee to use their shop to make fish and chips for 500.[39] Wood described a similar arrangement from a bakery:

> The local bakers, my mum knew the baker and my mum made the pies on these big boards, corned beef pies, but we had nowhere to cook them. So she went to see Duncan who had the cake shop and she explained, and he said 'Myrtle just as I'm switching the ovens off they'll still be hot enough to cook those pies'. So it wasn't costing him any more money. 'But send them down. We'll cook them and we'll send them up hot'. So the women had the veg to do up there, my mum had prepared the pies. It was a doddle in the end.[40]

The work retailers did was recognized by those on strike. At the end of the strike, the men marched to the pit to return to work and they passed the fish shop that had allowed fish and chips to be made in its facilities. The owner was given a lamp.[41]

As well as their involvement in the day-to-day strike relief, retailers were also involved in the push to ensure that there was a present for every child at Christmas. Presents were stored and organized at an empty space within the local co-op. The support group received donations of wood from local retailers and miners, used to make toys. The women's support group used the dense network of relationships to make sure that anything a retailer could offer, even if it was only a small contribution, could be brought together with other donations of time and money to meet local needs. Wood described how the women's group approached particular gaps:

> But one of my big memories is going into one of the local shops, Pennywise, and I said to the manager 'we've run out of presents for teenage girls and we've got no money', and he said 'Heather just help yourselves off the shelf and pay me afterwards', and we got all these things off the shelf, all these cosmetics and things off the shelves. We took them for these girls.[42]

This story shows the extent to which those most involved in the women's support group could take assistance from local retailers for granted and explicitly ask for what they needed. Retailers were enmeshed in personal social relationships of the village, and these were mobilized throughout the strike.

During the strike, the women's support group saw themselves as actively supporting local retailers, as well as the other way round. The women's support group was a major customer for food in Easington. The support group was receiving significant donations of money from around the United Kingdom and the world, and they were spending that money locally.[43] The women's support group made a conscious decision to make sure that when they had to purchase goods, their money went to local retailers. Heather Wood said: '[W]e started the meals, and we just said to the union, "give us the money" and we decided that we needed to help all the shopkeepers in Easington because they were helping us.'[44] They carefully rotated the retail outlets where they shopped. Each of the fruit and vegetable shops, and each of the butchers received orders. At the end of the dispute, the Easington Chamber of Trade, which had actively supported the strike, wrote to the women's support group to thank them for all they had done.[45]

Easington provides a stark example of local retailers' economic interest in the 1984/1985 strike. Before during and after the strike, retailers knew that their businesses were dependent on the work and jobs at Easington Colliery. When Easington Colliery closed, in 1993, local retailers followed. One of the dominant themes in oral histories with miners from Easington and their families was the loss of the shops after the pit closed. Interviewees compared the thriving Easington high street when the pit was open with the boarded-up shops when they were interviewed 30 years later. One miner was clear about how quick the transition was: 'The economy up that main street pretty much was thriving, and then it died as soon as the colliery shut. Because, I think it was in about six months of the colliery closing shops were just going to the wall, because nobody had any money to spend then.'[46] Mavis Farrell, an Easington midwife and miner's wife, was explicit about how much had been lost:

> But the whole community collapsed on itself. Like the shops. When the pits were all working you needn't go out of Easington. You could buy anything you wanted in Easington. There were furniture shops, there were shops for everything. ... Shoe shops, everything you could buy in Easington. You didn't need to get on a bus or drive or go anywhere. And then the economy just collapsed, so now all you've got down there is betting shops and take-aways and the Co-op.[47]

The shopkeepers who joined the Save the Easington Area Mines campaign and supported strike relief knew where their interests lay. The defeat of the 1984/1985 strike sealed the fate of many of Easington shops.

More than any other example discussed in this chapter, the impact of the closure of Easington Colliery on retailers lays bare the economic motivation for retailers. However, it also demonstrates that support of retailers cannot be reduced to that economic motivation. This case study shows the importance of the physical location of the retailers; the canteen could use the bakery's cooling oven and the fish and shop's deep friers because of their physical location. It also demonstrates the way that local relationships ensured that retailers were embedded into the relief effort. Everything retailers could offer was used and those involved in the committee asked for what they needed. The physical location, economic imperative and social relationships were intertwined and Easington retailers were a fundamental part of the strike.

Retailers in Easington stated again and again that striking miners would not starve and also that their children would experience Christmas. Hosgood ended his study of retailers' roles in their community in 1914 and argued that by that period, both the moral and the social dynamics of that relationship had begun to change. However, his claim that shopkeepers had an ideology that included a responsibility to working-class communities rings true in this moment of crisis seven decades later.[48] Retailers' commitment was strengthened by the shared local moral economy that saw pit closures as illegitimate, except under specific circumstances.[49] Local retailers in Easington did not operate and did not see their role entirely in market terms. Intertwined economic and social relationships led to their actions in support of the Miners' Strike, as did a moral economy that was grounded in the communities they lived in and an ideology of working-class retail that had its origins in the previous century and had survived significant changes.

Conclusion

This chapter has looked at two case studies, separated by time and place, and used secondary material to suggest that these case studies should not be treated as rare and exceptional. One advantage of the differences in these case studies, in terms of time and location, is that it demonstrates the ways that a strike or lockout can reveal aspects of working-class retail culture that are difficult to access. As well as exploring these two case studies, this chapter is making a methodological argument about the ways historians who study industrial disputes can reveal aspects of working-class life and culture that are usually difficult to access. First, because participants in industrial disputes often commit to remembering them and this means that aspects of working-class life that do not normally survive are documented. Second, because studying how a community functions under stress can reveal aspects that are usually hidden. The support retailers in working-class communities offered during industrial disputes demonstrates the interrelated social and economic relationships, and the moral understanding that framed those relationships.

'They shall not starve' was a key slogan during the Miners' Strike. It was fundamentally a moral framework – asserting people's right to food. Not long after this slogan was displayed in every shop in Easington, Hosgood argued that before the First World War shopkeepers were bound to their community through both social relationships and an ideology of responsibility to their community. The ideology Hosgood discussed is still woven into the retail practices discussed in this chapter, despite the significant change in retailing since 1914. These case studies showed the importance of the physical location of a shop, and the social relationships between shops and customers. The shops described in this chapter did not only exist within the market economy, but were also physically and socially embedded within particular communities. Understanding Hosgood's sense of obligation as a moral economy helps in understanding the actions of retailers to maintain both social and economic relationships when the communities they were part of were under stress.

Acknowledgements

Research for this chapter was part of the 'On Behalf of the People: Work, Community and Class in the British Coal Industry 1947–1994' project funded by the Arts and Humanities Research Council. We would like to thank the many former industry employees and their families who have shared their memories with the project and welcomed us in to their homes. We are also grateful to the many archivists and librarians who provided valuable support.

Notes

[1] C. Hosgood, 'The "pigmies of commerce" and the working-class community: small shopkeepers in England, 1870–1914', *Journal of Social History*, 22:3 (1989), 439–460.

[2] Hosgood, 'Pigmies of commerce', 443.

[3] Z. Lawson, 'Shops, shopkeepers and the working-class community: Preston, 1860–1890', *Transactions of the Historic Society of Lancashire and Cheshire*, 141 (1991), 309–328; S. Phillips and A. Alexander, 'An efficient pursuit? Independent shopkeeping in 1930s Britain', *Enterprise and Society*, 6:2 (2005), 278–304.

[4] A. Alexander and S. Phillips, '"Fair play for the small man": perspectives on the contribution of the independent shopkeeper 1930–c. 1945', *Business History*, 48:1 (2006), 69–89.

[5] A. Portelli, 'The peculiarities of oral history', *History Workshop Journal*, 12:1 (1981), 96–107.

[6] A. Richards, *Miners on Strike: Class Solidarity and Division in Britain* (Oxford: Berg, 1996).

[7] A. Booth and R. Smith, 'The irony of the iron fist: social security and the coal dispute 1984–85', *Journal of Law and Society*, 12:3 (1985), 365–374.

[8] D. Kelliher, *Making Cultures of Solidarity: London and the 1984–5 Miners' Strike* (Abingdon: Routledge, 2021). See also contemporary discussions such as D. Massey and H. Wainwright, 'Beyond the coalfields: the work of the miners' support groups', in H. Benyon (ed), *Digging Deeper: Issues in the Miners' Strike* (London: Verso, 1986), 149–168.

[9] Tony Twibey interview with Grace Millar, 24/04/2019, 'On Behalf of the People' Oral History Project.

10 John Walton interview with Grace Millar, 07/03/2019, 'On Behalf of the People' Oral History Project.

11 Wm Morrison Supermarket PLC, 'Annual report and financial statements for the 53 weeks ending 2 February' (1985), 21, Companies House, https://find-and-update.comp any-information.service.gov.uk/company/00358949/filing-history?page=58 (accessed 08/02/2024).

12 S. Burt and L. Sparks, 'Structural change in grocery retailing in Great Britain: a discount reorientation?, *International Review of Retail, Distribution and Consumer Research*, 4:2 (1994), 195–217; C. Morelli, 'Explaining the growth of British multiple retailing during the golden age: 1976–94', *Environment and Planning A: Economy and Space*, 36:4 (2004), 667–684.

13 G. Shaw, L. Curth and A. Alexander, 'Selling self-service and the supermarket: the Americanisation of food retailing in Britain, 1945–60', *Business History*, 46:4 (2004), 568–582; A. Alexander, S. Phillips and G. Shaw, 'Retail innovation and shopping practices: consumers' reactions to self-service retailing', *Environment and Planning A: Economy and Space*, 40:9 (2008), 2204–2221; Morelli, 'Explaining the growth of British multiple retailing'; G. Shaw and A. Alexander, 'British co-operative societies as retail innovators: interpreting the early stages of the self-service revolution', *Business History*, 50:1 (2008), 62–78; A. Alexander, D. Nell, A. Bailey and G. Shaw, 'The co-creation of a retail innovation: shoppers and the early supermarket in Britain', *Enterprise & Society*, 10:3 (2009), 529–558.

14 S. Bruley, 'The politics of food: gender, family, community and collective feeding in south Wales in the general strike and miners' lockout of 1926', *Twentieth Century British History*, 18:1 (2007), 54–77; S. Thompson, 'That beautiful summer of severe austerity: health, diet and the working-class domestic economy in south Wales in 1926', *The Welsh History Review*, 21:3 (2003), 552–574.

15 S. Bruley, *The Women and Men of 1926: A Social and Gender History of the General Strike and Miners' Lockout of 1926 in South Wales* (Cardiff: University of Wales Press, 2010), 74–75, 139.

16 Hosgood, 'Pigmies of commerce'.

17 E. Eklund, 'The "anxious class"? Storekeepers and the working class in Australia, 1880– 1940', refereed paper, Labour History Conference: Labour & Community, 1999, https:// ro.uow.edu.au/labour1999/proceedings/refereed/11/ (accessed 08/02/2024).

18 A. Taylor, ' "Funny money", hidden charges and repossession: working-class experiences of consumption and credit in the inter-war years', in J. Benson and L. Ugolini (eds), *Cultures of Selling: Perspectives on Consumption and Society since 1700* (Aldershot: Ashgate, 2018), 153–182.

19 A. Green, *British Capital, Antipodean Labour: Working the New Zealand Waterfront, 1915– 1951* (Dunedin: University of Otago Press, 2001); D. Grant, *The Big Blue: Snapshots of the 1951 Waterfront Lockout* (Christchurch: Canterbury University Press, 2004).

20 'The Waterfront Strike Emergency Regulations 1951', *Statutory Regulations 1951* (Government Printing Office, 1951), 65–73.

21 'Hutt Valley Consumers' Co-operative Society Director's Report for Period 30th September, 1950 to 31st March 1951', 8572-01, Dick Scott Papers, Alexander Turnbull Library (ATL).

22 Ian Church interview with Grace Millar, 11/02/2011, Families and the 1951 Waterfront Dispute Oral History Project.

23 Trade Union History Project, 'A Dissenting New Zealand: a Seminar on the Life of Rona Bailey', December 1993, audio recording, OHC-01451, ATL.

24 NZWWU Auckland Branch, Minutes of Special Meeting of Executive & Chairmen of Committees, 16/03/1951, 94-106-11/01, Roth Papers, Alexander Turnbull Library (ATL).

25   Relief Committee, Auckland Branch, NZWWU, 'Report', 1951, 94-106-11/06, Herbert Roth Papers, ATL.

26   'Retiring Presidential Address', New Zealand Master Grocers Federation Annual Conference, 1951, MSY-5085, National Association of Retail Grocers and Supermarkets of New Zealand Inc., Records, ATL.

27   Maureen Martin interview with Liam Martin, September 1999, Transcript, OHColl-0458/1, ATL.

28   Detective D.S. Paterson, 'Relative to NZ Waterfront Dispute, February–March 1951', 29/03/1951, (R10074981), ADMO-21007-W5595-25/9/20/12, Part 1, Restricted Files, Archives New Zealand.

29   'Hutt Valley Consumers' Co-operative Society Director's Report for Period 30th September, 1950 to 31st March 1951', 8572-01, Scott Papers, ATL.

30   Kevin Ford interview with Grace Millar, 13/03/2011, Families and the 1951 Waterfront Dispute Oral History Project.

31   Maureen Martin, interview.

32   Maureen Martin, interview.

33   E.P. Thompson, 'The moral economy of the English crowd in the eighteenth century', *Past & Present*, 50 (1971), 76–136.

34   E.P. Thompson, *Customs in Common* (London: Merlin, 1991), 340.

35   N. Götz, ' "Moral economy" its conceptual history and analytical prospects' *Journal of Global Ethics*, 11:2 (2015), 147–162.

36   N. Potamianos, 'Do shopkeepers have their own moral economy? Profiteering, unfair competition and the black market in Greece, 1916–1945', *Social History*, 47:1 (2022), 35–59.

37   P. Hetherington, 'The town behind them', *The Guardian*, [1984], Newspaper clipping, Heather Wood Papers, 2009–133 (a), BA.

38   Heather Wood interview with Grace Millar, 07/02/2019, 'On Behalf of the People' Oral History Project.

39   Heather Wood, interview.

40   Heather Wood, interview.

41   Heather Wood, interview.

42   Heather Wood, interview.

43   S.E.A.M. Miners Relief, Summary of Accounts, Heather Wood Papers, 2009–133 (a), Beamish, the Living Museum of the North, Archives (BA).

44   Heather Wood, interview.

45   Easington Chamber of Trade to 'Girls', [1985], Heather Wood Papers, 2009–132 (b), BA.

46   Ian Hanson interview with Grace Millar, 25 April 2019, 'On Behalf of the People' Oral History Project.

47   Mavis Farrell interview with Grace Millar, 19 June 2019, 'On Behalf of the People' Oral History Project.

48   Hosgood, 'Pigmies of Commerce'.

49   For a discussion of moral economy and pit closures see J. Phillips, 'Deindustrialization and the moral economy of the Scottish coalfields, 1947 to 1991', *International Labor and Working-Class History*, 84 (2013), 99–115; E. Gibbs, 'The moral economy of the Scottish coalfields: managing deindustrialization under nationalization c. 1947–1983', *Enterprise & Society*, 19:1 (2018), 124–152; A. Perchard and J. Phillips, 'Transgressing the moral economy: Wheelerism and management of the nationalised coal industry in Scotland', *Contemporary British History*, 25:3 (2011), 387–405.

13

Understanding the 'Gift' in the Post-Economic Downturn Charity Shop

Triona Fitton

Introduction

The modern British charity shop has served many purposes. For some, it has been a place of work or a volunteering opportunity. For others, a recycling hub for offloading unwanted goods, a community nexus for sharing chit-chat, or a low-cost shopping site. The shops have also provided a lucrative fundraising revenue stream for charitable organizations and a means of promoting the charity's brand on the high street. Charity shops have been a core element of everyday social life for many people – not only those who clean, organize and sell items, but also for those who use the shops out of necessity or in the search for sartorial individuality. These shops have existed in multiple incarnations, from temporary vendors set up within churches or community buildings, to nationwide chains of multiple stores, causing Suzanne Horne to describe them as retail in an 'untraditional distributive form'.[1]

While research has explored the forms charity shops take around the world, as discussed in the opening chapter, the unique and colourful identity of the British high street charity shop, with its unique and colourful identity as a high street staple, is perhaps the most widely researched of all.[2] Selling goods for a charitable purpose in a relatively formal shop setting is a staple of the British high street, most often found in city centres and their backstreets rather than in suburbs, and distinct from the large airport-hangar-style warehouses favoured by comparative charitable retail ventures in countries like the United States in terms of their size and positionality. British charity shops are often small (rarely larger than two rooms) and closely in tune with their surrounding community in terms of stocked goods, charitable purpose and volunteer cohort. As a result, they offer a compelling insight into how local communities navigate broader social changes, and how the shops themselves are required to evolve and respond to such change.[3]

The evolution of the British charity shop has been considered by Gosling in Chapter 8 and the limits of its international adoption addressed by Field in Chapter 9. This chapter adds to our historical understanding of British charity shops by focusing on a recent period of societal upheaval. I examine the use of terminology of the 'gift' within the context of the post-economic downturn charity shop. Using ethnographic research findings from a British charity shop, I explore how the idea of the charitable gift was subverted, primarily by the power and influence of the state and private businesses, through two national initiatives within charity shops that were primarily executed and negotiated at the local shop-floor level. Global economic crises can be most interesting when examined in terms of the minutiae of their impacts: the mundane interactions and exchanges that take place day in, day out. Under wider influences, these interactions can take on new meanings, and even the language used to define them can become problematic.

The ethnographic research undertaken consisted of six months of participant observation and interviews with shop workers in a British charity shop that raised funds for a national children's charity. This took place in 2010, as these two initiatives – Retail Gift Aid and Retail Gift in Kind – were playing out in what was at the time the charity's highest earning shop. The shop was in Manchester's bustling city centre, near a railway station that serves as an important cross-country transport hub. When the research took place, the site was representative of the 'demise of the high street'.[4] Customary high street chain shops closed down and left vacant spaces that became occupied by pawn brokers, cash-for-gold shops, betting shops – as well as charity shops. This change was identified across the United Kingdom, particularly in places with high levels of deprivation, after the economic crash of 2008. Subsequent socioeconomic change at the macro level spurred a process of gentrification in Manchester city centre and 'the production of urban space for progressively more affluent users'.[5] The charity shop that was studied has long since been swallowed up by chain coffee shops and commuter eateries, along with the greasy spoon café and betting shops that formerly surrounded it. This change can be seen in its infancy in the findings of this research, in the intrinsic co-dependency of public, private and charitable services.

The example of these local changes and specific developments in the practice of charity retailing can therefore be viewed in a wider frame through the impact the fluctuating global economy has had on the functions, identity and processes of the traditional British charity shop. In this way, the chapter uses micro-level analysis (ethnography) to understand meso (the shop and its parent charity) and macro (global economic context) changes to charity retail in the 21st century.

Charity shop economics, circa 1990–2010

Researchers first identified the influence of global economic trends upon the British charity shop in the 1990s, when an extended period of affluence that began in the 1980s served to boost the supply of surplus used items available to charity shops.[6] Over the course of a decade, the number of charity shops in the United Kingdom almost doubled from circa 3,200 in 1990 to 6,220 in 2002.[7]

Academic interest in charity retail mirrored this increase. Some of the earliest work specifically on charity retail was undertaken by Suzanne Horne and Adelina Broadbridge, who began exploring a classification of charity shops for a working paper in 1993. At this point, there had not been a great deal of research into charity shops, and much of their data was informed by statistics gathered from retail sector surveys and information from newspaper articles. Many other theorists refer to Horne and Broadbridge's early work as indicative of the period of growth and evolution charity shops experienced, reflecting their responsiveness to national and global socioeconomic change.[8]

Charity shop economics were scrutinized in the fields of retail management and non-profit organization theory, representing the development of charity from being seen as outmoded, to something modern, adaptive and potentially profitable that responded to changes in the economic climate. By becoming dynamic and responsive in a way that mimicked for-profit retailers, charity shops experienced increased competition; between themselves, and increasingly with budget retailers such as Primark and Poundstretcher. As a result, charity shops had to work harder to raise funds, sometimes by dropping prices, or by aesthetic investments such as shop-floor revamps.[9]

The global economic recession in the late 2000s resulted in a period of generalized upheaval, risk and rapid change. There was a sense of increased trepidation and cynicism about many areas of social life. The full force of the economic downturn was felt both on the traditional British high street, and in the public perception of charities and their role within society. Their practices were scrutinized heavily in subsequent years.[10] Negative public attitudes towards charities grew, fuelled by reports of sky-high charity executive pay packets, soaring operational costs, the involvement of many charities in widely criticized government workfare schemes, the prevalence of aggressive street fundraising, and a general lack of transparency in how charitable funds were being spent. Public concerns about the British charity sector were exacerbated by austerity measures brought in by the then newly elected Conservative-Liberal Democrat coalition government: in particular their political ideology of a Big Society which emphasized the importance of individual voluntary action to address social issues.

Despite the controversies, this was a momentous time for charity retail in Britain, as other high street outlets went bust and space emerged for a reimagined form of second-hand retail. Globally, the trajectory for the retail environment was not promising: job losses, a rising cost of living and an increase in personal debt converged to affect consumer spending, alongside the continued growth of online shopping impacting upon physical retail stores' profits. Formerly well-performing shops struggled, and popular British retail chains such as Woolworths and British Home Stores failed to survive the period. However, shops that were able to adapt to the crisis ended up benefiting from the economic downturn.[11] Charity shops had been previously lauded for emerging unscathed from periods of recession in the 1980s, and many of them moved into the vacant high street spaces provided by the closure of chain stores during this time.[12] Post-2008, retail markets were depressed because the average British citizen was 'trading down, staying home, eating in, and "making do"',[13] and charity shops were thriving. Pamela Nickel paraphrased *The Economist* in stating that while austerity was in, so also was thrift, as shoppers gravitated towards second-hand chic as a style choice as well as a necessity.[14]

The resilience of the charity shop sector in this period can be partly attributed to the savvy way in which they adapted to serve local communities and help out suffering businesses. Cross-sectoral partnerships between charity and the for-profit sector began to emerge, partially to alleviate the burden of unsold stock as high street stores struggled to shift goods. Carrigan and de Pelsmacker described a partnership between Oxfam and Marks & Spencer (M&S) where clothing donors to Oxfam stores received a £5 M&S voucher, providing their donation contained clothing with M&S labels. The scheme increased donations to Oxfam at a time when charity shops were struggling for donations, as frugal former donors sought to make extra money from unwanted items via car boot sales or eBay. It resulted in £1.7 million in extra sales for the charity.[15]

Cross-sectoral partnerships at the meso-level were one way charity retail adapted and evolved to the post-recession economic landscape. However, partnerships were not only built between businesses and charities. The state has also played a significant role in charity retail success, even prior to the global economic crash. Charity shops received a statutory 80 per cent rate relief, which could be upped to 100 per cent at the discretion of local councils.[16] They also were not required to pay Value Added Tax (VAT) on goods sold. Charity shops in Britain, much like the wider charity sector, operated co-dependently with government.

The rest of this chapter will look in detail at two schemes that illustrate these cross-sectoral partnerships in the charity shop, and the bearing they had upon the shop's identity at a point when the impacts of the global financial crisis were acutely felt.

Retail Gift Aid

Gift Aid – a UK government scheme that tops up donations to charity – has been around since the 1990 Finance Act, and initially it applied to cash donations only. By completing a Gift Aid declaration, a charity could claim back the basic rate of tax paid: 25p for every £1 donated.[17] Gift Aid was worth over £1 billion to UK charities in 2009/2010.[18] Following an amendment to the Finance Act in 2006, charity shops were also able to claim Gift Aid by selling second-hand goods as an agent on behalf of the individual. The donor completes a form agreeing to donate the proceeds from the sale, plus the additional Gift Aid amount earned from it, in a process known legally as Retail Gift Aid (henceforth Gift Aid).[19]

Gift Aid was generally embedded within other processes that indicated the increased professionalization of charity retail. For instance, the circulation of stock between stores was only possible for charity shops that had gone through a phase of professionalizing and expanded into a chain. The shop in this study was part of a chain of charity shops for a large national children's charity, and therefore regularly circulated unsold stock. It also had the infrastructure to offer Gift Aid as it had organized and formalized the transactional process of selling goods and the donation and sorting process too. Items were tagged with different labels to enable both prices and subsequent Gift Aid donations to be tracked.

In the shop processes observed in this ethnography, this process began at the point of the donation, when the donor was asked if they would like to Gift Aid their donation. If they agreed, they were given a form to complete with their details, which confirmed that the shop could act as an agent in the sale of their donations. It also confirmed that the donor was a UK earner and taxpayer, as this additional amount would be claimed as a taxable deduction. This form was then attached to the bag of donations; a small card was detached from the top and given to the donor. This allowed them to Gift Aid donations again and again without repeatedly providing their details, thus simplifying future Gift Aid transactions. The card, the form and donated items were then tagged with the same unique identifying number, meaning sales and Gift Aid earned could be traced back to the individual, and the total amount raised including Gift Aid could be calculated. For the donor, the card both resembled and to some extent operated as a loyalty card, encouraging them to donate items again, mimicking for-profit retailers. For the charity, the card represented an additional bonus donation that came from the state, and thus the British taxpayer.

In the store, small green Gift Aid stickers adhered to the price tags were the only signifiers of this additional gift of donation top-ups by the state. The stickers remained on items that were circulated from other shops through stock rotation, when all other labels were replaced and items frequently re-priced according to the average unit price for that particular shop. Therefore the Gift Aid system superseded localized shop pricing systems, which tended to be more responsive to the needs of their customer base.

Gift Aid was not only a network that bridged state tax relief and the donor, it also related to an increased profit orientation in charities at the meso-level, and the professional ambitions of those running the shop. Consider this comment by the shop manager Maria, a paid employee, on the researcher's first day of volunteering in the shop: "We need to ask people who donate if they will Gift Aid their items when they give them to us. This is important, it can make me an extra £15–£20 grand per year if they do!" (Fieldnotes, 1 February 2010). Note the personal pronoun 'me' when Maria mentioned how much money the system can make. Gift Aid served as a tool to enhance the shop's earnings, but also the manager's own success in reaching her sales targets – again mimicking the for-profit sector. The terminology of the gift has been mobilized in relation to the pursuit of capital for the benefit of the individual, which is privileged over the charitable cause, its beneficiaries, or the needs of the local community. This is an identified tension of any gift relationship due to the intersection of market forces and personal relations.[20] In this instance, it shows the adaptive and subversive nature of how gift language is applied within the charity retail space.

The donors who completed the forms were also subject to this individualizing process. Their personal information was submitted into a database and the charity informed the donor how much money they had earned for the children's charity by sending letters headed 'Thank you for helping us to help them'.[21] An imaginary link was constructed between the donor and the beneficiary group, encouraging donors to feel they are participating in wider communal social action alongside the charity.

Although framed by the charity as a letter of thanks to donors, the letter was actually a legal requirement. The small print stated that the donor had the choice to donate the money and Gift Aid percentage or claim it back from the charity.[22] It also performed a secondary role as a marketing technique. The letter served to remind the donor of their gift and its impact, with an aim of inciting them to donate goods more regularly using their Gift Aid card. These letters of thanks often included instructions on easier ways to donate, including ways to arrange doorstep donation pick-ups from the donor's home.

Often, the donation figures stated on these letters were inaccurate. Despite efforts to streamline the process, the system of collecting Gift Aid in store was fallible and open to manipulation. The fieldnotes of this ethnography note instances of the same Gift Aid stickers being recorded into the system more than once, and of fallen stickers being picked up off the floor and stuck onto random items. Since it was the number on the sticker, and not the item itself, that was tracked on the system, subversions of the Gift Aid process were common:

> I bring some donations in to the shop … [Maria] asks me "Do you have your Gift Aid card?" [I do not have one as I am not working and therefore not a taxpayer].
>
> Maria says "It's OK. I have to get the form for these [she gestures to a bag of books on the side that another customer has just donated with Gift Aid] so I will just put those stickers on yours too". (Fieldnotes, 12 March 2010)

The act of using an unknown donor's Gift Aid status to earn additional profits improperly raised the question of the charity shop's moral responsibility in relation to the data they held about their donors. Misappropriation of this data was commonplace. The blithe way in which an anonymous donor's taxable status was exploited to claim additional Gift Aid on items donated by non-taxpayers meant that, like most bureaucratic systems, the Gift Aid process was open to contravention, and was manipulated through the contrived sense of communal identity that the charity fostered. This manipulation happened at the micro-level, in exchanges between local actors (such as shop volunteers and paid staff) who were responding in a relatively normative way to bureaucracy, and to broader endogenous and exogenous pressures upon the charity retail sector.

The Gift Aid process also removed one of the key appeals of charity shop donation: the distancing of an item from the individual when it is given away.[23] Historically, charity shop donations preserved the anonymity of the donor; once an item was donated, it could no longer be traced back to you.[24] However, Gift Aid donors were registered on a system where every penny earned on every item they donated was recorded and monitored. As the earlier excerpt illustrates, once the form was completed the donor had no knowledge of or control over what their Gift Aid tax relief was being used for. The assumption that charity was synonymous with accountability and acting in the public interest was taken for granted.[25] This was in spite of the profit-maximizing incentives that gained prominence as charity shops became gradually more professionalized and responded to the 2008 financial crisis.[26] Charity shops carry with them the symbolic power of charity as something that is regarded as unquestionably good, and acting in the interests of the general community.[27] The improper use of personal data and manipulation of tax systems to make money do not sit comfortably with this perception.

While Gift Aid capitalized on state support and databases of donors to maximize profits, the second case study of the 'Gift' in the post-downturn charity shop describes another profit-maximizing strategy that collected goods from the private sector and created a database of business donors: Retail Gift in Kind.

Retail Gifts in Kind

A Gift in Kind is any non-monetary donation that benefits an institution or an individual. Academics have discussed some examples of these donations, such as book collections donated to academic libraries, and donations of art heirlooms, antiques and furniture to universities.[28] Charity shop donations as a form of Gift in Kind have not been academically explored. In this study, Retail Gifts in Kind (henceforth Gift-in-Kind) referred to large donations of new stock from for-profit companies. In the United States, these kinds of non-monetary donations have been described as 'product philanthropy'.[29]

Gift-in-Kind deviated from the traditional heterogeneous stock of charity shops, in that they were often mass donations of similar items. This meant stock could be more rationally organized, distributed, monitored and sold. These large donations had significant impacts upon the stock make-up of the shop. Customers could select from different sizes and colours of the same item. Items were usually brand new, often with labels from the for-profit retailer still attached, occasionally from expensive brands. There were frequently more than one of the same item, reducing the opportunity for sourcing unique items (a hallmark of charity shops).[30] This homogeneity of stock resulted in a homogeneity of prices, and items were often labelled at a lower price to that on the original price tag. Gift-in-Kind items were clearly labelled in blue, distinguishing them from individual donations from the general public, which were labelled in purple. They were also recorded under a separate category on the itemized till.

Like Gift Aid, the Gift-in-Kind process was a professionally managed system that operated throughout the shop network. A Gift-in-Kind Account Manager, Mike, worked in an office above the shop with two administrative employees who developed and sustained Gift-in-Kind links with local businesses. Mike preferred to treat the management of this process as a commercial endeavour, something he illustrated by employing business language during his interview (he spoke of stock, profits, growth, margin and budgets). Despite having the word 'gift' in his job title, the relationships Mike was in charge of were purely transactional. A disconnect between acts of charity and the process of maintaining lucrative Gift-in-Kind networks was evident:

'We approach businesses to donate stock … it's almost like, I'm a supplier that [the charity] use to get stock, and it's almost like the shops are our customer. … The charity, touchy-feely end is at the other end of the spectrum … it's a good sentiment, but, it doesn't pay the bills.' (Interview with Mike, 21 April 2010)

The shop was aiming towards stocking 80 per cent Gift-in-Kind leaving only 20 per cent individually donated stock. This benchmark was being tested in the shop as it was the highest-earning shop in the charity's chain, and Gift-in-Kind played an important role in the day-to-day operations. Donations came regularly, usually several times a week, from large retailers. These included supermarket chains (Asda, Sainsbury's and Tesco gave large clothing donations), popular fashion outlets from the time (Topshop, Miss Selfridge, Burton and Zara all donated clothes), department stores (Debenhams donated bedding), sports brands (Bench donated jackets) and also occasionally independent retailers who sold online or on market stalls (everything from phone cases to brand new lingerie). Every time a company gave a Gift-in-Kind, the contact was recorded as a donor in the Gift-in-Kind spreadsheets by Mike's administrative team, and then approached at intervals to see if, as Mike stated, they needed any more stock 'taken off their hands'.

The retailers involved participated in these partnerships through regularly donating, but they did not wholly encourage visible association between the business and the charity. The charity shop was required to arbitrate the image of the donor brand or company within their shop space. This role of arbitration sometimes included altering Gift-in-Kind goods through the removal or defacement of labels, to ensure the business would not suffer monetary losses through customers attempting to return charity shop purchases to the original store. At a point in time when many retailers were going bust, this sensitivity was acute. Mike explained that charity shops ought to 'flaunt' Gift-in-Kind stock 'a bit', but emphasized the importance of doing so subtly. He reasoned that this was due to the 'negative connotations' charity shops hold for some: their historical association with lower social status and as a site populated by the disadvantaged or socially excluded.[31]

'With the Bench stock … you're relying on people paying £120 for that brand and that lifestyle … when we got it, we splashed it everywhere, and we probably de-valued their brand, I think, they got a lot of negative feedback from their legitimate customers, their retail customers, you know, the JJBs [a large sporting retailer]. … The story we were told is, the retail manager's got off the train … came down, saw obviously Bench all over the window, half the price of current season stock. Obviously, he's trying to achieve his targets, his objectives. They pretty much said that they won't be able to donate again.' (Interview with Mike, 21 April 2010)

Despite co-operative relations with businesses, the charity shops' association with the material constraints of poverty renders it as an abject space, somewhere that is risky for brands to associate with.[32] In referring to for-profit shops that sell Bench items as Bench's 'legitimate customers', Mike's reflection categorized charity shops as illegitimate, as if these items were attained unlawfully or are something to be hidden or disguised. Procedures such as the removal or defacing of the original labels in clothes reinforced the impression that brands were keen to distance themselves from where their items ended up. Due to these uncertainties, Gift-in-Kind relations with companies remained relatively ad hoc and vulnerable to being severed at any time due to the way the gift relationship interacted with market forces.

The abject nature of the charity shop space was compounded by another type of donation that was labelled, and classified on the till, as a Gift-in-Kind, however was not sourced from a commercial retailer. These gifts were from state sources – police evidence, stolen goods and the products of prison labour:

[The assistant manager, Emily] brings down a couple of clear plastic bags, inside are brown police evidence bags, some of them still inscribed with the details of who they were seized from. We go through it all, Emily tells me "Watch out. Some of this stuff might have blood on it. Because sometimes it's removed from people who have been in a fight or whatever." (Fieldnotes, 26 March 2010)

Emily warned the researcher about the riskiness, or liminality, of these items due to their association with an anonymous, criminalized *other*.[33] However, once they were taken from the bags, checked over, cleaned up and tagged like other Gifts-in-Kind, the taboo was lifted and these goods took on a new life with the customer who purchased them. The cleansing of prior meaning and creation of new meaning and purpose – or 'revalorising' – of second-hand goods has been widely theorized about, with particular reference to the 'moral' role of the shops in removing the negative connotations an item may have picked up.[34] Charity shop processes cleansed ambiguous items, concealing their association with illegal activities or marginalized individuals, just as they protected a corporate brand's reputation by cutting a label out of a jacket before selling it.

Invisible labour was involved in processing these liminal Gifts-in-Kind, but who undertook the labour in producing them was also not made explicit. For example, at one point during a shift, the researcher noticed the dump bins next to the till were filled with hand-sewn cloth tote bags, labelled with a sign that read 'Bags For Life'. These were priced relatively cheaply and were also recorded on the till as Gift–in–Kind:

> They are all mismatched, made from various swatches of materials. When I ask Emily about them, she says "Oh, we get them from the prison." I ask her to elaborate and she says, "They make them for us. At the women's prison. I guess it's something to keep them occupied and to fill up their day." (Fieldnotes, 19 April 2010)

As in the previous example, the past life of the item was completely hidden from the customer. There is a dark irony in the fact that prison labour produced something that was then labelled as a Bag For Life – the only subtle inference to the carceral origins of the item. Bags For Life, as with the Gift Aid loyalty cards mentioned previously, originated from the for-profit retail sector. However, the charity shop subverts the meaning of the terminology and plays with customers' normative assumptions of what they expect to encounter within a retail space.

The Gift-in-Kind system emphasized the role charity shops played in repurposing costly waste by-products of consumer society.[35] For-profit companies provided Gifts-in-Kind so readily because it was an easy and cost-free means of disposal of unsellable stock, and the company can reclaim any VAT they paid on goods they did not go on to sell. As a result, companies' Gift-in-Kind donations can be understood as merely a useful business deal, as opposed to a charitable act, or a gift. Items that were labelled as Gift-in-Kind, but originated from the criminal justice system, also enabled shop staff to achieve their high Gift-in-Kind targets. Gift-in-Kind therefore comprised of individualistic processes that disguised the origins and history of an item, rejuvenating it for future sale.

The charity shop 'gift': a subversive moral economy

At the heart of our understanding of gifts is the relationship between giver and recipient. Normatively, we equate gift giving with kindness or generosity – however social theorists understand the process to be something more than that. A 'gift' is regarded as being a process of exchange within non-market relations, a formal pretence according to the anthropologist Marcel Mauss, that it is fundamentally obligatory to return.[36] Gifts tend to be imbued with multiple meanings, and hold within them a history of the relationship between giver and receiver, as well as the identity of the giver and recipient themselves; in this sense they are unique, non-fungible and often irreplaceable.[37] For example, a jumper given by a mother to her daughter before she goes away to university is not the same as one purchased by the daughter for herself; alongside its practical utility it also represents maternal care, family protectiveness and security, perhaps a sense of loss, the continuation of the relationship beyond this disjuncture. This means that the word 'gift' can serve to rebrand a commodity and take it from being generic to exceptional. There is a moral imperative within a gift relationship, meaning we habitually treat these items differently to those that are purchased simply as commodities.

This case study involved two instances of 'gifts' that relied upon the appeal of that moral imperative, while being somewhat removed from the personal (and in the case of Gift-in-Kind from the state, deliberately eradicating it). These illustrations support Mauss' assertion that the gift relationship is dependent upon obligation and reciprocation. Donors receive something in return for their donations, whether a thank you letter and a warm glow (Gift Aid), a VAT rebate and reduced disposal costs, or the cleansing of tainted items gleaned from the criminal justice system (Gift-in-Kind). The explorations in this chapter also support theorists such as Blau, Levi-Strauss, Emerson, Gouldner and Bourdieu, who argued that gift giving is governed predominantly by rational self-interest.[38] These perspectives can be explored further by understanding the participation in these exchanges as individualized rather than communal – thus raising questions about the community-centric role charity shops are expected to play on the British high street, a role that would be presumed to be ever-more important during a period of post-recession austerity.

The prior section demonstrated how Gift Aid and Gift-in-Kind were beneficial for both the donor and the shop worker – the actual recipient of the charitable gift (the beneficiaries) for this particular charity were mostly absent in the relationship. This echoes major gift fundraising, where beneficiaries become objects within the gift relationship rather than participants.[39] Reciprocity in gift relationships is often not related to charitability, empathy, kindness or care, but is more a response to self-culture and the increased individualization of society during times of increased uncertainty and risk.[40] The detached and bureaucratic way that donations were solicited, recorded in databases and managed in the Gift Aid database, linking the individual back to the monetary value of their donations, was unprecedented in charity retail history. David Cheal describes a characteristic of gifts in general: that they operate as demonstrations of 'continued attachment'.[41] We give presents annually at Christmas or on birthdays to indicate our ongoing relationship with our loved ones. The Gift Aid and Gift-in-Kind databases represent ongoing relationships in an institutionalized form. They operated to encourage reciprocity and remind donors of their obligation to give, either through thank you letters, the Gift Aid loyalty card, or through solicitation by the Gift-in-Kind team, mimicking the way gifts are returned in Mauss' conceptualization. They also created and sustained an imagined, disparate, digital community of businesses and individuals that stretched beyond the local.

Charity shops have always maximized the potential of the leftovers of consumerism by reviving waste, in what O'Brien describes as the 'alchemist's dream' of turning useless products into gold.[42] Theories of object histories or 'cultural biographies' of things here move away from the intriguing individual backstories of traditional second-hand donations to homogeneous mass gifts that deal with the issue of unsold stock and erase the negative associations that are their by-product.[43] By understanding Gift-in-Kind as an opportunity for the reuse of otherwise waste goods at a time of economic crisis, the 21st-century British charity shop can be seen as an important redemptive space. The tendency for these leftovers of capitalism to be hidden out of sight in the charity shop space highlights the discomfort we feel with the amount of waste our system produces. Charity shop donating has previously been found to make people feel better about their own consumerism.[44] Gift-in-Kind merely removed the middle-man.

The same can be said of the unusual Gifts-in-Kind that were donated by the police or were the products of prison labour: these items lost their moral ambiguity when they were reclassified as Gift-in-Kind alongside other shiny new Gift-in-Kind donations. This pursuit of moral redemption holds similarities to the waste populations of Darkest England workshops discussed by Ruth McDonald in Chapter 6 of this volume, or Lucy Morris' discussion of the early charity ethos of religious reformation.[45] Transformative rituals of cleaning and relabelling serve to distance an item from its marginal roots. Importantly, many of these transformations, manipulations and adaptations in the Gift Aid and Gift-in-Kind processes happened behind the scenes, protecting customers and wider society from danger and risk. In doing so, they also shield the public from the uncomfortable reality that the charitable gift relationship obscures: a reality of predatory global capitalism, over-consumption, tax manipulation, waste and deviance.

What has emerged from this micro-examination of 'gift' terminology is a subversive moral economy of charity retail, based broadly on E.P. Thompson's, and David Cheal's, concept of moral economies in mass societies.[46] The ultimate aim of a moral economy is the obligation to provide assistance to your local community in some form, and it operates alongside political and exchange economies as a means of assuring order and balance. What is distinct about the moral economy in this setting is that the institutionalization of social ties (or professionalization processes that encompass Gift Aid and Gift-in-Kind) impacted upon the reliability of those ties, as was seen in manager Maria's manipulation of the Gift Aid system. The databasing of both Gift Aid and Gift-in-Kind donors provoked transgressions that revealed the 'irrationality of rationality' in charity shops. Efforts to rationalize, control and monitor the gift relationship had subtle perverse and counterintuitive effects.[47] These processes aimed to improve fundraising, but at the risk of destabilizing local ties, disrupting trust and damaging perceptions of what charity is. Nevertheless, enduring relationships – not capital – always lie at the heart of gift economies.[48]

Even prior to the economic downturn, charities were keen to take part in intersectoral co-operation with business. Due to the trust charities tend to engender within a local community, they provided a natural space for these kinds of 'helpful partnerships' to thrive.[49] With government support offering a degree of financial stability to charities in Britain, and the subsequent impact of the recession and austerity policies, it is evident why the public, private and charity sector invested so heavily in gift relationships. However, the charity retail environment is heterogeneous and so was participation in these formalized gift schemes. Gift Aid and Gift-in-Kind were mostly limited to larger charity shop chains, due to the difficulty and cost of universal implementation.[50] They provided an avenue for increasing charity revenue through increasing quantity and quality of stock donations. This increased the opportunities for shop workers to hit targets and encourage repeat donations, but only for stores that were sufficiently professionalized in their practices. Professionalization of charity shops is not a universal process. Many shops for smaller, local charities were left behind, only able to engage with Gift-in-Kind in an ad hoc way, and not able to implement Gift Aid at all. These changes in charity retail represented a bifurcation of charity shop forms and the processes they were able to engage with in order to make money, a full exploration of which is beyond the scope of this chapter. However, these processes caused a Matthew Effect within charity retail, whereby advantage begets advantage.[51] This enabled larger charities with chains of shops to raise more funds, while smaller charities raise less. Smaller charities with one-off shops tend to be focused upon local causes, but were not afforded the same opportunities to form gift relationships as national chains of shops. These national chains, with their highly professionalized operations, rely on individualization among staff and other mimicry of the for-profit sector.

The wording of the schemes studied here is important; as gifts are a means of asserting power within the system of capitalism.[52] The analysis in this chapter suggests that the gift described by these two processes proved mutually beneficial to the charity and to first-sector businesses, while utilizing the flexibility of state tax allowances to maximize the money earned. Therefore power remained exactly where it was before – situated with those who already own the means within the capitalist system. The loss was on the behalf of the taxpayer, who indirectly footed the bill for the co-operations between charity and businesses. Also losing out were nearby small businesses such as second-hand junk shops and pawn shops, whose positions as the detritivores of capitalist surplus were threatened by the ubiquity of charity retail – another side effect of post-recession charity shops on their local community.[53]

Conclusion

The case study examples of Gift Aid and Gift-in-Kind have been highlighted here as indicative of the wider sectoral networks that charity shops have become increasingly reliant upon. This chapter offers a reassessment of the claims of authors writing before the downturn that the charity sector operates relatively independently of governmental or corporate interests.[54] Instead, relationships between charities and private firms have led to the suggestion that charities are merely for-profits in disguise, particularly at times when the competition for resources becomes more severe.[55] These two applications of the terminology of gifts on the shop floor of this Manchester charity shop further complicate this assertion of independence when we reflect upon the site today. A city-wide project to rejuvenate run-down central shopping sites erased all evidence of this shop and replaced it with a gleaming, generic sandwich shop owned by a US company. The aims of Gift Aid and Gift-in-Kind to improve profits at a local level, therefore, were unsuccessful. Nevertheless, the parent charity continues to thrive and operate many hundreds of national shops.

This chapter demonstrates that local, micro-level subversion of moral economies can become naturalized as part of social routines, such as shopping and donating. This operates hand-in-hand with our common sense understanding of what a gift is. The people who worked in the charity shop negotiated gift relationships and subverted the moral economy in order to retain the shop's position on the high street during a period of severe macro-societal flux. As is noted in Cheal's work, gift relations are 'powerfully affected by economic and demographic change, and by the hopes and fears of ordinary people faced with personal crises'.[56] The gift as observed in this shop in the early 2010s was, at least in part, governed by global market forces, businesses and the state, rather than a sense of local solidarity, empathy or charitable care.

Acknowledgements

The author would like to thank the editors and other authors of this volume for their helpful feedback, and all of the participants from the original 2010 research project.

Notes

[1] S. Horne, 'Charity shops in the UK', *International Journal of Retail & Distribution Management*, 26:4 (1998), 155.

[2] M. Mitchell, R. Montgomery and D. Rauch, 'Toward an understanding of thrift store donors', *International Journal of Nonprofit and Voluntary Sector Marketing*, 14:3 (2009), 255–269; D. Wodon, N. Wodon and Q. Wodon, 'Opening a new nonprofit thrift store: performance, competition, pricing, and financial sustainability', *MPRA Paper*, 56943 (2013), https://mpra.ub.uni-muenchen.de/56943/1/MPRA_paper_56943.pdf

(accessed 13/02/2024); M. Mitchell and R. Montogomery, 'An examination of thrift store shoppers', *The Marketing Management Journal*, 20:2 (2010), 94–107; P. Nickel, 'Thrift shop philanthropy', *Cultural Politics*, 12:2 (2016), 173–189; R. Shearer and K. Carpentier, 'Determining the optimal donation acceptance policy for nonprofit stores', *Nonprofit Management and Leadership*, 26:1 (2015), 59–71; A. Podkalicka and J. Meese, ' "Twin transformations": the Salvation Army's charity shops and the recreating of material and social value', *European Journal of Cultural Studies*, 15:6 (2012), 721–735; S. Horne and A. Maddrell, *Charity Shops: Retailing, Consumption and Society* (London: Routledge, 2002); F. Larsen, 'Valuation in action: ethnography of an American thrift store', *Business History*, 61:1 (2019), 155–171; J. Le Zotte, ' "Not charity, but a chance": philanthropic capitalism and the rise of American thrift stores, 1894–1930', *The New England Quarterly*, 86:2 (2013), 169–195.

3   See Horne, 'Charity shops in the UK', 155–161; S. Horne, 'The charity shop: purpose and change', *International Journal of Nonprofit and Voluntary Sector Marketing*, 5:2 (2000): 113–124; N. Gregson, L. Crewe and K. Brooks, 'Discourse, displacement, and retail practice: some pointers from the charity retail project', *Environment and Planning A*, 34:9 (2002), 1661–1683; S. Horne and A. Maddrell, *Charity Shops: Retailing, Consumption and Society* (London: Routledge, 2003).

4   P. Hubbard, *The Battle for the Highstreet* (London: Palgrave Macmillan, 2017).

5   J. Hackworth, 'Postrecession gentrification in New York City', *Urban Affairs Review*, 37:6 (2002), 815.

6   E. Parsons, 'Charity retail: past, present and future', *International Journal of Retail & Distribution Management*, 30:12 (2002), 586–594.

7   A. Broadbridge and E. Parsons, 'Still serving the community? The professionalisation of the UK charity retail sector', *International Journal of Retail & Distribution Management*, 31:8 (2003), 418–427.

8   J. Brace-Govan and I. Binay, 'Consumption of disposed goods for moral identities: a nexus of organization, place, things and consumers', *Journal of Consumer Behaviour*, 9 (2010), 69–82; E. Parsons, 'Charity retailing in the UK: a typology', *The Journal of Retailing and Consumer Services*, 11:1 (2004), 31–40; Broadbridge and Parsons, 'Still serving the community?'; A. Broadbridge and E. Parsons, 'Trading up in charity retailing: managing in a climate of change', *The Institute of Retail Studies Working Paper Series*, 2:2 (2002), 1–22; Horne, 'The charity shop'; Horne, 'Charity shops in the UK'.

9   N. Gregson, K. Brooks and L. Crewe, 'Discourse, displacement and retail practise: some pointers from the charity retail project', *Environment and Planning A*, 34:9 (2002): 1665; Parsons, 'Charity retailing in the UK', 39.

10 J. Dean, *The Good Glow: Charity and the Symbolic Power of Doing Good* (Bristol University Press, 2020).

11 N. Wrigley and D. Lambiri, 'High street performance and evolution: a brief guide to the evidence', monograph, University of Southampton, 2014, 4, https://doi.org/10.13140/2.1.3587.9041

12 Horne, 'The charity shop'; Parsons, 'Charity retail'.

13 Nickel, 'Thrift shop philanthropy'.

14 Nickel, 'Thrift shop philanthropy', 176.

15 M. Carrigan and P. de Pelsmacker, 'Will ethical consumers sustain their values in the global credit crunch?', *International Marketing Review*, 26:6 (2009), 677.

16 N. Livingstone, 'The changing structure of charity retailers in Edinburgh's built environment', *Local Economy*, 26:2 (2011), 125.

17 J. Browne and S. Adam, 'A survey of the UK tax system', *Institute for Fiscal Studies*, 9 (2006), 1–39.

18 T. McKenzie and C. Pharoah, 'Gift aid: reform or inform', July 2010, http://www.cgap.org.uk/uploads/reports/CGAP_Briefing_Note_5.pdf (accessed 10/10/2020).

[19] HMRC, 'Gift aid rules in specific situations: selling goods on behalf of individuals', 2023, http://www.hmrc.gov.uk/charities/gift_aid/rules/retail.htm (accessed 20/04/2020).

[20] D. Cheal, *The Gift Economy* (New York: Routledge, 1988).

[21] Letter sent to Gift Aid donors, as observed by author 2010.

[22] HMRC, 'Gift aid rules in specific situations'.

[23] N. Gregson and V. Beale, 'Wardrobe matter: the sorting, displacement and circulation of women's clothing', *Geoforum*, 35:1 (2004), 689–700; N. Gregson, A. Metcalfe and L. Crewe, 'Moving things along: the conduits and practices of divestment in consumption', *Transactions of the Institute of British Geographers*, 32:2 (2007), 187–200; N. Gregson, A. Metcalfe and L. Crewe, 'Practices of object maintenance and repair', *Journal of Consumer Culture*, 9:2 (2009), 248–272.

[24] Gregson et al, 'Discourse, displacement and retail practise'.

[25] R. Goodall, 'Charity shops in sectoral contexts: the view from the boardroom', *International Journal of Nonprofit and Voluntary Sector Marketing*, 5:2 (2000), 106.

[26] Parsons, 'Charity retail'.

[27] Dean, *The Good Glow*.

[28] D.C. Paredes, 'Gift-in-kind in the academic library: the University of Saskatchewan experience', *Library Collections, Acquisitions, and Technical Services*, 30:1–2 (2006), 55–68; T. Fitton, *Hidden History: Philanthropy at the University of Kent* (Canterbury: University of Kent, 2015).

[29] C.M. Gray, 'Gift-in-kind and other illiquid assets', in D.R. Young (ed), *Financing Nonprofits: Putting Theory into Practice* (Lanham, MD: Altamira Press, 2007).

[30] Gregson et al, 'Discourse, displacement and retail practise'.

[31] E. Chattoe, 'Charity shops as second hand markets', *International Journal of Nonprofit and Voluntary Sector Marketing*, 5:2 (2006), 153–160.

[32] D. Sibley, *Geographies of Exclusion* (London: Routledge, 1995).

[33] M. Douglas, *Purity & Danger* (London: Routledge and Kegan Paul, 1966).

[34] J. Brace-Govan and I. Binay, 'Consumption of disposed goods for moral identities: a nexus of organization, place, things and consumers', *Journal of Consumer Behaviour: An International Research Review*, 9:1 (2010), 69–82. See also N. Gregson and L. Crewe, *Second-Hand Cultures* (London: Berg Publishers, 2003); G. McCracken, *Culture and Consumption* (Bloomington and Indianapolis: Indiana University Press, 1986); A. Appadurai (ed), *The Social Life of Things: Commodities in Cultural Perspective* (Cambridge University Press, 1988); G. McCracken, 'Culture and consumption: a theoretical account of the structure and movement of the cultural meaning of consumer goods', *Journal of Consumer Research*, 13 (1990), 71–84; N. Gregson, A. Metcalfe and L. Crewe, 'Moving things along: the conduits and practices of divestment in consumption', *Transactions of the Institute of British Geographers*, 32:2 (2007), 187–200; J. Botticello, 'Between classification, objectification, and perception: processing secondhand clothing for recycling and reuse', *Textile* 10:2 (2012), 164–183.

[35] Horne and Maddrell, *Charity Shops*, 127.

[36] M. Mauss, *The Gift: Forms and Functions of Exchange in Archaic Societies* (London: Cohen & West, 1970), 2.

[37] J. Carrier, *Gifts and Commodities: Exchange and Western Capitalism Since 1700* (London: Routledge, 2005).

[38] D.W. Light, 'Toward an economic sociology of compassionate charity and care', *Working Papers*, 331 (2007); Cheal, *The Gift Economy*.

[39] L. Alborough, 'Lost in translation: a sociological study of the role of fundraisers in mediating gift giving in non-profit organisations', *International Journal of Nonprofit & Voluntary Sector Marketing*, 22:4 (2017), 1–6.

[40] U. Beck and E. Beck-Gernsheim, *Individualization: Institutionalized Individualism and Its Social and Political Consequences* (London: SAGE, 2002), 42.

[41] Cheal, *The Gift Economy*, 147.

[42] M. O'Brien, *A Crisis of Waste? Understanding the Rubbish Society* (London: Routledge, 2007), 5.

[43] I. Kopytoff, 'The cultural biography of things: commoditization as process', in A. Appadurai (ed), *The Social Life of Things: Commodities in Cultural Perspective* (Cambridge University Press, 1986), 64–94.

[44] L.R. Morgan and G. Birtwhistle, 'An investigation of young fashion consumers' disposal habits', *International Journal of Consumer Studies*, 33:2 (2009), 195; E. Coverly, L. O'Malley and M. Patterson, 'Hidden mountain: the social avoidance of waste', *International Centre for Corporate Social Responsibility Research Paper Series* (2003), 17.

[45] L. Morris, 'The economics of charity: who cares?', *Third Sector Review*, 15:1 (2009), 44.

[46] E.P. Thompson, 'The moral economy of the English crowd in the eighteenth century', *Past & Present*, 50 (1971), 76–136; Cheal, *The Gift Economy*, 15.

[47] G. Ritzer, *The McDonaldization of Society*, 6th edn (London: SAGE, 2011).

[48] Cheal, *The Gift Economy*, 40.

[49] D. Phelan, 'The 1999 charity shops survey', *NGO Finance*, 9:6 (1999), 16–29.

[50] For a discussion of how smaller, local, independent charity shops are not so able to adopt 'professionalized' characteristics see T. Fitton, 'Pricing up & haggling down: value negotiations in the UK charity shop', *JOMEC Journal*, 17 (2022), 55–78.

[51] R. Merton, 'The Matthew effect in science: the reward and communication systems of science are considered', *Science*, 159:3810 (1968), 56–63.

[52] G. Bataille, *The Accursed Share: An Essay on General Economy*, trans. R. Hurley, vol 1 (New York: Zone, 1988); Nickel, 'Thrift shop philanthropy'.

[53] Fieldnotes; see also Horne and Maddrell, *Charity Shops*, 35.

[54] J. Bryson, M. McGuiness and R. Ford, 'Chasing a "loose and baggy monster": almshouses and the geography of charity', *Area*, 34:1 (2002), 49.

[55] B. Weisbrod, 'The nonprofit mission and its financing: growing links between nonprofits and the rest of the economy', in B. Weisbrod (ed), *To Profit or Not to Profit: The Commercial Transformation of the Nonprofit Sector* (New York: Cambridge University Press, 1998).

[56] Cheal, *The Gift Economy*, ix.

14

Reflections

George Campbell Gosling, Alix R. Green and Grace Millar

This collection had its beginnings at academic workshops and discussions that took place before the COVID-19 pandemic. The chapters were largely written, read and revised over phases of lockdown and of shifting restrictions in the United Kingdom. The long process of the authors and editors preparing the book for publication began in 2022, as clearer pictures were forming of the pandemic's ongoing impact. Government policy, both directly in terms of lockdown measures, furlough schemes and so on, and the ripple effects of interpretation and response at local level, intervened in people's lives in sudden and profoundly disruptive and dislocatory ways. At the same time, particular forms of connection emerged amid the general disconnection from everyday patterns of life. Entering the final stages of assembling the manuscript in 2023, it seemed to us important to reflect on how the book's themes and questions may look now – and where research in the field could go next. We do so in an open and provisional, but also, we hope, generative way; the production of this volume in the pandemic context has, if anything, brought the value and potential of 'retail and community' as an agenda for multi- and interdisciplinary inquiry into sharper relief.

COVID-19 may appear to fit with, even to reinforce, a familiar phasing of modern retail history with a rapid acceleration of trends already well established by the turn of the century: the decline of the high street in favour of the scale, choice and standardization of out-of-town malls, chains and online shopping. Non-essential shops were closed for extended periods and subject to restrictions when open. In 2021, 11,449 shops across the United Kingdom ceased trading. The following year, this figure had increased dramatically to 17,145. Where on average more than 31 shops a day were closing for good in 2021, this had increased to nearly 47 in 2022, two-thirds of which (11,090) were independent retailers. In sharing these figures, the

Centre for Retailing Research positioned the pandemic as one episode within a 'perma crisis' of over a decade's standing, which began with the financial crash of 2008 and deepened as online retailing undermined the viability of bricks-and-mortar stores.[1] Even charity shops, which might usually benefit from wider economic difficulties, were hit hard by the pandemic. Operating losses led to shop closures for all the largest chains, while those reopening after lockdown saw difficulties in recruiting volunteers exacerbated, with a 24 per cent fall in the number of charity shop volunteers across the United Kingdom in just three years.[2]

In this collection, we have sought to question and complicate too neat categorizations and periodizations. Writing these concluding reflections with the pandemic as an inescapable context, these efforts seem more relevant, not less so. On closer inspection, COVID-19 is not easily integrated into narratives of perma crisis nor does it serve as a moment of complete rupture. The complexities we foregrounded in the introduction and that authors explored in their chapters are also to be found as we consider the enmeshment of retail and community during and 'after' the pandemic. If a central task of this volume has been to examine assumptions of what has been lost in the transition from traditional to modern retailing – and, indeed, what we understand to be traditional or modern – then they are and will remain live issues for researchers for decades to come.

Even as those job losses and store closures were headline news, shop assistants and delivery drivers were grouped with NHS and care home staff as keyworkers, clapped for on doorsteps or thanked on the home-made posters displayed in front room windows. Narratives of service on the 'front line' reanimated once again nostalgic tropes of wartime resolve and postwar resilience so amenable to propagandist ends. This sits uncomfortably with a tripling of violence and abuse directed at shop staff, reaching 1,301 incidents daily.[3] Yet this designation of retail staff as 'heroes', however fragile and provisional, was bottom up at least as much as top down. When neighbours collected groceries, medicines and other necessities for those unable to leave their homes, the shops that could stay open became nodes of new, sometimes hyper-local networks as communities mobilized and coordinated on Facebook and WhatsApp groups.[4]

Supermarkets and many online retailers saw profits – and dividends to shareholders – increase, not without challenge, but the acceleration of the shift to online retailing did not just happen at scale.[5] Some small producers and local shops quickly shifted to sell online; social media allowed not just retail businesses but also private individuals and creatives to sell items and share content directly with customers locked down in their homes. Delivery to the doorstep or a timed collection from a hatch could follow an online purchase from a home-based sole trader or a local shop as from a global retailer or national chain.

So, the pandemic offered both a suspension of normal ways of living (and shopping) and an acceleration of already established trends – but also some reconfigurations of retail and community that mixed and blended elements of continuity, change and adaptation in combinations that are still unstable. Rather than attempting to accommodate COVID-19 within existing periodizations, or, indeed, to announce the advent of a new phase in the history of retail, we perhaps need to look for different ways to pattern time. One such option is to work with the idea of *practice*, a concept that has proved useful and malleable in a wide range of disciplines. Its very openness is its strength, giving interdisciplinary research a lens through which to view and explore the ways in which different practices – social practices, working and professional practices, charitable and gifting practices, buying and consumption practices – layer and enmesh in and between specific contexts.

Thinking about what themes a practice-oriented approach might suggest in a post-lockdown context, after Brexit and during a cost of living crisis, inequality seems among the most pressing. Retail, as some chapters have explored, provides spaces and contexts in which inequalities are experienced and managed, displayed and hidden. What does the shopkeeper as 'banker to the poor', or community level solidarity between retailer and customer, look like in Britain today? Analysis by the Institute for Fiscal Studies recognized that the 'specific nature of the economic shock associated with COVID 19 has interacted with many old and deep inequalities', including gender, race, socioeconomic background and region.[6] History has something important to offer here in understanding the interactions between deeper histories of inequality and the moments in which those histories are refracted through the lens of policy crisis. That means, perhaps, historians writing more explicitly about the contemporary, political lenses through which we inevitably view our sources. It may also mean casting our nets widely, for example, drawing on the diversity of research undertaken on and with communities 'in real time' on the effects of COVID-19, incentivized by funders' rapid pivoting of schemes towards pandemic-focused research.[7]

Practices are not easily defined nor their boundaries demarcated, but therein lies the strength of such an approach; to ask about practice is to move beyond the retail transaction to attend to lived experiences, affective worlds, senses of agency and identity and so on. Thematic work on inequality inevitably does this, and we see many opportunities to bring the lens of practice to the study of retail and community. It may, for example, lend a different cast to ideas such as professionalization, particularly prominent in literature on charity retail. For the local retailer or small charity moving online, recreating a sense of particularity and place in digital spaces to build connections with potential customers may be a form of professionalization without the implications of scale and infrastructure the term may conventionally carry. Perhaps of particular interest to historians are collectively held understandings of fairness in buying and selling, which may be more elusive when locality and community are enacted across in-person and online spaces, or as profit-seeking businesses mobilize notions of the collective good or partner with charitable causes.

Notions of practice may prove illuminative in thinking through the meanings of buying and selling. Chapters in this volume have touched on how the retail transaction – in many different settings – can signify something important: a display of loyalty or solidarity, an enactment of compassion or empathy (or, indeed, of patriotism, evangelism or enlightened self-interest); a sense of mutual benefit or interdependence, albeit at times uneasy or unwelcome. Sites of consumption may also be sites of retailing. The 'encounter at the counter', to borrow Keval's phrase from Chapter 11, is structured by the space in which it happens, as well as by political cultures, social codes and expectations and economic judgements, behind which many pasts and their meanings are layered. Such approaches offer rich potential for bringing spatial and historical attention together to broader retail contexts.

Such a nuanced layering of retail as practice requires continued interdisciplinary effort, particularly in terms of collaboration between historians – understood inclusively – and social scientists. The present collection lays some foundations here. In attempting to outline an agenda for histories of retail and community in the 21st century, however, we see the potential for moving from conversations among disciplines to a more engaged approach at methodological and conceptual levels. For example, future histories would undoubtedly benefit from sustained attention to shared concerns with categories of experience such as class, race and gender, and to concepts that help us explain the phenomena we study, for example, inequality or globalization. Interdisciplinary dialogue can only aid efforts to understand and move between the myriad levels at which the social contexts and meanings of retail are made and remade.

We need each other more than ever, as such efforts have acquired new complexities in recent years. Deep-rooted debates on what immigration and global trade say about Britain and its place in the world were placed firmly on the agenda by Brexit, framed and guided by contrasting and contested views of the British past.[8] It was in this context that we compiled this collection of English retail histories in global contexts, guided by an understanding that not only does locality not preclude globality but that the two are inseparable. The end of empire was the central change of our period in Britain's relationship with the rest of the world and we cannot understand the social contexts within which contemporary retail is embedded without grappling with colonialism and its ongoing legacies. These wider implications and resonances have not always been a feature of the increased interest in Britain's global history. 'Even as imperial historians offered interpretations of the 2016 referendum on Britain's membership in the European Union', the editors of *Twentieth Century British History*'s 2023 special issue on *Marking Race* noted, 'few confronted directly the deep investment in whiteness behind fantasies of "Global Britain"'.[9]

'How might historians narrate Britain's past', they asked, 'if we centre imperial racial formation and its contestations?' Historians of retail surely have much to offer in response. Taking, as this collection has, a broad understanding of retail – buying and selling, charitable, cooperative and commercial, shop floor and behind the scenes, working lives and customer conduct – creates many spaces to think 'with and through race'.[10] The racialization of staff behind the counter, of recipients of charity shop proceeds or of imagined producers of imperial goods are immediate examples. *Centring* race and racialization as an essential analytical tool, however, invites all those concerned with retail and community to rethink and reframe their working practices.

As part of such an undertaking, we can actively and critically engage with the power asymmetries built into the collections we use. Archivists have, rightly, critiqued historians and the humanities scholars using archival collections for their disinclination to engage with 'actually existing archives' or with the literature and professional knowledge and practice emerging from the field.[11] Historians willing to develop a working knowledge of archival practice and a foundational grasp of critical archives scholarship acquire tools to identify and interrogate the multiple interventions in the journey of a record from creation to access. There are vital interpretive clues and insights to be gained from considering a document's *archivality* – description, organization, arrangement – not least in enabling us to see power dynamics at work, whether in terms of racialization or other forms of minoritization and marginalization. When we are working on the records of an operational retailer that holds its own archives, the expertise of the business archivist is invaluable to help understand the historical organizational contexts in which the records we use were created and designated archival. As noted in Chapter 8, the same issues are at play in charity archives, within which we find fragmentary and obscured traces of charity retail's history.

The archival record is inevitably a partial one, in both senses of the word. Where few archival sources exist, reading 'against the grain' has been a technique employed to reveal and centre hidden and silenced lives in the documents created by their oppressors and in defiance of the record creator's original intentions.[12] For those working within living memory, addressing gaps and silences in existing collections by recording new oral histories and developing proactive donation plans with staff networks and community groups holds rich potential (and companies prizing their equality, diversity and inclusion credentials may even fund their archives to pursue such projects). Historians of retail have much to gain from contributing to and engaging with these welcome enrichments of the archival record.

The foregoing reflections offer possibilities rather than prescriptions for writing histories of retail and community in the 21st century. The three overarching themes of the collection – the social and community dimensions of retailing, the place of charity alongside commercial and co-operative retailing, and the significance of wider international connections and global contexts – remain, we would argue, relevant and resonant for historians, sociologists, anthropologists, archivists and others engaged in such a task. The importance of these histories is not confined, however, to scholarship concerned with retail or business history more broadly. It is the enmeshment of retail within social relationships at every scale that ensures connection to a wide range of major questions and concerns across the humanities and social sciences. Modern retailing and consumption encounters have not entirely lost their social, cultural, moral and political dimensions, even if they are sometimes well hidden by economic ones. Buying and selling remain rarely, if ever, purely transactional. Economic activity continues to be not only shaped by its social embeddedness, but also inscribed with social meaning. The transformations of the long 20th century changed but did not end the deep relationship between retail and community. What trends and transitions the rest of the 21st century brings will, we hope, be the subject of the kind of rich, interdisciplinary conversations that have animated this book.

Notes

[1] Centre for Retailing Research, 'The crisis in retailing: closures and job losses' (2023), https://www.retailresearch.org/retail-crisis.html (accessed 19/06/2023).

[2] L. Legraien, 'Number of charity shop volunteers drops by nearly a quarter in three years', *Civil Society*, 03/10/2022, https://www.civilsociety.co.uk/news/number-of-charity-shop-volunteers-drops-by-nearly-a-quarter-in-three-years.html (accessed 17/07/2023).

[3] British Retail Consortium, *Crime Survey 2022 Report*, https://brc.org.uk/media/679954/crime-survey-2022.pdf (accessed 14/07/2023).

[4] For a discussion of local community organizing, including hyper-local coordination on social media platforms, see A.R. Green, R. Warren, S. Woodward and D. Wiltshire, *North East Essex Communities Responding to Crisis COVID 19, Social Action and Our Local Neighbourhood* (2021), https://www.community360.org.uk/wp-content/uploads/2022/12/Covid-Report-Final.pdf (accessed 14/07/2023).

[5] Oxfam, *Not in This Together: How Supermarkets Became Pandemic Winners While Women Workers Are Losing Out*, Briefing Paper, 22/06/2021, https://policy-practice.oxfam.org/resources/not-in-this-together-how-supermarkets-became-pandemic-winners-while-women-worke-621194/ (accessed 14/07/2023).

[6] R. Blundell, M. Costa Dias, R. Joyce and X. Xu, 'Covid-19 and Inequalities' (Institute for Fiscal Studies, 2022), 3.

[7] See, for example, https://www.ukri.org/what-we-do/what-we-have-funded/find-covid-19-research-and-innovation-supported-by-ukri/ (accessed 14/07/2023).

[8] D. Thackeray, A. Thompson and R. Toye (eds), *Imagining Britain's Economic Future, c. 1800–1975: Trade, Consumerism and Global Markets* (London: Palgrave Macmillan, 2018), 4–5.

[9] M. Matera, R. Natarajan, K. Hammond Perry, C. Schofield and R. Waters, 'Introduction: marking race in twentieth century British history', *Twentieth Century British History*, 34:3 (2023), 407–414.

[10] Matera et al, 'Introduction', 409.
[11] M. Caswell, '"The archive" is not an archives: acknowledging the intellectual contributions of archival studies', *Reconstruction*, 16:1 (2016).
[12] M. Fuentes, *Dispossessed Lives: Enslaved Women, Violence and the Archive* (University of Pennsylvania Press, 2016); R. Carter, 'Of things said and unsaid: power, archival silences, and power in silence', *Archivaria*, 61 (2006), 215–233.

Index

References to figures appear in *italic* type; those in **bold** type refer to tables. References to endnotes show both the page number and the note number (231n3).